GIULIANO
BUGIALLI'S
FOODS OF
TUSCANY

GIULIANO
BUGIALLI'S

FOODS OF
TUSCANY

Photographs by John Dominis

Stewart, Tabori & Chang   New York

To the "Maledetti Toscani"

"Maledetti Toscani," or Damned Tuscans, is the ironic but affectionate phrase that the great twentieth-century Tuscan writer Curzio Malaparte used as the title of one of his books.

Text and recipes copyright © 1992 Giuliano Bugialli
Photographs copyright © 1992 John Dominis
Edited by Melanie Falick
Map by Liz Schweber

Published in 1992 by
Stewart, Tabori & Chang, Inc.
575 Broadway, New York, New York 10012

Library of Congress Cataloging-in-Publication Data
Bugialli, Giuliano.
  [Foods of Tuscany]
  Giuliano Bugialli's foods of Tuscany /
  by Giuliano Bugialli ; photographs by John Dominis.
     p.   cm.
  ISBN 1-55670-200-0
  1. Cookery, Italian—Tuscan style.   2. Tuscany (Italy) —Social life and customs.   I. Dominis, John.   II. Title.
TX723.2.T86B84   1992   92-9783
641.5945'5—dc20   CIP

Distributed in the U.S. by Workman Publishing,
708 Broadway, New York, New York 10003
Distributed in Canada by Canadian Manda Group,
P.O. Box 920 Station U, Toronto, Ontario M8Z 5P9

Printed in Japan
10 9 8 7 6 5 4 3 2 1

Frontispiece: All the ingredients for Salsa d'agresto (Sauce of Unripe Grapes) sitting on the wall of the aia, the area in front of a farmhouse that is used for such tasks as shelling legumes and separating the wheat from the chaff after the harvest. Notice the tiny immature grapes, which must be peeled one by one, and the freshly picked red onion still attached to its stem. The recipe is on page 290.

C O N T E N T S

It seems like another era when I think back to the time when I was searching for a name for my first cookbook, which was made up of recipes drawn from my own culinary life and that of my family's, and was therefore almost completely Tuscan. The publishers recoiled in horror at the suggestion that the title should include the words Tuscan or Tuscany as they implied too specialized a subject. And so it became The Fine Art of Italian Cooking. How things have changed! Today's readers are fascinated with the idea of cookbooks that uncover the riches of specific regions.

I decided to undertake this second book on Tuscan cooking because I wanted the opportunity not only to share more recipes from the inexhaustible Tuscan repertoire, but because I wanted to immerse my readers in my vision of Tuscany, with its unique and varied landscape, its great villas, palaces and gardens, its vineyards and olive groves, and its art. I also wanted to try to re-create some of the wonderful festivals of my early life.

For my research, I set out on a journey all around Tuscany. Family connections drew me through the countryside and the towns and villages. I experienced many little-known culinary triumphs—some of them in restaurants but most of them in private homes. Because my grandmother was from Siena, my family still belongs to a Sienese contrada and I was able to enter into all the rites connected to the famous Palio horse race, including the huge grilled dinner that is served the evening before the race. I visited an old country priest in a mountain village, a childhood friend of my mother's. I went to Arezzo, where my father spent part of his early life. I also drew upon my mother's memories of her grandparents' life at the court of the last Hapsburg Grand Duke of Tuscany and my own memories of my childhood in Florence, my visits to my Sienese grandmother, my summers on the Tuscan coast and the time I spent during my adolescence living on one of the greatest wine estates in Chianti.

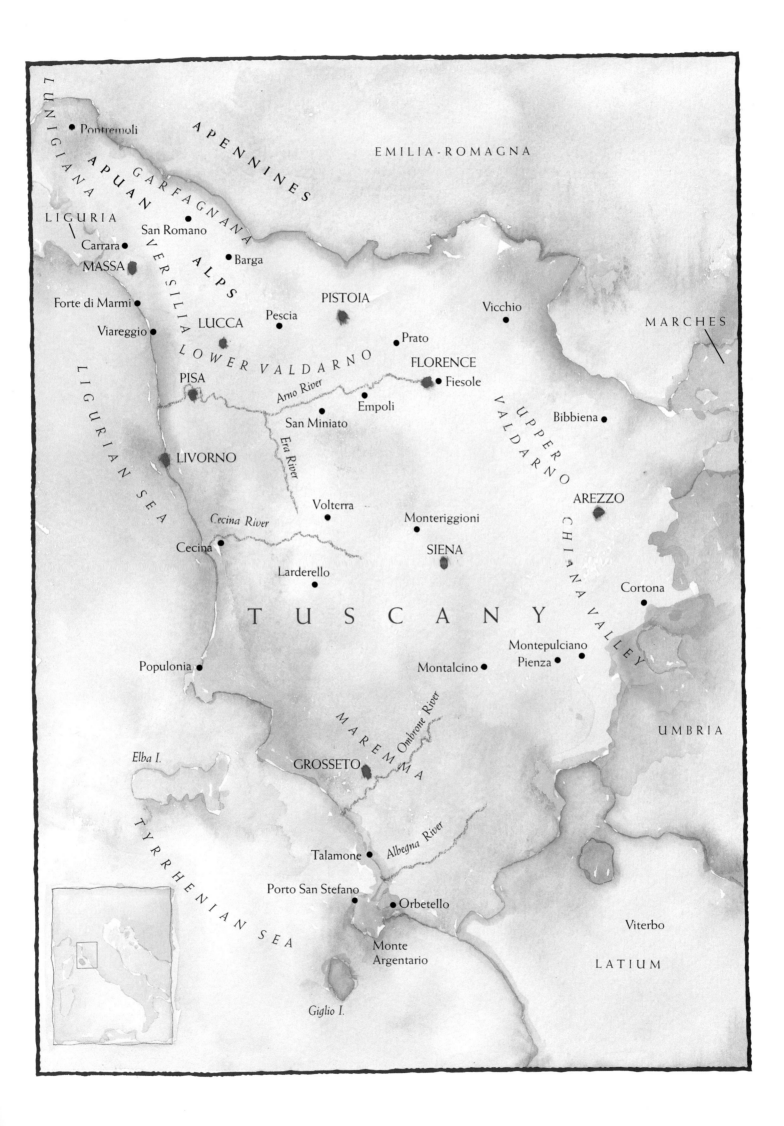

One of several Medici family-tree paintings now hanging in Florentine museums.

It was during the reign of this family, from the late fourteenth century until 1741, that the greatest flowering in Tuscany took place and a very large percentage of the Western world's significant art and culture was produced. In the early eighteenth century, the family faced a crisis when the last generation had no heirs, legitimate or otherwise. Even a woman, Anna Maria Luisa, was allowed to rule informally, but when she died in 1741, the Medici family was finally extinguished. And of all the people in Italy who have the enviable but quite common name of Medici, not a single one is related to the great ruling family of Florence, though naturally many claim to be.

I present the fruits of my labor. In addition to the well-known dishes from Florence, there are dishes from Lucca and its rich countryside, the Chianti area, and the Arno Valley as well as Arezzo, the Valdichiana and the culinary gold mine of Siena. I present specialties from Tuscany's southern coast and one-time marshlands, called Maremma, home to water buffalo and wild boar, and the distinctive cucina of Livorno, one of the repositories of Italian-Jewish cooking. The northern coast, including Viareggio, Massa and Carrara, as well as Pisa, founded by the Greeks or Etruscans and for over a millennium the dominant city of what is now Tuscany, is not ignored. And then there are the two mountainous areas, Casentino and Garfagnana, both boasting many unique recipes, and Pistoia and Pescia, so rich in flowers and vegetables. Nor do I overlook Montalcino and Montepulciano, the great wine centers that offer food of equal merit.

What is most fascinating is that all of these areas of Tuscany have maintained separate culinary traditions. To understand how and why, one must only be reminded that this region, the largest in Italy aside from the island of Sicily, has the greatest density of once-independent political units. The union of all of these into modern Tuscany, which occurred for the most part in the fifteenth century, is only a short epoch in their long histories. The people of these areas have an individuality that they do not intend to change. In addition, they have never lost confidence in the virtues of their gastronomy. After all, they have always had superb products: olive oil, sheep's cheeses, grains, wines, pork and beef, to name a few. And that same natural sense of aesthetics that produced their unsurpassed art also helped Tuscans to formulate their celebrated cucina.

Throughout this book are photos of not only the finished dishes but also the colorful Tuscan festivals, the famed markets and vineyards as well as the incomparable Tuscan architecture, monuments and fine art. Tuscan cucina is forever connected to this landscape, art and history, and that is the way I have tried to present it in this book.

APPETIZERS

The antipasto course, which precedes the so-called first course, has been part of festive Italian meals since as early as the sixteenth century. Its components vary greatly depending on where you are in Tuscany and whether you are eating in a home or a restaurant. The antipasto course may consist of a mixed platter of local preserved meats and crostini or, for a special dinner prepared at home, it may be a single elaborate hot or cold dish, such as a galantina or torta.

For this chapter, I have chosen a variety of dishes: The two crostini toppings merely hint at the wide variety of toppings that are enjoyed in Tuscany. In connection with the Crostini alle erbe, *I present our first Tuscan festival,* Calcio in costume, *at which I serve this type of* crostini. *I have also included two* frittate—*eggs that are mixed with vegetables, meat, fish or herbs, then cooked into a kind of large pancake and sliced like a pie.* Frittate, *which can be served warm or at room temperature, can be presented as an appetizer or a simple main course.* Cold antipasto *dishes include* Panzanella *in its Valdarno incarnation,* Trippa alla pisana, *and* Zampine di vitella all'agro. *As an example of hot* antipasti, *I present* Dadolata di polenta. *The* Torta di pomodoro, *like most* torte, *may be served either warm or at room temperature.*

CROSTINI

The rustic canapés called crostini are a Tuscan specialty, and a mixed antipasto for a festive dinner may include more than one kind—together with regional sausages and salamis and the local prosciutto. Cheeses are not included, as the Tuscans are reluctant to combine cheese with cured meats. Cheese antipasti exist on their own; for example, Pecorino paired with fresh fava beans or dressed with olive oil and black pepper.

Although crostini toppings vary throughout the region, there are some that one is likely to find all over, such as liver pâté seasoned with juniper berries or anchovies and/or capers, and butter flavored with mashed anchovies. At the seaside, one naturally finds crostini with seafood toppings. Among the vegetarian variations are bean purées or the wonderful chopped tomato-and-herb topping that I have included in the recipe for Crostini alle erbe on page 18.

In late August, when the Tuscan wheat harvest is over and the fields are covered with the stalks of cut grain, hunters begin their search for the fleet-footed hare, which moves so fast that it can hardly be seen. This is when the favorite Tuscan hare dishes are served, and a variation of one of them, Hare in Sweet and Spicy Sauce, is used as a topping for crostini (as well as a sauce for pasta). Once the hare is cooked and ready to be served as a main course, a portion of it is left on the stove until some of the bones actually dissolve. The result is a very rich sauce that works extremely well on crostini as well as pasta.

The Crostini alle erbe are the most summery of the crostini and seem to me very appropriate for the Calcio fiorentino, the Renaissance football games that are played each June between teams representing the four quarters (called quartieri) of Florence. Most Tuscan festivals have particular dishes associated with them, and the most obvious specialty for the Calcio would seem to be one featuring ox, since the prize for the winning team is one of these beautiful white animals. However, in typical Florentine fashion, the teams refuse to agree on such a dish, each of them having their own ideas about what to serve after the game.

Taking the photographs of the Calcio fiorentino was very exciting, as the savagery of the games is displayed against a back-drop of history and culture. The game itself takes place in the Piazza Santa Croce, filled with Medieval and Renaissance architecture. To watch this fierce battle, we were based in the Palazzo Piccolomini, which is still occupied by the Piccolomini family, one of whose ancestors was a Renaissance pope. The exterior of this palace is graced with frescoes by the great Vasari. During the Renaissance and Baroque periods, most Florentine palaces were covered with colorful frescoes like these, but very few of them remain.

Preceding pages: Each of the four quarters of Florence is named after the principal church of the area. In this match, the Santo Spirito team, dressed in white, was pitted against Santa Croce, the home team, in blue. Crostini alle erbe (Canapés with Herb Topping) sit on a serving platter on the ledge of the Palazzo Piccolomini, the palace where we were stationed for the game.

A pine cone with its nuts, the famous pignoli, still in their shells.

Interestingly, this Florentine savagery, while exhibited physically each year at the Calcio, is more often translated into words. It was said of the poet Dante, a Florentine if there ever was one, that he had "a perceptive eye and a wicked tongue." The typical Florentine has not changed much since that time in the thirteenth century, and it is for this "wickedness" that he is known, if perhaps not loved.

CROSTINI DI LEPRE

Hare Canapés

FLORENCE

1 small hare (about 4 pounds)
1 cup red wine vinegar
1 medium-sized red onion, cleaned
1 medium-sized carrot, scraped
2 celery stalks
10 sprigs Italian parsley, leaves only
4 ounces prosciutto or pancetta
½ cup olive oil
Salt and freshly ground black pepper
1 heaping tablespoon unbleached
    all-purpose flour
About 4 cups chicken or meat
    broth, preferably homemade

FOR THE SWEET AND
SPICY SAUCE
4 ounces semisweet chocolate,
    cut into pieces
1 cup red wine vinegar
4 ounces raisins
4 ounces pine nuts (*pinoli*)
4 ounces glacéed citron
¼ cup granulated sugar

PLUS
15 (5-inch) slices crusty Tuscan
    bread, about 1 inch thick

Remove the head and liver from the hare and discard. Wash the hare carefully, under cold running water, then place it in a bowl with 2 cups of cold water and the vinegar. Let it soak for 2 hours to remove the very strong gamey flavor.

Coarsely chop the onion, carrot, celery and parsley all together on a board. Cut the prosciutto into tiny pieces.

Drain the hare and rinse it under cold running water. Pat the hare dry with paper towels. Place a large casserole over medium heat, add the hare, cover the skillet and cook for 10 minutes. By that time a lot of off-white liquid will have come out of the hare. Remove the casserole from the heat, rinse the hare under cold running water again and pat it dry with paper towels. Cut the hare into 4-inch pieces.

Place a large casserole with the oil over medium heat and when the oil is warm, add the chopped ingredients along with the prosciutto. Sauté for 10 minutes, stirring with a wooden spoon, or until the onion is translucent. Add the hare and sauté for 20 minutes, stirring every so often with a wooden spoon. Season with salt and pepper. Sprinkle the flour over the hare, then heat the broth and add it, ½ cup at a time, to the casserole. When all the broth is used up, the hare should be almost cooked and quite soft.

Meanwhile, place the chocolate, vinegar, raisins, pine nuts, citron and sugar in a small bowl and mix very well. Add the mixture to the casserole with the hare, mix very well, cover and cook for 20 minutes more, stirring every so often with a wooden spoon. If the hare is not yet soft, continue cooking, adding lukewarm water as needed. (Cooking time for game is very unpredictable. Stop cooking when the meat starts detaching from the bones and some of the very thin bones start to dissolve.) Remove and discard all the bones, place the meat back in the casserole, add about 1 cup lukewarm water and continue cooking until the sauce is homogeneous, about 10 minutes.

Transfer the solid part of the sauce to a board and finely chop. Put the chopped solids back in the casserole, taste for salt and pepper and reduce for 5 minutes more. Spread 1 heaping tablespoon of this very thick sauce over each slice of bread or use it as a sauce for pasta, such as homemade *pappardelle*.

Serves 5 to 10.

CALCIO FIORENTINO ·
THE SOCCER GAME
IN RENAISSANCE COSTUME

The annual Calcio fiorentino or Calcio in livrea—*soccer in costume*—is celebrated in June as part of the observances in honor of San Giovanni, the patron saint of Florence. The event starts the moment the procession leaves the ancient Church of Santa Maria Novella and begins its march through the city to the playing field, the sounds of trumpets and drums transporting the crowds to a time long gone of imperial troops and republics, of Florentine neighborhood strongholds and loyalties. As the colorful, richly costumed procession enters the field, the men lead in a large white ox, who is very important, for he is the prize. On the field, spectators see not only soccer games between teams representing different quarters of the city, but also a Calcio in costume— a lively mix of colors, luxurious fabrics, and poses and profiles reminiscent of the very real history behind the game.

The game (or calcio) traces its history back to Greek and Roman times. The Romans saw it as a preparation for real combat, requiring robust physical health and the use of the whole body. Even today, the game's structure and movements recall the order of the Roman army. In early Greece, the game was considered a mock-war between two teams, each intent on possession of the ball.

Later references to the Calcio fiorentino appear in poems, diaries and historical documents of the Middle Ages and Renais-

The flag throwers, accompanied by drummers, signal the beginning of the game. The emblems on the flags represent the major and minor guilds, or arti maggiori and arti minori, of the city of Florence during the Middle Ages. Butchers, bakers and wine and oil merchants had their guilds among the arti minori, but the butcher's guild had more power than some of the arti maggiori because they owned all of the shops along the Ponte Vecchio, the famous covered bridge that today hosts only exclusive jewelry shops.

Typically, by the end of this vigorous battle, the players have destroyed their clothing, not once but several times. There is actually an umpire whose job it is to replace the players' garments, but he can never work quickly enough to keep them all fully clothed. The game ends in full battle, and often spreads over the tribune to the excited fans, who battle one another.

After marching through the city, the parade enters the Piazza Santa Croce playing field. The last costumed marchers bring in the prize: a white ox.

sance. The game had its "hooligan" aspects even in those days, for vigilant groups were assigned to block intruders from interfering. They were supposed to keep the peace if things got out of hand and to see that the games did not violate the standards of proper conduct.

There was also prestige attached to the games: Only the most physically fit youths of noble families could participate. They were expected to demonstrate forcefulness and courage, but also to show elegance and sumptuousness in their dress. The object was to be respected for their show of manhood on the field, but just as important for a Florentine, also to be admired by the the ladies present, who were themselves most elegant. Today, the aesthetic aspect of the game is preserved, with all the flourishes of costume, coat of arms, banners and courtly standards.

Ever since the game that took place on February 17, 1530, while Florence was under siege by the troops of the Holy Roman Emperor, the Calcio fiorentino has become a symbol of Florence's contemptuous resistance to outside domination. The game was held not only to continue a longtime tradition, but as an act of "innocent" defiance. When the officials of the supposedly "beleaguered" republic entered, the Florentine crowd greeted them with shouts and cheers, and the musicians who had stationed themselves on the roof of the church added to the fervor. In response to the uproar, the troops fired a cannon at the church, but they missed their target and the cannonball passed overhead, producing additional merriment.

Sometime in the eighteenth century the Florentines stopped this celebration, but the tradition was restored in 1930 on the anniversary of the siege. While the costumes and the procession transport the crowd to times long gone, the games that they watch are very much a part of the present, the outcome being quite important not only to the teams involved but also to the fans who live in the quarters that these teams represent.

CROSTINI ALLE ERBE

Canapés with Herb Topping

Finely chop the parsley, capers, tarragon and hard-boiled egg all together on a board. Transfer the chopped ingredients to a crockery or glass bowl, season with salt and pepper and mix in all the oil except for 1 tablespoon. Refrigerate, covered, until needed.

Cut the tomatoes into tiny pieces, place them in a crockery or glass bowl and season with salt and pepper. Add the remaining tablespoon of oil and the mint leaves. Refrigerate, covered, until needed.

When ready, put some of the parsley mixture on top of each slice of bread, arrange some of the tomato pieces on top and serve with a fresh mint leaf.

Serves 6.

25 sprigs Italian parsley, leaves only
8 tablespoons capers, preserved in wine vinegar, drained
½ tablespoon fresh tarragon leaves
1 extra-large hard-boiled egg
Salt and freshly ground black pepper
½ cup olive oil
2 large ripe tomatoes, blanched and seeded
5 large fresh mint leaves, torn into fourths

PLUS
18 (3-inch) slices crusty Tuscan bread, about 1 inch thick

TO SERVE
Fresh mint leaves

FRITTATE

Considering how often they appear on restaurant menus today, it is hard to imagine that not too long ago, frittate *were so little known outside of Italy that one had to struggle to describe how they differed from omelettes.*

Frittata di bianchi, *the first frittata I present in this chapter, is bound to become even more popular as it uses only egg whites, eliminating the cholesterol problem associated with other egg dishes. This traditional dish was not conceived for this purpose, however. In the days of the Grand Duchy a farm system was adopted that was considered quite progressive: Most land was owned by the nobility and rich merchants, but each farmer was guaranteed half of his own production, which was more than enough to fulfill his family's needs and still leave him with something to sell for his own profit. Naturally, the other half of the farmer's yield went to the* padrone, *the owner of the land. Because Tuscan land was so fertile and produced such bountiful crops, the farmers prospered. A few inequities remained, though. In the wintertime, when the hens laid few eggs, the* padrone *could take as many yolks as he wished, and, because of this, a whole repertoire of dishes using egg whites was developed by the farmers. And, when there were no eggs left at all, they developed the second type of* frittata *in this chapter,* Frittata di patate senza uova, *which omits eggs altogether and uses potatoes instead.*

Throughout the spring and early summer, the perfume of the acacia tree fills the Tuscan air. Entire roads are covered with them and when they shed their flowers it looks like falling snow. These flowers are edible, and it is traditional to make frittate *and even sweet fritters with them.*

FRITTATA DI BIANCHI

Egg-White Frittata

Cut the vegetable of your choice into pieces that measure less than 1-inch and soak them in a bowl of cold water for ½ hour.

Bring a medium-sized casserole of cold water to a boil over medium heat, then add coarse salt to taste. Drain the vegetable, add it to the casserole and cook until soft, 2 to 10 minutes, depending on the vegetable. Drain and cool under cold running water.

Finely chop the garlic and coarsely chop the parsley on a board. Heat 3 tablespoons of the oil in a skillet over medium heat and when the oil is warm, add the garlic and parsley and sauté for 30 seconds. Put in the cooled vegetable, season with salt, pepper and the hot red pepper flakes, and sauté for 15 minutes, stirring with a wooden spoon. Transfer the sautéed vegetable to a crockery or glass bowl and let cool for ½ hour before using.

1 pound of a vegetable, such as
    carrots, string beans, celery,
    long beans or cauliflower,
    cleaned
Coarse-grained salt
1 medium-sized clove garlic, peeled
10 sprigs Italian parsley, leaves only
4 tablespoons olive oil
Salt and freshly ground black pepper
A large pinch of hot red pepper
    flakes
6 extra-large egg whites

Use a fork to lightly beat the egg whites in a crockery bowl. Add the cooled vegetable to the egg and mix very well.

Prepare the *frittata:* Heat the remaining tablespoon of oil in a 10-inch no-stick omelette pan over low heat. When the oil is hot, add the beaten eggs. As the eggs set in the pan, keep puncturing the bottom with a fork in order to allow the liquid on top to seep through to the bottom. When the eggs are set and the *frittata* is detached from the bottom of the pan, place a plate, upside-down, over the pan and, holding the plate firmly, flip the plate and pan over so that the *frittata* comes out on the plate. Return the pan to the heat and carefully slide the *frittata* into the pan and cook the other side.

When the eggs are well set on the second side, after about 1 minute, transfer the *frittata* to a serving dish. Serve hot or at room temperature.

Serves 6.

FRITTATA DI PATATE SENZA UOVA

Giant Potato Pancake

Place a medium-sized casserole of cold water over medium heat. When the water reaches a boil, add coarse salt to taste and the potatoes, and cook until very soft, 35 to 45 minutes, depending on the size of the potatoes.

Meanwhile, coarsely chop the onions and finely chop the garlic on a board. Heat 3 tablespoons of the oil in a medium-sized saucepan over low heat and when the oil is warm, add the chopped ingredients and sauté for 10 minutes, stirring every so often with a wooden spoon. Season with salt and pepper. Add ½ cup cold water, raise the heat and let cook for 10 minutes more. By that time the onions should be translucent and the water completely evaporated. Transfer the contents of the saucepan to a crockery or glass bowl and let stand until needed.

When the potatoes are ready, peel them while they are still very hot, and pass them through a potato ricer into the bowl with the onions. Add 2 tablespoons of the oil and taste for salt and pepper. Coarsely chop the parsley, add it to the potato mixture and mix very well.

Heat a 14-inch no-stick omelette pan over low heat. When the pan is uniformly warm, use the remaining tablespoon of oil to lightly grease the whole surface. Transfer the potato mixture to the pan and use a rubber spatula to evenly spread out the mixture to form a thick pancake. Let the *frittata* cook for 5 minutes, shaking the pan several times to be sure the *frittata* is completely detached from the pan. Since there are no eggs or cheese to bind the *frittata,* be sure no large cracks form. If they do, still using the rubber spatula, press down on the mixture to patch them. After 5 minutes you will feel that a quite thick crust has formed.

Lightly oil a flat rimless serving dish (the same size as the pancake or the inside part of the lid of the pan) and gently slide out the *frittata.* Immediately invert the dish and slide the *frittata* back into the pan; if it breaks (since it is very fragile), reconstitute it by pressing down on the mixture with your spatula. Cook for 5 minutes more, shaking the pan several times. When ready (when the crust has formed on the bottom), slide the *frittata* out onto a serving dish, sprinkle on the parsley and serve.

Serves 12.

Coarse-grained salt
2 pounds all-purpose potatoes
2 medium-sized red onions, cleaned
2 medium-sized cloves garlic, peeled
6 tablespoons olive oil
Salt and freshly ground black pepper
20 large sprigs Italian parsley,
    leaves only

TO SERVE
10 large sprigs Italian parsley,
    leaves only

PANZANELLA DEL VALDARNO

Bread Salad

1 pound crusty Tuscan bread,
     preferably whole-wheat,
     several days old
6 tablespoons strong red wine
     vinegar
2 medium-sized red onions, cleaned
3 very large ripe tomatoes
1 celery heart
15 large fresh basil leaves, torn
     into thirds

TO DRESS THE SALAD
Salt and freshly ground black pepper
¾ cup olive oil

TO SERVE
15 large fresh basil leaves

OPTIONAL
4 whole anchovies preserved in
     salt or packed in olive oil,
     rinsed if in salt and drained if
     preserved in oil, or 8 anchovy
     fillets, packed in oil, drained

Unlike the classic Tuscan bread salad, the Panzanella *of the Arno Valley calls for soaking the bread in a combination of water and red wine vinegar, instead of water alone, and then omitting the vinegar from the dressing. Celery is added to the standard onion, tomato and basil; anchovies and hard-cooked eggs are optional additions. The Tuscans hate to waste any of their crusty country bread, and this salad, along with* pappa *(bread soup), is among their favorite dishes.*

Cut the bread into large pieces and place in a crockery or glass bowl. Pour 6 cups of cold water and the vinegar over the bread. Soak the bread for ½ hour.

Meanwhile, cut the onions into small pieces and let rest in a bowl of cold water for ½ hour. Cut the tomatoes into 2-inch pieces, without removing the seeds or skin, and place them in a large crockery or glass bowl. Cut the celery into small pieces and add it to the bowl with the tomatoes.

When ready, squeeze the water-vinegar out of the bread and place the bread on top of the tomato-celery mixture. Do not mix. Drain the onions and arrange them all over the bread, then sprinkle over the basil. Cover the bowl with plastic wrap and refrigerate for at least ½ hour.

Dress the salad with salt, pepper and the olive oil. Mix the salad very well and sprinkle on the basil leaves. If using the anchovies, coarsely chop them and add them at the last moment before serving.

Serves 6.

TRIPPA ALLA PISANA

Tripe Salad

There are so many treatments of tripe throughout Italy that an entire book could be compiled on the subject. Trippa alla fiorentina, *tripe (sometimes combined with calves' feet) cooked in tomato sauce,* is one of the most famous of these dishes and is often served with cannellini beans. In Trippa alla pisana, *a summery dish from old Pisa,* the precooked tripe is combined with a classic uncooked green sauce. Green sauces are still current in Italy, especially in Tuscany where they probably originated; this version is made with a large amount of chopped parsley leaves thickened with ground walnuts and almonds. In some recipes, vinegar, capers and/or anchovies are added. This dish is unusual in that the tripe is not recooked in the sauce. Cooked tripe is a staple in Italian markets and is usually sold at its own stand. Warm tripe sandwiches, made from tripe fresh from its broth, are a common snack.

The photograph of this dish was taken in front of the famous Palazzo dei Cavalieri *in the old Piazza dei Cavalieri,* which was the site of the old republic of Pisa's main government buildings during the Middle Ages and Renaissance. The palace was redesigned by Vasari for Grand Duke Cosimo I after the Florentine conquest in the late Renaissance. Since 1810, it has been home to the Scuola Normale Superiore, *the seat of humanistic and scientific studies of the ancient University of Pisa, where Galileo once taught.*

2 pounds completely cooked tripe
4 large cloves garlic, peeled
1 celery stalk
1 small red onion, cleaned
1 carrot, scraped
1 medium-sized ripe tomato or
    4 cherry tomatoes
Coarse-grained salt

FOR THE SAUCE
20 sprigs Italian parsley, leaves only
5 fresh basil leaves
2 ounces shelled walnuts
3 medium-sized cloves garlic, peeled
1 ounce almonds, blanched
Salt and freshly ground black pepper
¾ cup olive oil

TO SERVE
Boiled carrots and boiled potatoes

Place a medium-sized stockpot of cold water over medium heat.

Soak the tripe in a bowl of cold water for ½ hour.

When the water reaches a boil, add the garlic, celery, onion, carrot and tomato to the boiling water, along with coarse salt to taste. Let simmer for ½ hour.

Meanwhile, prepare the sauce: Place the parsley, basil, walnuts, garlic and almonds in a blender or food processor and grind until very fine, or finely chop all the ingredients on a board.

Transfer the parsley mixture to a crockery or glass bowl, season with salt and pepper, then pour in the olive oil and mix very well with a wooden spoon. Let the sauce rest in the refrigerator, covered, until needed.

Add the tripe to the pot in which the vegetables are simmering and simmer for 10 minutes. Remove the tripe, transfer it to a board and cut into ½-inch strips. Discard the garlic, onion, celery and tomato.

Arrange the tripe, boiled potatoes and boiled carrots on a serving platter, and pour some of the prepared sauce over the tripe. Serve, passing more sauce at the table.

Serves 6.

Trippa alla pisana *(Tripe Salad), with the Palazzo dei Cavalieri, home to the Scuola Normale Superiore, in the background. It was Napoleon who moved the university facilities to this building in 1810. The Bonapartes were Tuscans—they came from the nearby coast but moved to Corsica to work as administrators—and Napoleon never forgot his allegiance to this area.*

Tomato Tart

Dating back to Renaissance times, torte—vegetables, fish or meat enclosed in a bottom crust—form one of the oldest categories of antipasti, and were probably the precursors to the French quiche. Today, if the cook goes to the trouble of preparing a torta, it will usually make up the entire antipasto course. As during the Renaissance, torte are eaten both warm and at room temperature. The beautiful and flavorful Torta di pomodoro makes an impressive opener for a festive meal.

Prepare the crust: Sift the flour onto a board and arrange it in a mound. Cut the butter into pieces and place them over the mound. Use a metal dough scraper to incorporate the butter into the flour, adding the water, 1 tablespoon at a time, and seasoning with the salt and nutmeg. When all the water is used up, a ball of dough should be formed. Place the ball in a dampened cotton dish towel and refrigerate for at least 2 hours before using. Or, leave the crust in the refrigerator overnight.

Prepare the filling: Coarsely chop the celery, carrot, onion, garlic, parsley and basil all together on a board. If using fresh tomatoes, cut them into large pieces.

Place the fresh or canned tomatoes in a non-reactive casserole, then arrange all the prepared vegetables over the tomatoes. Pour the olive oil on top. Cover the casserole, set it over medium heat and cook for at least 1 hour, without stirring, but shaking the casserole to be sure the tomatoes do not stick to the bottom of the pan.

Pass the contents of the casserole through a food mill, using the disc with the smallest holes, into a second casserole. Add the butter and season with salt and pepper.

Place the casserole over medium heat and let the sauce reduce for 15 minutes more, or until a rather thick sauce forms. Transfer the sauce to a crockery or glass bowl and let cool completely.

Butter a 9½-inch tart pan with a removable bottom. Flour a pastry board. Unwrap the pastry and knead it for about 30 seconds on the board, then use a rolling pin to roll out the dough into a 14-inch disc.

Roll up the disc on the rolling pin and unroll it over the buttered pan. Gently press the dough into the bottom of the pan. Cut off the dough around the rim of the pan by moving the rolling pin over it. Using a fork, make several punctures in the pastry to keep it from puffing up. Fit a piece of aluminum foil loosely over the pastry, then put pie weights or dried beans in the pan (over the foil). Refrigerate the pastry for ½ hour.

FOR THE CRUST
8 ounces unbleached all-purpose flour
8 tablespoons (4 ounces) cold sweet butter
Pinch of salt
Pinch of freshly grated nutmeg
5 tablespoons cold water

FOR THE FILLING
1 medium-sized celery stalk
1 carrot, scraped
1 medium-sized red onion, cleaned
1 small clove garlic, peeled
10 sprigs Italian parsley, leaves only
5 large fresh basil leaves
1½ pounds very ripe fresh tomatoes or 1½ pounds drained canned tomatoes, preferably imported Italian
2 tablespoons olive oil
2 tablespoons (1 ounce) sweet butter
Salt and freshly ground black pepper

PLUS
3 extra-large eggs
½ cup grated *Parmigiano*
1 large very ripe fresh tomato
(optional)

TO SERVE
Fresh basil leaves

Preheat the oven to 375 degrees. Place the tart pan in the oven and bake for 35 minutes. Remove the pan from the oven, lift out the foil and weights or beans, return the pan to the oven and bake until the crust is golden, about 10 minutes.

Meanwhile, finish preparing the filling: Add the eggs and *Parmigiano* to the cooled tomato sauce. Taste for salt and pepper and mix very well with a wooden spoon.

Remove the tart pan from the oven (leaving the oven on). Let the crust cool for at least 15 minutes, then pour in the prepared filling. If desired, very thinly slice the tomato, remove all the seeds and arrange all the slices over the filling in the crust.

Bake the tart for 20 minutes longer. Remove the pan from the oven and let the tart cool for 15 minutes before transferring it from the tart pan to a serving dish. Slice the tart like a pie and serve it with the fresh basil leaves.

Serves 6 to 8.

DADOLATA DI POLENTA

Polenta "Cubes" in Spicy Sauce

Fried polenta is often used as the basis for an appetizer. It can be cut into slices (like crostini *) and embellished with chopped wild mushrooms or other toppings (called* Crostini di polenta*) or, as in* Dadolata di polenta, *it can be cubed, tossed in a piquant sauce and sprinkled with uncooked chopped garlic and parsley. In either case, the polenta should be prepared in advance because it must cool before it can be cut. In contrast, the finished dish must be served hot. Not even the most adventurous of the* nuova cucina *cooks has suggested eating polenta "salad." Both of the above are delicious and unclichéed appetizers.*

Prepare the polenta: In a large pot, bring the broth to a boil, then add salt to taste. In a very slow but steady stream, add the cornmeal, simultaneously stirring with a wooden spoon, preferably a flat wooden polenta spoon. Stir slowly, without stopping, for about 40 to 50 minutes, until the polenta is smooth, beginning to time from the moment when all the polenta has been added to the pot. If lumps form, push them against the side of the pan to crush them. Spread the cooked polenta out on a lightly oiled smooth surface, such as marble or aluminum foil, until completely cooled. The thickness of the layer of polenta should not exceed 1 inch.

Prepare the sauce: Finely slice the onion and finely chop the garlic. Heat the oil in a medium-sized casserole over low heat and when the oil is warm, add the prepared aromatic vegetables and sauté for 10 minutes or until the onion is translucent. Add the anchovies and mash them with a fork. Season with salt, pepper and the hot red pepper flakes. Add the vinegar, let it evaporate for 15 minutes, then put in the water and simmer for 20 minutes, or until the sauce is reduced by one third.

Meanwhile, cut the polenta into 1-inch cubes. Combine the vegetable and olive oils in a fryer and heat the oil to 375 degrees. Fry the polenta cubes until lightly golden all over. Drain them on a dish covered with paper towels.

When all the polenta cubes are ready, coarsely chop the parsley and finely chop the garlic and mix them together. Pour the hot sauce over the polenta, sprinkle on the chopped parsley and garlic, mix well and serve.

Serves 8.

2 quarts cold chicken or meat broth, preferably homemade
¾ pound coarse yellow cornmeal, preferably imported Italian
Salt and freshly ground black pepper

FOR THE SAUCE
1 small red onion, peeled
2 medium-sized cloves garlic, peeled
⅓ cup olive oil
2 whole anchovies, packed in salt, boned and rinsed, or 4 anchovy fillets, packed in oil, drained
Salt and freshly ground black pepper
A large pinch of hot red pepper flakes
¼ cup red wine vinegar
1½ cups cold water

TO FRY THE POLENTA
1 quart vegetable oil (⅔ corn oil, ⅓ sunflower oil)
4 tablespoons olive oil

TO SERVE
20 sprigs Italian parsley, leaves only
3 large cloves garlic, peeled

ZAMPINA DI VITELLA ALL'AGRO

Calves' Feet Salad

8 pounds calves' feet (yields about
    2 pounds of meat)
Coarse-grained salt
1 medium-sized carrot, scraped
1 medium-sized red onion, cleaned
1 celery stalk
10 sprigs Italian parsley

TO SERVE
6 tablespoons olive oil
Salt and freshly ground black pepper
Juice of 1 large lemon
10 sprigs Italian parsley, leaves only

*C*alves feet, which are eaten warm in Bollito misto (a main course of mixed boiled meats) are also eaten cold as a salad. Most often this salad is simply dressed with olive oil, but in Campi Bisenzio, outside of Florence, lemon juice is added to the oil to make the traditional all'agro dish presented here. Campi was for many centuries a center for raising sheep, and these were the sheep that provided the wool for the fine cloth that earned Florence its wealth. Campi has existed for such a long time that even though it is considered a suburb of Florence, it has developed its own unique cuisine. Both this dish and a pasta specialty made with a sauce of pecora (full-grown sheep, not lamb or mutton) are unknown in Florence.

During Roman times, when Florentia was a military town, merchants lived outside the city's walls and villages grew up along the main roads leading out of town. For example, Sesto Fiorentino was named after the sixth marker on the Roman road. The next town, Prato, meaning meadow, dates back to at least the seventh century. As Florence grew over the centuries, these towns grew also, so that today there is just one large urbanized area in which one town leads into the next. Despite this melding, the many centuries of separate existence cannot be forgotten as each place retains totally independent traditions. This is perhaps the most difficult concept for non-Italians to grasp—that places that are so close together can, as a result of their long, separate histories, remain so distinct.

Soak the calves' feet in a bowl of cold water for 1 hour.

Place a medium-sized pot of cold water over medium heat and when the water reaches a boil, add coarse salt to taste, then all the vegetables. When the water returns to a boil, drain the calves' feet and add them to the pot. Let cook, discarding the foam that forms on top, for at least 2 hours, or until the meat is very soft.

Transfer the meat to a serving dish and let cool completely. Discard all the bones and the poaching broth. Cut the meat into 1-inch pieces and dress it with the olive oil, salt, black pepper and lemon juice. Let marinate for at least ½ hour before serving with the parsley leaves sprinkled all over.

Serves 6.

BREADS · FOCACCIAS · PIZZAS

Bread is perhaps the most precious food for the Tuscans, and the supremacy of Tuscan bread in Italy comes from its combination of lightness, great flavor, variety and versatility. By using a simple base of flour, yeast and water, and making a few additions and substitutions, Tuscans have developed an enormous number of recipes. In their breads, they commonly employ whole-wheat flour, chestnut flour, farro flour and chick-pea flour as well as cornmeal. Added to the dough are such flavorful ingredients as olives, herbs—rosemary and sage, for example—and nuts. There is also the additional category of flat breads, with variations in form (focacce, pizze and schiacciate) as well as seasonings (such as garlic, garlic paste, olive paste, basil and cracklings).

Since hard wheat was probably unknown in Roman times, the bread of that era was most likely made with a soft wheat flour like farro. Pane toscano, which utilizes a flour that is harder than farro, is made with a very similar technique to that employing the older farro flour, indicating that the technique for making bread has not changed significantly over the centuries.

As was the case in the ancient world, in modern Tuscany left-over bread is never thrown away. It is reused for soups, salads, the much-used bread crumbs, crostini and croutons.

Light, crusty Pane toscano *is the basic bread of all Tuscany. Its yeastiness echoes that of the great Tuscan wines, but in order to maintain its adaptability, its flavor is kept neutral. The pinch of salt added to the sponge is not for flavor, but to interact with the yeast; indeed, the bread tastes saltless. It is this bread's neutrality, though, that makes it so versatile. With the slightest alteration— some salt and a little olive oil dripped over it, for example, or the addition of an herb to the dough—it metamorphoses into a whole other magnificence, some examples of which follow.*

FOR THE SPONGE
¾ cup plus 1 tablespoon
    unbleached all-purpose flour
1 ounce fresh compressed yeast or
    2 packages active dry yeast
½ cup lukewarm or hot water,
    depending on the yeast
Pinch of salt

FOR THE DOUGH
5 cups unbleached all-purpose flour
1¾ cups lukewarm water

Prepare the sponge: Place the ¾ cup of flour in a small bowl and make a well in the center. Dissolve the yeast in the water, stirring with a wooden spoon. Add the pinch of salt. Pour the dissolved yeast into the well and mix very well with the wooden spoon, until the flour is incorporated. Sprinkle the additional tablespoon of flour over the sponge, then cover the bowl with a cotton dish towel and let rest, in a warm place away from drafts, until the sponge has doubled in size, about 1 hour. (Two signs that the sponge has doubled in size are the disappearance of the tablespoon of flour or the formation of large cracks on top.)

Arrange the 5 cups of flour in a mound on a board, then make a well in the center. Place the sponge in the well, along with ½ cup of the water. With a wooden spoon, carefully mix together all the ingredients in the well, then add the remaining water and start mixing with your hands, gradually absorbing the flour from the inside rim of the well. Keep mixing until all but about ½ cup of the flour is incorporated, then knead the dough with the palms of your hands, in a folding motion, until it is homogeneous and smooth, about 15 minutes, incorporating the remaining flour, to keep the dough from sticking. Give the dough the shape you prefer (a long or round loaf), then place it in a floured cotton dish towel. Wrap the dough tightly in the towel and let it rest, in a warm place away from drafts, until doubled in size, about 1 hour.

To improvise a brick oven, line the bottom shelf of your oven with unglazed terra-cotta tiles. Preheat the oven to 375 degrees. In order to adequately heat the tiles, you must preheat the oven for twice as long as is normally necessary.

When the dough is ready, quickly unfold the wrapped dough directly onto the tiles. Bake the bread for about 55 minutes, until it sounds hollow when tapped. Do not open the oven for 30 minutes after you have placed the dough inside it.

Let the bread cool on a rack before serving.

Makes 1 loaf.

HARD AND SOFT WHEAT

The ancient soft wheat called farro in Italian, spelt or emmer in English, was the predominant wheat of ancient Rome, and was used both whole and ground for cereals and breads. Though this wheat has become less common since hard wheat has become so popular, it is still used in Tuscany: whole, as the basis of a famous soup from Lucca (Minestra or Zuppa di farro) and ground, in Pane di farro, a rustic bread from the mountainous Garfagnana in the Lucchesia area of northern Tuscany. Interestingly, even pasta does not depend on the use of the hard-wheat flour, as pasta was made in Roman times and is today still made with farro flour in these same areas of Garfagnana. And couscous, of course, is simply coarsely ground wheat.

P A N E   D I   F A R R O

Lucca Soft Wheat Bread

GARFAGNANA

Prepare the sponge: Place the 1½ cups of flour in a small bowl and make a well in the center. Dissolve the yeast in the lukewarm or hot water and pour it into the well along with the salt. Mix very well with a wooden spoon until a very smooth sponge forms. Sprinkle the remaining tablespoon of flour over the sponge, cover the bowl with a cotton towel and let rest, in a warm place away from drafts, until the sponge has doubled in size, about 1 hour. (Two signs that the sponge has doubled in size are the disappearance of the tablespoon of flour or the formation of large cracks on top.)

Arrange the 2 cups of all-purpose flour in a ring on a board. Place the farro flour inside the ring, and when the sponge is ready, place it over the farro flour. Using a wooden spoon, start incorporating the sponge and the farro flour, then start adding the water, little by little. Add the salt. When all the water is added, start incorporating the all-purpose flour and continue to mix until a dough forms. Sprinkle the remaining ¼ cup of flour on the board and knead the dough with the palms of your hands, in a folding motion, for 5 minutes.

Heavily flour a cotton towel. Shape the dough into a 12-inch loaf and place it in the prepared towel. Wrap the towel all around

FOR THE SPONGE
1½ cups plus 1 tablespoon
    unbleached all-purpose flour
1 ounce fresh compressed yeast or
    2 packages active dry yeast
1 cup lukewarm or hot water,
    depending on the yeast
A large pinch of salt

FOR THE DOUGH
2 cups plus ¼ cup unbleached
    all-purpose flour
1 cup farro flour
1 cup lukewarm water or milk
Pinch of salt

The same straw that is used to make the famous Florentine hats is used in the countryside to stop flasks of young wine.

and tuck in the ends. Let the dough rest, in a warm place away from drafts, until doubled in size, about 1 hour.

Place one or more large unglazed terra-cotta tiles over the middle shelf of your oven and preheat the oven to 375 degrees. When ready, transfer the dough onto the terra-cotta tiles and bake for 50 minutes. Remove from the oven and let the bread rest for at least 1 hour before serving.

Makes 1 loaf.

PANE SCURO ALLE NOCI

Whole-Wheat Nut Bread

Pane scuro alle noci *is a Tuscan bread enriched with chopped nuts—harking back to the days when chopped or ground nuts were used more often in cooking—and just a little whole-wheat flour. Unlike the more usual Tuscan dark bread, the whole-wheat flour is kept to a minimum and is sifted in order to remove some of the bran. (In Italy, the wheat kernels are not pulverized—which turns the bran to powder—but are put through a cylindrical grinder that allows some of the larger pieces of bran to remain in the flour.) Tuscan breads made with a large amount of whole-wheat flour are simply called* Pane scuro. *When the bread is made predominantly with whole-wheat flour, it is referred to as* Pane integrale.

Place the cup of flour in a small bowl and make a well in the center. Dissolve the yeast in the water, then pour it into the well along with the salt. Mix with a wooden spoon until a very smooth sponge forms. Sprinkle on the remaining tablespoon of flour, cover the bowl with a towel and let rest, in a warm place away from drafts, until the sponge has doubled in size, about 1 hour. (Two signs that the sponge has doubled in size are the disappearance of the tablespoon of flour or the formation of large cracks on top.)

    Arrange the 4½ cups all-purpose flour in a mound on a board. Make a large well in the center, then place the whole-wheat flour, walnuts, salt and pepper to taste in the well. When the sponge is ready, place it in the well with the other ingredients, then gradually add the water, mixing with a wooden spoon. When all the water is used up, a quite thick batter should be formed. Start taking some of the flour from the edges of the well, then, working with your hands, incorporate more of the flour. When a dough is formed, start kneading it with the palms of your hands in a folding motion, until all the flour is used up, about 5 minutes.

    Heavily flour a cotton dish towel, then tightly wrap the dough in the towel and let it rest, in a warm place away from drafts, until doubled in size, about 1 hour.

    Place one large or several smaller unglazed terra-cotta tiles on the middle shelf of your oven and preheat the oven to 400 degrees. When the dough is ready, transfer it onto the tile and bake for 1 hour 20 minutes. Remove the bread from the oven and cool for 1 hour before serving.

Makes 1 loaf.

FOR THE SPONGE
1 cup plus 1 tablespoon
    unbleached all-purpose flour
2 ounces fresh compressed yeast or
    4 packages active dry yeast
½ cup lukewarm or hot water,
    depending on the yeast
Pinch of salt

FOR THE DOUGH
4½ cups unbleached all-purpose
    flour
1 cup whole-wheat flour, sifted to
    remove any large pieces of bran
½ cup walnuts, coarsely chopped
A large pinch of salt
Freshly ground black pepper
2 cups lukewarm water

36 BREADS · FOCACCIAS · PIZZAS

OLIVE BREADS

The following two olive breads, though different, start with similar ingredients. The Pane di olive *calls for finely chopped black olives and black pepper and uses enough yeast to keep it refined and light. In contrast, the* Pane alla Garfagnana con olive, *made with coarsely chopped olives, uses less yeast and incorporates corn-meal into the white flour, making it rather rough and countrified.*

P A N E   D I   O L I V E

Bread with Chopped Olives

25 large black Greek olives
1 tablespoon olive oil

FOR THE SPONGE
1 cup plus 1 tablespoon
    unbleached all-purpose flour
3 ounces fresh compressed yeast or
    6 packages active dry yeast
¾ cup lukewarm or hot water,
    depending on the yeast
Pinch of salt

FOR THE DOUGH
5½ cups unbleached all-purpose
    flour
1½ cups lukewarm water
2 teaspoons salt
1 teaspoon freshly ground black
    pepper

Pit the olives and finely chop them on a board. Transfer them (about 6 ounces of chopped olives) to a crockery or glass bowl, then add the olive oil and mix very well with a wooden spoon.

Prepare the sponge: Place the cup of flour in a small bowl and make a well in the center. Dissolve the yeast in the water, then pour it into the well, along with the salt. Mix with a wooden spoon until all the flour is absorbed. Sprinkle the remaining tablespoon of flour over the sponge. Cover the bowl with a cotton towel and let rest, in a warm place away from drafts, until the sponge has doubled in size, about 1 hour. (Two signs that the sponge has doubled in size are the disappearance of the tablespoon of flour or the formation of large cracks on top.)

When the sponge is ready, arrange the flour in a mound on a board. Make a large well in the flour, then add the risen sponge, along with the olives, water, salt and pepper. With a wooden spoon, start mixing all the ingredients in the well, then start incorporating some of the flour from the edges of the well, a little at a time, until a rather thick batter forms. Use your hands to incorporate more flour, until a dough is formed, then knead with the palms of your hands, in a folding motion, until the dough is homogeneous and smooth, about 5 minutes. By that time all the flour should be used up.

Shape the dough into a long loaf, completely wrap the dough in a very well floured cotton towel and let rest, in a warm place away from drafts, until doubled in size.

Line the middle shelf of your oven with unglazed terra-cotta tiles and preheat the oven to 400 degrees. When the dough is ready, transfer it onto the tiles in the oven and bake for 1 hour 20 minutes, or until the loaf produces a hollow sound when tapped. Let the bread cool on a rack for at least 1 hour before serving.

Makes 1 loaf.

PANE ALLA GARFAGNANA CON OLIVE

Garfagnana-Style Bread with Olives

Prepare the sponge: Place 1½ cups of the white flour and the cornmeal in a large bowl, mix very well and make a well in the center. Dissolve the yeast in the water and pour it into the well, along with the olive oil and salt. Mix very well with a wooden spoon, then start incorporating the flour from the edges of the well, until all the flour is absorbed. Sprinkle on the tablespoon of flour, cover the bowl with a towel and let the sponge rest, in a warm place away from drafts, for at least 5 hours.

Arrange the remaining 2 cups of flour on a board, scatter the olives all over it, then add the risen sponge. Mix very well, incorporating the flour a little at a time, then start kneading, in a folding motion, for 2 minutes, or until smooth.

Lightly oil a 14-inch round baking dish. Transfer the dough to the dish and use your fingers to spread out the dough to cover it. Cover the dish with a cotton towel and let rest, in a warm place away from drafts, until the dough has doubled in size, about 1 hour.

Preheat the oven to 375 degrees. When ready, bake the bread for 1 hour. Let the bread cool on a rack for at least 1 hour before serving.

Makes 1 loaf.

3 ½ cups plus 1 tablespoon
    unbleached all-purpose flour
1 ¼ cups coarse yellow cornmeal,
    preferably imported Italian
1 ounce fresh compressed yeast or
    2 packages dry active yeast
2 cups lukewarm or hot water,
    depending on the yeast
5 tablespoons olive oil
Salt
6 ounces large black Greek olives,
    pitted and coarsely chopped

As an alternative to using pesticides, bottles of sugared water are placed in the olive branches to catch the flies that can harm the olives.

Bread from Lucca

Although today in Lucca Pane toscano *is the standard, at one time this area was known for its own bread called* Pane lucchese. *A slightly sweet loaf that counts milk and a little sugar among its ingredients, it is now confined to breakfast— if it is served at all, as it has become quite rare. Because* Pane lucchese *is baked on a baking pan, not directly on hot bricks, its crust is much softer than that of* Pane toscano. *It would be a great shame if this bread were to disappear, as it adds further variety to the Tuscan repertoire.*

4 cups plus 1 tablespoon
    unbleached all-purpose flour
1 cup whole-wheat flour

FOR THE SPONGE
1 teaspoon sugar
3 teaspoons salt
1½ ounces fresh compressed yeast
    or 3 packages active dry yeast
1 cup lukewarm or hot whole milk,
    depending on the yeast

FOR THE DOUGH
1 cup lukewarm whole milk
¼ cup unbleached all-purpose flour
    for kneading

TO BAKE THE BREAD
1 tablespoon (½ ounce) sweet
    butter

Mix the all-purpose and whole-wheat flours together. Place the sugar, salt and yeast in a crockery or glass bowl and pour the milk over it. Mix very well to dissolve the yeast completely, then, 1 cup at a time, add 2 cups of the mixed flour, mixing very well with a wooden spoon. When the 2 cups of flour are incorporated, sprinkle on the tablespoon of flour and cover the bowl with a cotton dish towel. Let the sponge rest, in a warm place away from drafts, until doubled in size, about 1 hour. (Two signs that the sponge has doubled in size are the disappearance of the tablespoon of flour or the formation of large cracks on top.)

When ready, add the milk to the sponge, mix very well, then add 2 more cups of the mixed flour and keep mixing with a wooden spoon until a dough forms. Spread out the remaining mixed flour on a board and transfer the dough from the bowl onto the flour. Start kneading, using a folding motion, until all the flour is used up. Sprinkle the ¼ cup of flour on the board and knead the dough for 10 minutes more. Shape the dough into a loaf about 15 inches long, heavily flour a cotton towel and tightly wrap the dough. Let rest, in a warm place away from drafts, until doubled in size, about 1 hour.

Preheat the oven to 375 degrees and lightly butter a cookie sheet. When ready, transfer the dough onto the prepared sheet and bake for 55 minutes. Remove from the oven, transfer the bread to a rack and cool for at least 2 hours before serving.

Makes 1 loaf.

Following pages: Focaccia alle erbe *(Herb-Flavored Focaccia),* La Mantovana *(the antique pound cake) and candy-covered almonds, called* confetti, *on a table in front of the Ospedale del Ceppo in Pistoia. The arcade, with its beautiful glazed terracotta frieze from the workshop of the Della Robbia, was added in 1514 when this hospital became a branch in the Florentine hospital system. The frieze is said to reflect the influence of the great Florentine sculptors Verrocchio, Michelangelo's teacher, and Benedetto da Maiano. The word "ceppo" means tree trunk, and it is part of the hospital's name because the carved stump of a tree trunk once sat in this piazza and served as a container in which people could place contributions to the hospital.*

Rustic Cornmeal Bread

The ring-shaped Ciambella toscana, a very rustic loaf made with cornmeal and boiled mashed potatoes, is one of the few Tuscan breads that are baked in a mold rather than directly on hot bricks in the oven. Although potato has some of the qualities of yeast since the alcohol it gives off when cooked makes flour rise (one of the best pizza doughs calls for potato instead of yeast), here it is used more for the full-bodied texture it creates when combined with cornmeal. The majority of Tuscan dishes that include cornmeal among their ingredients—aside from polenta itself—come from this same area of the Garfagnana, the mountains north of Lucca.

1 large all-purpose potato
(about 6 ounces)
Coarse-grained salt

FOR THE SPONGE
1½ cups plus 1 tablespoon
unbleached all-purpose flour
2 ounces fresh compressed yeast or
4 packages active dry yeast
1 cup lukewarm or hot water,
depending on the yeast
Salt

FOR THE DOUGH
4 cups unbleached all-purpose flour
1 cup fine or coarse stone-ground
yellow cornmeal, preferably
imported Italian
Salt
1½ cups lukewarm water

Boil the potato, with the skin on, in salted water, until very soft. While still hot, peel the potato and rice it with a potato ricer into a crockery or glass bowl, using the disc with the smallest holes. Let the potato rest until needed.

Meanwhile, prepare the sponge: Place the 1½ cups of flour in a bowl and make a well in the center. Dissolve the yeast in the lukewarm or hot water. Pour the dissolved yeast in the well of the flour, add salt and mix with a wooden spoon, until all the flour is incorporated and a very smooth dough forms. Sprinkle the remaining tablespoon of flour all over the sponge, cover the bowl with a towel and let the sponge rest, in a warm place away from drafts, until doubled in size, about 1 hour. (Two signs that the sponge has doubled in size are the disappearance of the table-spoon of flour or the formation of large cracks on top.)

Prepare the dough: Arrange the flour in a large ring on a board. Place the cornmeal and the riced potato in the center of the ring, along with the salt. When the sponge is ready, transfer it to the center of the ring. Using a wooden spoon, start com-bining all the ingredients in the center of the ring. Start adding the water, a little at a time and, when all the water is used up, little by little, using your hands, start incorporating the flour from the edges of the ring. When all but about ¾ cup of the flour is incorporated, start kneading the dough, using the palms of your hands, in a folding motion, until all the flour is amalga-mated, about 10 minutes.

Lightly flour a 20-cup ring mold. Shape the dough into a ring and transfer it to the prepared mold. Cover the mold with a towel and let the dough rest until doubled in size, about 1 hour.

Preheat the oven to 375 degrees. When ready, bake the bread for 1 hour, or until a toothpick inserted in the center comes out dry. Remove from the oven, unmold the bread onto a rack and let cool for about 1 hour before serving.

Makes 1 ring loaf.

Covaccine, *the tiniest and thinnest of the pizza variations, used to be made by Tuscan farmers in order to test whether their wood-burning ovens were hot enough for bread-baking. When making* covaccine, *neither oil nor salt is added until after baking. In the recipe that follows semolina flour is added to the dough to create an even more countrified* covaccine.

Although Tuscan, mainly Florentine, is the basis of the classic Italian language, there are still many regional words that are used only in Tuscany and are not considered "good" Italian. Covaccine, *Tuscan vernacular for* schiacciata, *is one of them. While other regions admit to having dialects, Tuscans admit only to having a vernacular.*

Mix the semolina flour and the unbleached flour together. Place the flours in a mound on a board and make a well in the center. Dissolve the yeast in 1 cup of the water and dissolve the coarse salt in the remaining cup. Pour the dissolved yeast into the well of the flour and start mixing with a wooden spoon, incorporating some of the flour from the edges of the well. When a rather thick batter is formed, add the cup of salted water to the well, and keep working with the spoon, incorporating more flour. When a dough is formed, start kneading with your hands in a folding motion, until all but ¼ cup of the flour is incorporated.

Divide the dough into 16 pieces. Knead each piece for 30 seconds, giving it the shape of a roll. Cover each roll with a cotton dish towel and let rest, in a warm place away from drafts, until doubled in size, about 1 hour.

When ready, start rolling out the *covaccine*, one at a time, with a rolling pin, giving each the shape of a disc; the thickness of the layer of dough should not exceed ¼ inch. Let the *covaccine* rest between cotton towels, in a warm place away from drafts, until doubled in size, about 1 hour.

Line the middle shelf of your oven with unglazed terra-cotta tiles and preheat the oven to 400 degrees.

When ready, bake the *covaccine*, one or more at a time, according to the capacity of your oven, for 4 to 5 minutes on each side, until crisp. Remove from the oven, pour some olive oil all over and sprinkle on some salt. Serve hot.

Serves 16 as an appetizer.

1 pound very fine semolina flour
3 cups unbleached all-purpose flour
2 ounces fresh compressed yeast or
    4 packages active dry yeast
2 cups lukewarm or hot water,
    depending on the yeast
2 teaspoons coarse-grained salt

TO SERVE
Olive oil
Fine salt

FOCACCINE AL SALE GROSSO

Salted Little Focaccine

The small focaccine of the Versilia coast use butter or lard (rather than oil) plus coarse-grained salt in the dough. The olive oil plus additional salt are reserved for sprinkling over the bread after baking, the usual procedure for Tuscan flat bread. Focaccine are available inland as well, thanks to the residents of the large Tuscan cities who frequent the coastal resorts during the summer and call for focaccine upon their return home. You can see the focaccine in the photograph of the feast for the Fireworks in Florence on page 69.

FOR THE SPONGE

1½ cups plus 1 tablespoon
    unbleached all-purpose flour
1 ounce fresh compressed yeast or
    2 packages active dry yeast
1 cup lukewarm or hot water,
    depending on the yeast
Pinch of salt

FOR THE DOUGH

2 cups unbleached all-purpose
    flour
4 tablespoons (2 ounces) sweet
    butter or lard, at room
    temperature
1 tablespoon coarse-grained salt

TO BAKE

6 tablespoons olive oil
2 tablespoons cold water

TO SERVE

4 tablespoons olive oil
About 1 tablespoon coarse-
    grained salt

Prepare the sponge: Place the 1½ cups of flour in a small bowl and make a well in the center. Dissolve the yeast in the water, then pour it into the well, along with the salt. Mix very well with a wooden spoon, incorporating all the flour. Sprinkle the remaining tablespoon of flour on top. Cover the bowl with a cotton towel and let rest until the sponge has doubled in size, about 1 hour. (Two signs that the sponge has doubled in size are the disappearance of the tablespoon of flour or the formation of large cracks on top.)

When the sponge is ready, arrange the 2 cups flour in a mound on a board and make a large well in the center. Transfer the risen sponge to the well, along with the butter. Mix the sponge and the butter together very well, then start incorporating some of the flour from the edges of the well. When a ball of dough is formed, start kneading it with the palms of your hands, until the dough becomes very smooth and elastic, about 4 minutes. At that moment, add the coarse salt and knead the dough for 30 seconds more.

Divide the dough into 12 pieces and stretch each piece, using your hands or a rolling pin, into a disc about 6 inches in diameter. Transfer the discs onto two lightly oiled cookie sheets. When all the *focaccine* are on the sheets, mix the oil and the water in a small bowl, brush some of the oil mixture on each *focaccina* and prick the surface of each *focaccina* with a fork. Cover the cookie sheets with plastic wrap and place cotton towels over the wrap. Let the *focaccine* rest, in a warm place away from drafts, until doubled in size, about 1 hour.

Preheat the oven to 375 degrees. When ready, bake the *focaccine* for 20 minutes. Lightly oil their surface with the oil and sprinkle on a little coarse salt. Serve hot.

Serves 12 as an appetizer.

SCHIACCIATE AND FOCACCE

Full-sized schiacciate and focacce, which can be rectangular or round in shape (though focacce are a bit higher), are both cooked in heavily greased baking dishes as opposed to Tuscan breads, pizzas or covaccine, which are baked directly on hot tiles. Schiacciate and focacce are both made with oil, butter or lard in the dough and may be seasoned with a variety of herbs or other flavorings.

I begin this grouping of recipes with Schiacciata coi siccioli. Siccioli are little pieces of pork rind that are rendered until crisp. These very flavorful "cracklings" are inserted into the dough before baking. Rosemary (or sage) leaves, olive oil and black pepper complete the flavorings. This dough may also be used to make loaves of bread.

Next come the focacce recipes, the first of which—Focaccia alle olive—recalls our olive breads. Chopped black olives, butter or lard and black pepper are included in the dough, on which olive oil is sprinkled before it is left to rise. Once risen, the dough is studded with large pieces of olive. Focaccia all'aglio saltato is made with sautéed chopped garlic while Focaccia al ramerino calls for fresh rosemary (or rosemary preserved in salt or dried and blanched), but can be made with sage instead.

The Schiacciata coi siccioli and Focaccia al ramerino, as well as the ingredients for another focaccia, appear in the photograph of the magnificent medieval kitchen of the abbey of Badia a Passignano on pages 48–49. Note the immense stone table, which is built into the floor, and the fireplace around which the entire community of monks used to sit. Not visible in the photo are the large flues that carry the heat of the fire to the upper floors. The ceiling of the kitchen is dome-shaped and very high. The abbey, which dates back to 1049, is surrounded by vineyards and olive groves, and has a working wine cellar that may date back to ancient Rome.

Schiacciata or Bread with "Siccioli"

FOR THE SPONGE

1¾ cups plus 1 tablespoon
    unbleached all-purpose flour
½ ounce fresh compressed yeast or
    1 package dry active yeast
1 cup lukewarm or hot water,
    depending on the yeast
Pinch of salt

FOR THE DOUGH

1 tablespoon rosemary leaves,
    fresh, preserved in salt, or
    dried and blanched or
    10 large sage leaves, fresh or
    preserved in salt
3 cups unbleached all purpose flour
1 tablespoon olive oil
¾ cup lukewarm water
Salt and freshly ground black pepper
1 ounce *siccioli* (or *ciccioli*)
    cracklings, crumbled (see
    instructions at end of recipe)

FOR THE *SCHIACCIATA*

6 tablespoons olive oil
Coarse-grained salt

FOR THE *SICCIOLI* (SEE NOTE)

12 ounces pork skin, cut into
    1-inch pieces
2 tablespoons olive oil
1 tablespoon salt

Following pages: Schiacciata coi
siccioli *(Bread with "Siccioli")* and
Focaccia al ramerino *(Focaccia with
Rosemary) topped with sage in the kitchen
of the* Badia a Passignano *in the
Chianti area. Also shown are the sponge,
oil and flour for another* focaccia.

Prepare the sponge: Place the 1¾ cups of flour in a medium-sized bowl and make a well in the center. Dissolve the yeast in the water, then add the dissolved yeast and salt to the well. Mix very well with a wooden spoon until all the flour is absorbed. Sprinkle on the remaining tablespoon of flour, cover the bowl with a cotton dish towel and let rest, in a warm place away from drafts, until doubled in size, about 1 hour. (Two signs that the sponge has doubled in size are the disappearance of the tablespoon of flour or the formation of large cracks on top.)

Coarsely chop the rosemary or sage on a board. Place the flour on a pastry board and make a large well in the center. Place the chopped herbs in the well, then the olive oil and the sponge. Add the water and the salt and pepper to taste. With a fork, start mixing all the ingredients in the well, then incorporate some of the flour from the edge, constantly mixing with the fork. Add the *siccioli*, then more flour, until a dough is formed. Start kneading with your hands until all the flour is absorbed, always in a folding motion. Knead for 5 minutes.

If preparing a loaf, shape dough into a long loaf, flour a cotton towel and wrap it tightly around the loaf. Let rest, in a warm place away from drafts, until doubled in size, about 1 hour.

If preparing a *schiacciata*, use 2 tablespoons of the oil to grease a 15½-by-10½-inch jelly-roll pan. Stretch the dough into a rectangle that is the same size as the pan, place the dough in the pan and pour the remaining olive oil all over. Prick the dough with a fork in several places and sprinkle on coarse salt. Cover the *schiacciata* with a piece of plastic wrap and a cotton dish towel and let rest, in a warm place away from drafts, until doubled in size, about 1 hour.

Preheat the oven to 400 degrees. When ready, bake for 40 minutes if preparing the *schiacciata* and 1 hour 5 minutes if preparing the bread, until it sounds hollow when tapped. The bread is better eaten at room temperature, the *schiacciata* quite hot.

Makes 1 loaf or 1 schiacciata.

Note: *Siccioli* (cracklings) can be purchased in markets selling ingredients for "soul food," or made at home as follows:

Place the pork skin, olive oil and salt in a medium-sized skillet (preferably iron) over very, very low heat; cover and let cook for 2 hours. Stir every so often with a wooden spoon, but be very careful to stay out of the way of splattering fat.

When the cracklings are ready, remove the skillet from the heat, let cool for 1 minute before uncovering, then, with a slotted spoon, transfer the cracklings to a dish to cool completely. Cracklings should be very crisp and chewy. Wait until the fat in the skillet is cool before discarding.

Olive Focaccia

CHIANTI AREA

Chianti landscape.

Prepare the sponge: Place the 2 cups of flour in a medium-sized bowl and make a well in the center. In a small bowl, dissolve the yeast in the water, stirring with a wooden spoon. Then pour the dissolved yeast into the well of the flour, add the salt and stir with a wooden spoon until all the flour is incorporated. Sprinkle the remaining tablespoon of flour over the sponge. Cover the bowl with a cotton dish towel and let the sponge rest, in a warm place away from drafts, until it has doubled in size, about 1 hour. (Two signs that the sponge has doubled in size are the disappearance of the tablespoon of flour or the formation of large cracks on top.)

When the sponge is ready, spread the 1¾ cups of flour all over a board, then spread the sponge over it, along with the olives and butter, seasoning with the salt and pepper. Start mixing the dough with your hands, incorporating all the flour, and knead until all the butter is completely amalgamated and dissolved.

Use 4 tablespoons of the oil to heavily grease a 15½-by-10½-inch jelly-roll pan. Use a rolling pin to stretch the dough into a rectangle that is the same size as the pan. Transfer the sheet of dough to the prepared pan, drip the remaining oil over the top, prick the dough all over with a fork, then cover with a piece of plastic wrap and a cotton towel, and let rest, in a warm place away from drafts, until doubled in size, about 1 hour.

Preheat the oven to 375 degrees. When the dough is ready, remove the plastic wrap, press the olive pieces into the dough, sprinkle on some coarse salt and bake for 40 minutes. Remove from the oven, transfer the *focaccia* to a board, cut into squares and serve.

Serves 12 as an appetizer.

FOR THE SPONGE
2 cups plus 1 tablespoon
　　unbleached all-purpose flour
1 ounce fresh compressed yeast or
　　2 packages active dry yeast
1¼ cups lukewarm or hot water,
　　depending on the yeast
Pinch of salt

FOR THE DOUGH
1¾ cups unbleached all-purpose
　　flour
15 large black Greek olives, pitted
　　and coarsely chopped (about
　　3 ounces)
4 tablespoons (2 ounces) sweet
　　butter or lard, at room
　　temperature
Salt and abundant freshly ground
　　black pepper

TO COOK THE *FOCACCIA*
8 tablespoons olive oil
6 large black Greek olives, pitted
　　and cut into large pieces
Coarse-grained salt

FOCACCIA ALL'AGLIO SALTATO

Focaccia with Sautéed Garlic

FOR THE SPONGE
1½ cups plus 1 tablespoon
    unbleached all-purpose flour
1 ounce fresh compressed yeast or
    2 packages active dry yeast
1 cup lukewarm or hot water,
    depending on the yeast
Pinch of salt

FOR THE DOUGH
6 large cloves garlic, peeled and
    coarsely chopped
5 tablespoons olive oil
2 cups unbleached all-purpose flour
¼ cup lukewarm water
½ tablespoon salt
Freshly ground black pepper

TO COOK THE *FOCACCIA*
6 tablespoons olive oil

TO SERVE
3 tablespoons olive oil
Coarse-grained salt and freshly
    ground black pepper

Prepare the sponge: Place the 1½ cups of flour in a medium-sized bowl and make a well in the center. Dissolve the yeast in the water in a small bowl, stirring with a wooden spoon. Pour the dissolved yeast into the well of the flour, add the salt and stir with a wooden spoon until all the flour is incorporated. Sprinkle the remaining tablespoon of flour over the sponge, then cover the bowl with a cotton dish towel and let the sponge rest, in a warm place away from drafts, until doubled in size, about 1 hour. (Two signs that the sponge has doubled in size are the disappearance of the tablespoon of flour or the formation of large cracks on top.)

When the sponge is ready, place the garlic with the oil in a small saucepan over medium heat and sauté until the garlic is very lightly golden. Remove from the heat and let rest for 10 minutes before using.

Arrange the 2 cups flour on a board, make a well in the center and put in the sponge, water, salt and pepper followed by the sautéed garlic and oil. Start mixing with a wooden spoon, incorporating all but 2 or 3 tablespoons of the flour, then start kneading the dough with your hands until it becomes elastic.

Use 2 tablespoons of the oil to heavily grease a 15½-by-10½-inch jelly-roll pan. Use a rolling pin to stretch the dough to the same size as the pan. Transfer the sheet of dough to the prepared pan, drip the remaining oil over the top and prick the dough all over with a fork. Cover with a piece of plastic wrap and a cotton towel, and let rest, in a warm place away from drafts, until doubled in size, about 1 hour.

Preheat the oven to 375 degrees. When the dough is ready, remove the plastic wrap and the cotton towel and bake for about 40 minutes. Remove the *focaccia* from the oven and transfer it to a board. Drip the 3 tablespoons of olive oil all over, season with salt and pepper and cut into squares.

Serves 12 as an appetizer.

FOCACCIA AL RAMERINO SALTATO

Focaccia with "Sautéed" Rosemary

Prepare the sponge: Place the 2 cups of flour in a large bowl and make a well in the center. Dissolve the yeast in the water, then pour it into the well along with the salt. Use a wooden spoon to incorporate the flour, little by little, until it is all used. Sprinkle on the remaining tablespoon of flour, cover the bowl with a cotton dish towel and let rest, in a warm place away from drafts, until the sponge has doubled in size, about 1 hour. (Two signs that the sponge has doubled in size are the disappearance of the tablespoon of flour or the formation of large cracks on top.)

Heat the oil in a small saucepan over low heat and when the oil is warm, remove the pan from the heat and add the rosemary.

Spread out the 2 cups of flour on a board and place the sponge in it. Make a well in the sponge, then pour in the oil with the rosemary, water and salt and pepper to taste. First mix all the ingredients in the well together, then start incorporating the flour, little by little, until a ball of dough is formed. Knead the dough in a folding motion, until all the flour is incorporated and the dough is elastic and smooth.

Use 4 tablespoons of the oil to grease a 15½-by-10½-inch jelly-roll pan. Use a rolling pin to stretch the dough into a rectangle that is the same size as the pan. Place the dough in the pan, spreading it out to reach the sides if necessary. Drip the remaining olive oil all over, then sprinkle on coarse salt to taste. Prick the dough all over with a fork, then cover the pan with plastic wrap and a cotton towel, and let rest, in a warm place away from drafts, until doubled in size, about 1 hour.

Preheat the oven to 400 degrees. When the dough is ready, bake it for 30 minutes. Remove the *focaccia* from the oven and sprinkle with more coarse salt and olive oil. Cut into squares and serve hot.

Serves 12 as an appetizer.

FOR THE SPONGE
2 cups plus 1 tablespoon
    unbleached all-purpose flour
½ ounce fresh compressed yeast or
    1 package active dry yeast
1½ cups lukewarm or hot water,
    depending on the yeast
Pinch of salt

FOR THE DOUGH
4 tablespoons olive oil
3 tablespoons rosemary leaves,
    fresh, preserved in salt or dried
    and blanched or sage leaves,
    fresh or preserved in salt
2 cups unbleached all-purpose flour
¼ cup lukewarm water
Salt and freshly ground black pepper

TO BAKE THE *FOCACCIA*
7 tablespoons olive oil
Coarse-grained salt

FOCACCIA DEL CAVATORE

Focaccia of the Marble Workers

Focaccia del cavatore (Focaccia of the Marble Workers) is associated with the marble workers of the great quarries of Carrara, which are still active today, and from which so much of the beautiful white marble of Florentine sculpture was cut. The chopped walnuts in the Focaccia of the Marble Workers are believed to give the hardworking quarrymen additional energy for their labor.

Workers at Carrara have been digging since Roman times and the mountaintops have acquired a snow white color and peculiar shapes that the people have given such names as "The Sleeping Beauty" and "The Monster." The marble for Michelangelo's David came from Carrara, and in 1991, the quarries were searched for a piece of marble to replace the toe that had been damaged. It took nine months to find a matching piece because the marble cut for the sculpture had acquired a patina over the centuries.

FOR THE SPONGE

1½ cups plus 1 tablespoon
    unbleached all-purpose flour
1 ounce fresh compressed yeast or
    2 packages active dry yeast
1 cup lukewarm or hot water,
    depending on the yeast
Pinch of salt

FOR THE DOUGH

2½ cups unbleached all-purpose
    flour
½ cup lukewarm water
Salt and freshly ground black pepper
3 ounces shelled walnuts,
    coarsely chopped

TO BAKE THE *FOCACCIA*

4 tablespoons olive oil
2 tablespoons rosemary leaves,
    fresh, preserved in salt or dried
    and blanched

TO SERVE

Fine salt
Olive oil

Prepare the sponge: Place the 1½ cups of flour in a bowl and make a well in the center. Dissolve the yeast in the lukewarm or hot water and pour it into the well of the flour along with the salt. Mix with a wooden spoon, incorporating all the flour. Sprinkle the remaining tablespoon of flour over the sponge, cover the bowl with a cotton towel and let rest, in a warm place away from drafts, until the sponge has doubled in size, about 1 hour. (Two signs that the sponge has doubled in size are the disappearance of the tablespoon of flour or the formation of large cracks on top.)

Arrange the flour for the dough on a board, transfer the risen sponge onto the flour, then start kneading, incorporating the flour and gradually adding the water. When almost all the flour is used up, add a little salt and pepper and the walnuts to the dough and knead a little more.

Use 2 tablespoons of the oil to grease a 15½-by-10½-inch jelly-roll pan. Lightly stretch the dough with a rolling pin, transfer it to the prepared pan and stretch it to the size of the jelly-roll pan, using your fingers. Drip the remaining olive oil over the *focaccia*, sprinkle the rosemary leaves all over and cover the pan with plastic wrap. Place a cotton towel on top of the plastic wrap and let the dough rest, in a warm place away from drafts, until doubled in size, about 1 hour.

Preheat the oven to 375 degrees. When ready, bake the *focaccia* for 40 minutes. Remove from the oven, sprinkle with the fine salt and drizzle with olive oil. Cut into squares and serve.

Serves 8.

FOCACCIA AL BASILICO

Focaccia with Basil

To *achieve the basil flavor in* Focaccia al basilico, *fresh basil leaves are placed on the dough while it rises, then discarded; after the focaccia is baked, it is cut into squares and served in a basket with new basil leaves, allowing it to absorb additional flavor.*

Prepare the sponge: Place the 2 cups of flour in a large bowl and make a well in the center. Dissolve the yeast in the cup of water, then pour it into the well along with the salt. Use a wooden spoon to gradually incorporate the flour. Sprinkle on the remaining tablespoon of flour, cover the bowl with a cotton dish towel and let rest, in a warm place away from drafts, until the sponge has doubled in size, about 1 hour. (Two signs that the sponge has doubled in size are the disappearance of the tablespoon of flour or the formation of large cracks on top.)

When the sponge is ready, spread out the 1 ¼ cup of flour on a board and place the sponge in it. Add the butter, water and salt and pepper, and start incorporating all the ingredients into the sponge, kneading in a folding motion, until all the flour is incorporated and the dough is elastic and smooth.

Use 2 tablespoons of the oil to grease a 15½-by-10½-inch jelly-roll pan. Use a rolling pin to stretch the dough to the same size as the jelly-roll pan, then place the dough in the pan, spreading it out to reach the sides, if necessary. Use your index finger to make 15 indentations all over the top of the dough. Place a basil leaf in each one, then sprinkle coarse salt all over and drip the remaining 4 tablespoons olive oil to cover the entire surface. Prick the dough all over with a fork, then cover the pan with a piece of plastic wrap. Place a cotton dish towel over the pan and let the dough rest, in a warm place away from drafts, until doubled in size, about 1 hour.

Preheat the oven to 400 degrees. When the dough is ready, remove the towel, the plastic wrap and all the basil leaves, and bake for 35 minutes. Remove from the oven and cut into squares. Serve hot with more olive oil and coarse salt and the additional 20 fresh basil leaves.

Serves 12.

FOR THE SPONGE
2 cups plus 1 tablespoon
    unbleached all-purpose flour
½ ounce fresh compressed yeast or
    1 package active dry yeast
1 cup lukewarm or hot water,
    depending on the yeast
Pinch of salt

FOR THE DOUGH
1¼ cups unbleached all-purpose
    flour
4 tablespoons (2 ounces) sweet
    butter or lard, at room
    temperature
¼ cup lukewarm water
Salt and freshly ground black pepper

TO COOK THE *FOCACCIA*
6 tablespoons olive oil
15 large fresh basil leaves
Coarse-grained salt

TO SERVE
Several tablespoons olive oil
Coarse-grained salt
20 fresh basil leaves

FOCACCIA ALLE ERBE

Herb-Flavored Focaccia

The Focaccia alle erbe *from Empoli gets its name from the sage and rosemary added to the dough. This focaccia is presented with some of its raw ingredients and two desserts in the photograph on pages 40–41. The photo was taken in the* piazza *of the Ospedale del Ceppo in Pistoia, and the desserts come from this town, which is not far from Empoli. La Mantovana, to the right, is probably an ancestor of the modern pound cake, and despite its name, is typical of Prato and Pistoia, not Mantova. The little almond-covered candies are Pistoia's own special* confetti, *and are traditionally presented by the bride and groom to their wedding guests. The candies symbolize fertility, and I am not sure why the married couple gives these to the guests rather than the other way around.*

Prepare the sponge: Place 1 cup plus 2 tablespoons of the flour in a bowl and make a well in the center. In a small bowl, dissolve the yeast in the lukewarm or hot water and pour it into the well, along with the salt. Use a wooden spoon to, little by little, incorporate the flour from the inner part of the well. When all of it is incorporated, sprinkle the remaining tablespoon of flour over the sponge. Cover the bowl with a cotton dish towel and let rest, in a warm place away from drafts, until the sponge has doubled in size, about 1 hour. (Two signs that the sponge has doubled in size are the disappearance of the tablespoon of flour or the formation of large cracks on top.)

Finely chop the sage, rosemary and garlic all together on a board. Transfer the chopped ingredients to a small bowl and add the oil and salt and pepper to taste. Mix very well with a wooden spoon and let stand until needed.

When the sponge is ready, spread out the flour and cornmeal on a board. Transfer the sponge to the board and start mixing with your hands, incorporating more flour. Add the prepared herbs, then start adding the water a little at a time, until all the flour is incorporated. Knead the dough for 2 minutes more.

Heavily oil a 14-inch round baking dish or a 15½-by-10½-inch jelly-roll pan. Use your fingers or a rolling pin to spread out the dough in the prepared dish. Brush with a little oil, then

FOR THE SPONGE
1 cup plus 3 tablespoons
     unbleached all-purpose flour
1 ounce fresh compressed yeast or
     2 packages active dry yeast
¾ cup lukewarm or hot water,
     depending on the yeast
Pinch of salt

FOR THE DOUGH
10 large sage leaves, fresh or
     preserved in salt
2 tablespoons rosemary leaves,
     fresh, preserved in salt or dried
     and blanched
2 large cloves garlic, peeled
2 tablespoons olive oil
Salt and freshly ground black pepper
2¼ to 2½ cups unbleached
     all-purpose flour
1 cup coarse stone-ground
     yellow cornmeal, preferably
     imported Italian
¾ cup lukewarm water

TO BAKE THE *FOCACCIA*
2 tablespoons olive oil

TO SERVE (OPTIONAL)
Coarse-grained salt
2 tablespoons olive oil

cover with plastic wrap and a cotton towel. Let rest, in a warm place away from drafts, until doubled in size, about 1 hour.

When ready, preheat the oven to 375 degrees and bake the *focaccia* for 45 minutes. Remove from the oven and cool for a few minutes before transferring the *focaccia* to a board. Sprinkle with coarse-grained salt and 2 tablespoons olive oil, if desired. Cut into squares and serve warm.

Serves 8 to 10.

FOCACCIA VARIATIONS

Focaccia viareggina, from the port of Viareggio, is distinctive in that malt is added to the dough, which makes it unnecessary to prepare a sponge before mixing the dough. The Italian word malto *derives from the English word* malt, *a word of Anglo-Saxon rather than Latin origin, which makes it seem likely that malt was brought to Italy by the British. The question is, when? Britain and Florence maintained close relations from the ninth century because Florence needed British wool in addition to its own to make its famous cloth. Chaucer was ambassador to Florence in the fourteenth century, and the British fleet was the protector of Tuscany's independence for a time in the eighteenth century. Perhaps it was the British fleet at Viareggio or Livorno that gave the Italians malt, hoping to teach them how to make beer. Of course, wine has always remained supreme, but malt, derived from grains, could be used for its fermenting capabilities in breads as well as beverages. And so Italy does have several breads that use malt.*

Farther down the coast, below Livorno, we have the Maremma, where they make a type of stuffed focaccia called Focaccia ripiena alla maremmana. The "stuffing," which is actually incorporated into the dough rather than between two layers, is made with anchovy fillets and sautéed red onions. Anchovies are plentiful in the Tuscan seas, and, because of their ability to lift a flavor without dominating it, they form an important seasoning element in Tuscan cooking. Used in small quantities, they lend very little salt to a dish, and I am often surprised when I must put in additional salt.

FOCACCIA VIAREGGINA

Viareggio-Style Focaccia

Place the flour in a large bowl and make a well in the center. Put the butter, malt and salt in the well. Place the yeast in a medium-sized bowl, add the water and mix very well. Pour the dissolved yeast into the well of the flour with the other ingredients and mix with a wooden spoon, incorporating some of the flour. Keep incorporating the flour until a quite firm dough forms. Transfer the contents of the bowl to a board and start kneading the dough, incorporating more flour. Keep kneading until all the flour is used up, about 4 minutes.

Use 2 tablespoons of the oil to grease a 15½-by-10½-inch jelly-roll pan, then stretch the dough, using a rolling pin, to the same size as the pan. Cover the pan with lightly oiled plastic wrap, then place a cotton towel over the plastic and let the dough rest, in a warm place away from drafts, until doubled in size, about 1 hour.

Preheat the oven to 375 degrees. Combine the remaining 6 tablespoons of oil, 1 tablespoon of cold water and a large pinch (almost 2 teaspoons) of coarse salt in a small container and mix very well with a wooden spoon, until the salt is almost dissolved.

When the dough is ready, immediately brush the whole surface of the *focaccia* with the prepared oil mixture, then use the point of your finger to make several depressions in the dough. Fill these small holes with the remaining oil mixture. Bake for 35 minutes. Serve hot.

Serves 12.

1¾ pounds unbleached all-purpose
    flour
1 tablespoon (½ ounce) sweet
    butter or lard
1 scant tablespoon malt
Salt
1 ounce fresh compressed yeast or
    2 packages active dry yeast
2 cups lukewarm or hot water,
    depending on the yeast

TO BAKE THE *FOCACCIA*
8 tablespoons olive oil
Coarse-grained salt

58 BREADS · FOCACCIAS · PIZZAS

FOCACCIA RIPIENA ALLA MAREMMANA

Focaccia with Onions

FOR THE STUFFING
1 pound red onions, cleaned
5 tablespoons olive oil
Salt and freshly ground black pepper
A large pinch of hot red pepper
    flakes
2 cups lukewarm water
4 whole anchovies, packed in salt,
    boned and rinsed, or 8 anchovy
    fillets, packed in oil, drained

FOR THE SPONGE
1½ cups plus 1 tablespoon
    unbleached all-purpose flour
1 ounce fresh compressed yeast or
    2 packages active dry yeast
Pinch of salt
1 cup lukewarm or hot water,
    depending on the yeast

FOR THE DOUGH
2½ cups unbleached all-purpose
    flour plus ½ cup for kneading
Salt and freshly ground black pepper

TO BAKE THE *FOCACCIA*
6 tablespoons olive oil

TO SERVE
4 tablespoons olive oil
Coarse-grained salt

Prepare the stuffing: Very thinly slice the onions and soak them in a bowl of cold water for ½ hour.

Meanwhile, prepare the sponge: Place the 1½ cups of flour in a bowl. Dissolve the yeast and salt in the water, then incorporate into the flour. Sprinkle the tablespoon of flour over the sponge. Cover and let rest, in a warm place away from drafts, until the sponge has doubled in size, about 1 hour. (Two signs that the sponge has doubled in size are the disappearance of the tablespoon of flour or the formation of large cracks on top.)

Drain the onions, then place them in a skillet with the olive oil and set the skillet over medium heat. Sauté the onions for 15 minutes, then season with salt, black pepper and hot red pepper flakes. Cook the onions for 45 minutes, adding the water as needed. By that time, the onions should be soft and there should be no liquid left in the skillet. Transfer the contents of the skillet to a crockery or glass bowl and let stand for ½ hour, until lukewarm. Coarsely chop the anchovies, add them to the bowl with the onions and mix very well.

When the sponge is ready, arrange the 2½ cups flour in a mound on a board and make a well in the center. Place the lukewarm onion mixture and its juices in the well, along with the sponge. Season with a little salt and pepper, then start incorporating the flour from the edges of the well, until a quite firm dough has formed. (The amount of flour needed depends on the amount of liquid in the onions. Onions with less liquid will require less flour.) Add the remaining ½ cup of flour and knead the dough for 2 minutes more.

Use 2 tablespoons of the oil to grease a 15½-by-10½-inch jelly-roll pan. Use a rolling pin to stretch the dough to the same size as the jelly-roll pan, then transfer the stretched dough to the pan and drip the remaining 4 tablespoons oil over the dough. Prick the *"schiaccia"* (as *focaccia* is known in Maremma) all over with a fork, then cover the pan with plastic wrap and a cotton towel. Let the *focaccia* rest, in a warm place away from drafts, until doubled in size, about 1 hour.

Preheat the oven to 375 degrees. When ready, bake the *focaccia* for 40 minutes. Remove from the oven, drip the oil all over the top and sprinkle on coarse salt. Cut into squares and serve hot.

Serves 12.

GRISSINI AL RAMERINO

Rosemary Grissini

FLORENCE

60 BREADS · FOCACCIAS · PIZZAS

The popular Italian breadsticks called grissini *are widely available commercially, but like so many foods, they are even more delicious when homemade. The best-known* grissini *are associated with Torino in Piemonte, and may well have originated there.* Grissini al ramerino *include the very Tuscan touch of rosemary in the dough.*

Most often, after the grissini *dough rises, it is cut with a knife into long strips that are stretched individually by hand, but by using the* tagliatelle *cutter of a pasta machine you can achieve better and more uniform results in one-tenth the time. When I invented this technique, grissini-making became an everyday routine for me.* Grissini *emerge from the oven crisp and flaky, and are delicious by themselves as a snack, or as an accompaniment to other foods.*

FOR THE SPONGE

2 cups plus 1 tablespoon
    unbleached all-purpose flour
½ ounce fresh compressed yeast or
    1 package active dry yeast
1½ cups lukewarm or hot water,
    depending on the yeast
½ teaspoon salt

FOR THE DOUGH

2 cups plus ½ cup unbleached
    all-purpose flour
4 tablespoons olive oil
4 tablespoons rosemary leaves,
    fresh, preserved in salt or
    dried and blanched, very
    coarsely chopped
Salt and freshly ground black pepper

Prepare the sponge: Place the 2 cups of flour in a large bowl and make a well in the center. Dissolve the yeast in the water, then pour it into the well with the salt. Use a wooden spoon to incorporate the flour, little by little, until it is all used. Sprinkle on the remaining tablespoon of flour, cover the bowl with a cotton dish towel and let rest, in a warm place away from drafts, until the sponge has doubled in size, about 1 hour. (Two signs that the sponge has doubled in size are the disappearance of the tablespoon of flour or the formation of large cracks on top.)

Spread 2 cups of the flour on a board and place the sponge in it. Make a well in the sponge, then pour in the olive oil, along with the rosemary and salt and pepper to taste. First incorporate the oil and the rosemary into the sponge, then, little by little, incorporate the flour, until a ball of dough is formed. Keep kneading the ball of dough with the remaining ½ cup flour.

Divide the dough into four pieces. Pass each piece through a pasta machine set at its widest setting three or four times. Fold each piece in half and press so that the two layers stick together well. Insert the *tagliatelle* cutter on the pasta machine. Pass each piece of dough through the cutter, immediately peeling off each individual strip by hand, as the machine cuts them but does not separate them completely.

Transfer the strips of dough onto a floured cookie sheet, being careful to place them far enough apart to keep them from sticking to each other once risen. When all the pieces of dough have been cut, cover the cookie sheets with cotton towels and let the *grissini* rest, in a warm place away from drafts, until doubled in size, about 1 hour.

Preheat the oven to 375 degrees. When ready, bake the *grissini* for 30 minutes, until very crisp and golden.

Makes about 40.

TORTA DI CECI O CECINA

Giant Chick-Pea Pancake

LIVORNO

Related to flat breads is the Torta di ceci or Cecina, which is a pancake made completely of chick-pea flour. Although this preparation goes back to ancient times, it is still quite popular in the Livorno area of the coast, and until about twenty years ago, Livorno was full of small stands baking and selling cecina on street corners. Cecina is made with a yeastless batter similar to the batter used in old Palermo, Sicily to make the famous fried panelle (chick-pea flour fritters). Cecina is most often eaten between two pieces of bread or inside a roll, and the Italians like to say that the ratio of bread to cecina should be two to one.

Do not sift the flour but be sure to crush any lumps. Place the flour in a crockery or glass bowl and make a well in the center. Start adding the water, little by little, mixing with a wooden spoon and taking some of the flour from the edges of the well, first trying to get a quite thick batter, then making it thinner by adding all the remaining water. This technique helps to keep lumps from forming. When all the water is used up, add the olive oil and salt. Let the batter rest in a cool place for at least 4 hours before baking.

Preheat the oven to 375 degrees. Pour the 2 tablespoons of oil in a 14-inch tin-lined round baking dish. As everybody in Livorno says, preparing the *cecina* is easy if you know how to pour the batter into the center part of the pan where the oil is: Without shaking the pan, drip the batter so that the pan remains completely oiled and the batter floats on top.

Bake for 35 minutes or longer, until a thin golden crust forms. Serve hot, slicing it like a pie, with freshly ground black pepper.

Most of the time, *cecina* is served like a sandwich between two slices of bread.

Serves 8 to 12 as a snack or appetizer.

¾ pound chick-pea flour
3 cups cold water
2 tablespoons olive oil
Salt

TO BAKE
2 tablespoons olive oil

TO SERVE
Freshly ground black pepper

A hot-from-the-oven Cecina (*Giant Chick-Pea Pancake*) in its typical tin-lined copper pan, set against Livorno's Fortezza Medicea.

PANINI DI RAMERINO ALL'OLIO

Rosemary Rolls

In the spring and early summer, the Tuscan hills are filled with golden broom flowers.

The recipe for the small Panini di ramerino, or rosemary rolls, calls for less oil than is required for the classic rosemary bread (Pan di ramerino); it also calls for sugar in addition to raisins, whereas the Pan di ramerino relies solely on raisins for sweetness. Before baking, a cross is cut into the top of each roll and then the dough is brushed with a mixture of egg, oil and sugar.

We took the photograph of the Panini di ramerino (see full-size photograph on pages 30–31) in the refectory of the monastery of the Badia a Passignano, which is located about 15 miles from Florence. We entered the evocative, peaceful thirteenth-century cloister, filled with the perfume of orange and lemon trees growing out of huge terra-cotta pots, from a very sunny hillside. We then found ourselves in the refectory, face-to-face with this wall-size

fresco, its rich coloring contrasting with the purity and simplicity of the setting. The fresco, called The Last Supper, *was executed by the fifteenth-century Florentine artist Domenico Ghirlandaio (with the help of his brother David). We attempted to reflect the table of the Apostles portrayed in the painting in our choice of table settings for the photograph. The fruits and nuts that surround the* panini *carry the same symbolism as those in the painting. The broom flowers came from the hills outside, which were blanketed with them.*

FOR THE SPONGE

1¾ cups plus 1 tablespoon
    unbleached all-purpose flour
½ ounce fresh compressed yeast or
    1 package active dry yeast
1 cup lukewarm or hot water,
    depending on the yeast
Pinch of salt

FOR THE DOUGH

3 tablespoons olive oil
5 heaping tablespoons raisins
4 tablespoons rosemary leaves,
    fresh, preserved in salt or dried
    and blanched
1 tablespoon granulated sugar
Pinch of salt
½ cup lukewarm water
1¾ cups unbleached all-purpose
    flour

TO BAKE

1 tablespoon olive oil
1 extra-large egg
2 tablespoons granulated sugar

Prepare the sponge: Place the 1¾ cups of flour in a small bowl and make a well in the center. Dissolve the yeast in the water and pour it into the well. Add the salt, then mix all the ingredients together, absorbing all the flour. Sprinkle the remaining tablespoon of flour over the sponge, cover the bowl with a cotton towel and let rest, in a warm place away from drafts, until doubled in size, about 1 hour. (Two signs that the sponge has doubled in size are the disappearance of the tablespoon of flour or the formation of large cracks on top.)

When ready, add the olive oil, raisins, rosemary, sugar and salt to the bowl with the sponge and mix very well. Add the water and mix well again.

Place the 1¾ cups of flour on a board and make a well in the center. Pour the contents of the bowl into the well and start mixing the ingredients in the well, using a fork and incorporating the flour from the rim of the well. When two-thirds of the flour is incorporated, start kneading with your hands, in a folding motion, until all the flour is incorporated and the dough is smooth and elastic, about 15 minutes.

Divide the dough into eight pieces. Knead each piece for a few minutes and shape into a roll about 5 inches in diameter. Place the prepared rolls in a very-well-floured cotton dish towel, keeping them far enough apart that they won't touch each other when the dough has risen. Cover with another towel and let rest, in a warm place away from drafts, until doubled in size, about 1 hour.

Preheat the oven to 375 degrees and line the bottom shelf of the oven with unglazed terra-cotta tiles.

When the rolls are ready, lightly beat the olive oil, egg and sugar in a small bowl, using a fork. With a sharp knife, make a cross on the top of each roll, brush the top of each roll with the egg mixture and transfer to the preheated oven, placing the rolls directly on the tiles. Bake for 40 minutes, until golden. Let the *panini* cool for at least 20 minutes before serving.

Makes 8 rolls.

FIRST COURSES

Since the order of courses was established in Renaissance Florence, this formal organization has remained in effect at Italian meals and indeed has spread throughout most of the Western world. Antipasti, which means "before the meal," was not given a place in the order. The official first course originally consisted of thickened and spiced soups to which dumplings were added. These dumplings, not usually enclosed in pasta, were called ravioli. Fresh pasta became a part of this course in the form of several lasagne dishes, called minestra di lasagne, and the occasional dumplings (or ravioli) enclosed in pasta, called tortelli. (Today, these stuffed pastas, still called tortelli in Tuscany, are generally known as ravioli elsewhere.) Dried pasta became popular in the early nineteenth century and swept through the peninsula, replacing many of the soup dishes. Despite this, a large number of soups still remain and are commonly eaten for the evening repast. Pasta, on the other hand, is usually part of the larger midday meal.

In this book, for the first time I am able to give some indication of the full range of these soup dishes. I begin with some of the simpler soups that are not served over bread and often feature vegetables. The minestroni *are thicker and include some type of grain, pasta, rice, cornmeal and/or beans. The largest category is the Tuscan* zuppe, *all of which are served over slices of Tuscan bread. The ultimate in this group is* pappa, *a kind of bread soup that is flavored in a variety of ways depending on the place of origin.*

Dried pastas have not been ignored, as there is no denying that an excellent selection of recipes has evolved over the last century-and-a-half, many of which are associated with specific places. However, it is perhaps the fresh pastas and fresh stuffed pastas that vary most from province to province, and I have tried to include a sampling of recipes that reflects the uniqueness of the different areas. And, finally, there are the rice dishes, generally risotti, *which entered Tuscan cooking several centuries ago, probably from Lombardy.*

VEGETABLE SOUPS

We begin with three vegetable soups: Garmugia, Lucca's signature soup, is made only in the spring-time and only with fresh vegetables, including peas, asparagus, and fresh fava beans. Also included in this light and refreshing recipe is wild fennel, which is so often associated with Sicilian and Sardinian cooking, but grows all over the Chianti and in other parts of Tuscany as well. Only a few toasted croutons thicken this light and refreshing soup and they are an optional addition.

The other two vegetable soups feature vegetable purées that are called creme in Italian, although they are not made with cream or milk. Bell peppers are the starting point for the Crema di peperoni, which is thickened with potato and flavored with thyme, clove and bay leaves. Passato di fagioli alla mugellese, from the mountainous Mugello directly north of Florence, features a bean purée seasoned with touches of marjoram, sage and scallions plus fresh pasta. As is the case with most Tuscan bean soups, a drop of olive oil is added just before serving.

Preceding pages: For a close-up view of the June 24th fireworks for the Feast of S. Giovanni, we stationed ourselves on the rooftop of the Hotel Continental. We set out this buffet for the celebration (from left to right): Pane di pollo (Chicken Bread), a large bowl of Spaghetti di S. Giovanni (Pasta for the Fireworks), Ciliege al vino rosso (Cherries Baked in Red Wine), Zuccotto all'Alkermes (Zuccotto with Alkermes), Coniglio ed insalata (Rabbit Salad), and Focaccine al sale grosso (Salted Little Focaccine).

G A R M U G I A

Spring Vegetable Soup

Coarsely chop the scallions and cut the pancetta into tiny pieces. Place a medium-sized stockpot with the olive oil over medium heat and when the oil is warm, add the scallions, pancetta and ground beef, and sauté for 15 minutes, stirring every so often with a wooden spoon.

Place the fava beans and peas in a bowl of cold water to soak for a few minutes. Soak the artichokes in a second bowl of

8 large scallions, green part removed
4 ounces pancetta, in one piece
4 tablespoons olive oil
8 ounces ground beef
4 ounces fresh fava beans (see Note)
4 ounces shelled peas
2 large artichokes, cleaned and cut into eighths

1 lemon
1 pound asparagus, white part
    discarded and green part
    divided into three mounds: the
    tips, the next 2 inches and
    what remains
10 fresh basil leaves
10 sprigs Italian parsley, leaves only
1 tablespoon chopped fresh wild
    fennel or 1 tablespoon
    chopped leaves of fennel bulb
Salt and freshly ground black pepper
8 cups chicken or meat broth,
    preferably homemade

TO SERVE
Fresh basil leaves
Toasted croutons (optional)

cold water with the lemon cut in half and squeezed. Soak each of the asparagus mounds in its own bowl of cold water.

Coarsely chop the basil, parsley and fennel all together.

Drain the fava beans and peas, then the artichokes and the bowl containing the lower part of the asparagus, and add to the stockpot. Cook for 10 minutes. Season with salt and pepper. Drain the middle part of the asparagus and add to the pot. Add the broth and simmer for 15 minutes. Drain the tips of the asparagus and add them to the pot. Simmer for 5 minutes more. By that time all the vegetables should be cooked and soft; not even one of the vegetables should be *al dente*. Add the chopped basil mixture, mix very well, taste for salt and pepper and cook for 1 minute more. Serve hot with fresh basil leaves and croutons (if using) on each individual serving.

Note: In this soup, the beans and each vegetable *must* be fresh. Do not use dried fava beans, preserved herbs or frozen peas. The herbs and peas are relatively easy to find. If fresh fava beans are not available, substitute additional fresh peas. Choose tiny spring peas when available; otherwise, the larger ones will work fine.

Serves 8.

C R E M A D I P E P E R O N I

Sweet Pepper "Cream"

ALL OVER TUSCANY

4 yellow or red bell peppers (all of
    one color)
1 medium-sized red onion, cleaned
1 medium-sized all-purpose potato
    (about 8 ounces)
About 6 cups chicken or meat
    broth, preferably homemade
¼ teaspoon dried thyme or a
    sprig fresh thyme
1 whole clove
2 bay leaves
Salt and freshly ground black pepper

TO SERVE
6 scant teaspoons olive oil
Fresh basil leaves

Remove the stem, pulp and seeds from the peppers, and cut them into small pieces. Soak the peppers in a bowl of cold water for ½ hour. Cut the onion into small pieces and soak it in a second bowl of cold water. Peel and cut the potato into pieces that are the same size as the onion and add to the bowl with the onion.

Bring the broth to a boil over medium heat. Drain the onion and potato, add them to the broth and cook for 15 minutes. Drain the peppers, add them to the pot and cook for 40 minutes more. If the broth reduces too much, add extra broth. After 40 minutes the "cream" should be quite smooth.

Pass the contents of the pot through a food mill, using the disc with the smallest holes, into a second pot.

Wrap the thyme, clove and bay leaves in cheesecloth and secure with a string to create a bag. Add the bag to the new pot and set it over medium heat to simmer for 25 minutes. Taste for salt and pepper. Serve the "cream" warm, with a sprinkling of olive oil and basil leaves.

Serves 6.

Mugello-Style Puréed Bean Soup

Soak the beans in a bowl of cold water overnight.

The next morning, drain and rinse the beans and put them in a heavy, medium-sized casserole.

Coarsely chop the onion, carrot, garlic, celery, sage and marjoram all together on a board. Clean the scallions, separating the green parts from the white. Place the white sections of the scallions in a bowl of cold water and let them stand until needed. Rinse the green sections very well, then coarsely chop them on a board. Transfer all the chopped vegetables and herbs to the casserole with the beans.

Cut the pancetta into tiny pieces and add it to the casserole, along with the peppercorns and oil. Add enough cold water to the casserole to reach 2 inches above the bean mixture. Cover the casserole, place it over low heat and let simmer for 45 to 50 minutes, or until the beans are cooked through but still retain their shape. Add salt to taste and mix very well. Remove 1½ cups of the beans, without liquid, from the casserole and put them in a crockery or glass bowl. Cover the bowl and let stand until needed.

Cook the bean mixture in the casserole for another ½ hour so that the beans become very soft. Pass the contents of the casserole through a food mill, using the disc with the smallest holes, into a clean casserole.

Place the second casserole over low heat, uncovered, and let simmer for 15 minutes more, stirring every so often with a wooden spoon to prevent the purée from sticking to the pot. Taste for salt and pepper. At this point all the ingredients should be very well integrated.

While the soup is simmering, prepare the pasta with the ingredients listed at right (see Appendix, page 293). Stretch the layer of pasta to a thickness of 1/16 of an inch and take the layer of pasta to the next to last notch on the pasta machine. With a *taglierini* cutter, cut the pasta into *spaghettini*.

Bring a large pot of cold water to a boil and add the reserved beans to the soup. Meanwhile, drain and coarsely chop the scallion whites.

Prepare the soup bowls by placing some chopped scallions in each one. When the water reaches a boil, add coarse-grained salt to taste, then the pasta, and cook for 30 seconds or less. Drain the pasta and add it to the bean soup. Mix well and ladle the soup and pasta into the individual bowls. Sprinkle a teaspoon of oil over each serving.

Serves 8.

2 cups dried cannellini beans
1 small red onion, cleaned
1 medium-sized carrot, scraped
1 large clove garlic, peeled
2 medium-sized celery stalks
2 large sage leaves, fresh or
    preserved in salt
1 teaspoon dried marjoram
15 scallions
2 ounces pancetta or prosciutto,
    in one piece
10 black peppercorns
4 tablespoons olive oil
Coarse-grained salt
Salt and freshly ground black pepper

FOR THE PASTA
2 cups unbleached all-purpose flour
3 extra-large eggs
Pinch of salt

TO COOK THE PASTA
Coarse-grained salt

PLUS
8 teaspoons olive oil

Goose is a traditional element in the dinner prepared to celebrate the end of the wheat harvest in Tuscany. Marinated Cucumbers (see page 258) are also part of this festive meal.

BORDATINO

Polenta Soup

In this recipe from Livorno, cornmeal and water are added to sautéed aromatic vegetables, pancetta and tomato paste to create a flavorful polenta that is so thin that it is really a soup.

Coarsely chop the onions, celery and carrots all together on a board. Cut the pancetta into tiny pieces.

Heat the oil in a medium-sized stockpot over low heat and when the oil is warm, add the pancetta and sauté for 5 minutes. Add the chopped ingredients and cook for 5 minutes more. Raise the heat to medium, add the tomato paste, stir very well and season with salt and pepper. Add the 1 cup cold water and cook for 10 minutes more, stirring every so often with a wooden spoon.

Add the 3 quarts cold water to the stockpot and when the water reaches a boil, start adding the cornmeal, in a slow steady stream, being sure no lumps form, always mixing with a flat wooden spoon (or polenta spoon) to prevent the cornmeal from sticking. When all the cornmeal is used up, lower the heat and let the soup simmer for 45 minutes, stirring every so often with the spoon. Just before the soup is ready, taste for salt and pepper.

Serve in soup bowls with a sprinkling of olive oil and use a spoon to eat. The consistency should resemble a rather thick minestrone.

Serves 8 to 10.

2 medium-sized red onions, cleaned
3 celery stalks
3 medium-sized carrots, scraped
4 ounces pancetta or prosciutto, in one piece
4 tablespoons olive oil
4 tablespoons tomato paste
Salt and freshly ground black pepper
1 cup cold water

PLUS
3 quarts cold water
½ pound coarse stone-ground yellow cornmeal, preferably imported Italian

TO SERVE
Olive oil

MINESTRA DI FARRO

Minestrone with Wheat Berries

Of all the minestrone recipes, Minestra di farro, which uses the ancient soft wheat berries called farro, is probably the oldest. In this version from Carmignano, an area of great vineyards and Etruscan tombs, the farro is left whole and becomes as soft as cooked barley. Unusual in this dish is the final touch of rosemary-flavored oil. Aside from the hot pepper-flavored olio santo (sacred oil) from Chianti, flavored oils are rarely used in Tuscan cooking.

On the road that leads from Florence to Carmignano is the fifteenth-century Medici villa of Poggio a Caiano, which was built by Lorenzo the Magnificent following the designs of Giuliano da Sangallo. In recent decades, the wine producers of this area have discovered that their traditional wine was originally made with just two red grapes and was not Chianti at all. They have, in turn, returned to making their full-bodied wine according to the methods recorded in documents from the fourteenth century.

3 medium-sized carrots, scraped
3 medium-sized celery stalks
1 large red onion, cleaned
2 cloves garlic, peeled
3 ounces pancetta or prosciutto,
    in one piece
4 tablespoons olive oil
1 medium-sized all-purpose
    potato, peeled and cut into
    ½-inch pieces
Salt and freshly ground black pepper
1½ quarts chicken or meat broth,
    preferably homemade

PLUS
Coarse-grained salt
¾ pound farro (soft wheat berries)

TO SERVE
Olive oil flavored with rosemary
    (see Note)

Coarsely chop the carrots, celery and onion all together on a board and finely chop the garlic. Cut the pancetta into tiny pieces. Place a medium-sized stockpot with the oil over medium heat and when the oil is warm, add the pancetta and sauté for 3 to 4 minutes, stirring with a wooden spoon. Add the chopped ingredients and sauté for 2 minutes more. Add the potato and sauté for 5 minutes more, or until the onion is completely translucent. Season with salt and pepper, then add the broth and let simmer, covered, for 1 hour.

Meanwhile, soak the farro in a bowl of cold water for 45 minutes.

Just before the farro is ready, place a medium-sized stockpot of cold water over medium heat. When the water reaches a boil, add some salt, then drain the farro and add it to the stockpot. Mix very well with a wooden spoon and simmer for 35 minutes, stirring every so often because the wheat has a tendency to stick. Drain the farro, saving the water.

When the broth with the vegetables is ready, add the farro and enough cooking water to yield a medium-thick consistency, keeping in mind that the farro must be cooked in the broth for 15 minutes more. After 15 minutes, taste for salt and pepper. Serve hot with a sprinkling of black pepper and a "C" of the rosemary-flavored olive oil over each serving.

Note: If you don't have any of the flavored olive oil on hand, place a tablespoon of rosemary leaves in a cheesecloth bag and add it to the broth just before adding the broth to the sautéed vegetables. Discard the cheesecloth bag before adding the farro to the soup; substitute plain olive oil when serving.

Serves 8.

Minestrone with Cannellini Beans

Minestrone ai fagioli del Valdarno *is based on* Risotto ai fagioli *(page 134), the Tuscan version of rice and beans. Valdarno, where this recipe originated, is part of the Arno Valley, which stretches from Arezzo, passing Florence, down to Pisa, and includes a number of historic towns. San Miniato, a hill town in the Florence-Pisa stretch of the valley, was an important capital of the Holy Roman Empire, and the ruins of Frederick Barbarossa's castle may be seen there. Perhaps Barbarossa picked this spot for his castle because it was one of the few places where fresh white truffles could be found.*

Cook the beans and prepare the sauce according to the risotto recipe (page 134), up to the point at which you have divided the sauce in half, pouring one portion over the beans and leaving the other in the casserole.

For the minestrone, add to the casserole holding the sauce both the water from the beans and the 4 cups of broth, and bring to a boil. Add the rice and cook for about 16 minutes. The rice should be completely cooked, not *al dente* as for risotto. Taste for salt and pepper, then add all the beans and sauce. Mix very well and simmer for 30 seconds more.

Serve with fresh basil leaves.

Serves 8 to 10.

Sage is one of the most commonly used herbs in Tuscan cooking.

1 cup dried cannellini beans
1 large clove garlic
2 sage leaves, fresh or preserved
    in salt
Salt and freshly ground black pepper

FOR THE SAUCE
2 medium-sized red onions, cleaned
2 medium-sized carrots, scraped
1 large clove garlic, peeled
1 celery stalk
10 sprigs Italian parsley, leaves only
10 basil leaves, fresh or preserved
    in salt
4 ounces pancetta or prosciutto,
    in one piece
5 tablespoons olive oil
Salt and freshly ground black pepper
A large pinch of hot red pepper
    flakes
1½ pounds very ripe fresh
    tomatoes or 1½ pounds
    drained canned tomatoes,
    preferably imported Italian

PLUS
4 cups chicken or meat broth,
    preferably homemade
1 cup raw rice, preferably Italian
    Arborio

TO SERVE
Several fresh basil leaves

ZUPPE

The word zuppa *does not simply mean "soup," but is more accurately translated as "soup poured over slices of bread," and it is in this category that most Tuscan soups fall. The bread used for zuppe should be several days old and a little hardened so it does not completely fall apart in the hot broth.*

Most zuppe are made with water (not chicken or beef broth), and such is the case with Cavolo nero con le fette, *in which the kale cooking water is the basis for the broth.* Zuppa di carciofi, *an exception to the rule, is made with chicken or meat broth, and features artichokes that have been sautéed with prosciutto, garlic and parsley.*

In Acquacotta maremmana, *which comes from the shores around Grosseto in the Maremma area, raw egg yolks are placed on top of the bread slices and are cooked by the boiling vegetable broth that is poured over them. Acquacotta, a term that is common in this part of Tuscany, translates as "cooked water," emphasizing the lack of meat broth. This is one of the rare recipes in Italian cuisine that includes both* Parmigiano *and red pepper. The combination works here because the pepper spices the broth and the cheese relates to the eggs.*

CAVOLO NERO CON LE FETTE

Kale with Tuscan Garlic Bread

Soak the kale in a bowl of cold water for ½ hour. Bring a large pot of cold water to a boil, then add coarse salt to taste and the lemon juice. When the water returns to a very rapid boil, drain the kale, add it to the water and cook for about 25 minutes or more, depending on the size and tenderness. In the winter, kale is generally tender and cooks quickly.

Preheat the oven to 375 degrees. Place the bread on a cookie sheet and toast until lightly golden on both sides.

Rub the toasted slices of bread with the garlic, then place them in four individual soup bowls. When the kale is ready, pour 1 tablespoon of the kale cooking water over each slice of bread, then with a strainer-skimmer, place the kale over the bread. Sprinkle each portion with 1 tablespoon of the oil and some freshly ground black pepper. Serve hot.

Serves 4.

3 pounds kale, cleaned, large
    stems removed
Coarse-grained salt
A few drops of lemon juice
4 (6-inch) slices Tuscan bread,
    about 2 inches thick
2 medium-sized cloves garlic, peeled
4 tablespoons olive oil
Freshly ground black pepper

ZUPPA DI CARCIOFI

Artichoke Zuppa

Place the artichokes in a bowl of cold water with the lemon cut in half and squeezed, and soak for ½ hour.

Meanwhile, cut the prosciutto into tiny pieces and finely chop the garlic and parsley all together on a board.

Clean the artichokes: Cut off the ends of the stems, then trim off all of the darker outer ring of the stems. Remove as many rows of the outer leaves as necessary until you arrive at those leaves in which you can see the separation between the green at the top and the light yellow at the bottom. Remove the top green part by pressing your thumb on the bottom yellow part of each leaf and, with your other hand, tearing off the top green part. When you reach the rows in which only the very tops of the leaves are green, cut off these tips completely with a knife.

To remove the hair and the choke, first cut the artichoke into quarters lengthwise; then cut out the inside choke and hair.

6 large artichokes
1 lemon
3 ounces prosciutto or pancetta,
    in one piece
2 medium-sized cloves garlic, peeled
20 sprigs Italian parsley, leaves only
4 tablespoons olive oil
Salt and freshly ground black pepper
10 cups chicken or meat broth,
    preferably homemade

PLUS
8 to 10 (6-inch) slices crusty Tuscan
    bread, not more than 1½ inches
    thick, lightly toasted

TO SERVE
Fresh basil leaves

Slice the artichokes vertically into six or eight wedges, depending on the size of the artichokes. Place the artichoke pieces back in the acidulated water until needed.

Heat the oil in a medium-sized casserole over medium heat and when the oil is warm, add the prosciutto and sauté for 2 minutes. Add the chopped ingredients and sauté for 1 minute more. Drain the artichokes and add them to the casserole while still very wet. Season with salt and pepper, cover the casserole and sauté for 15 minutes, stirring every so often with a wooden spoon. Add the broth and simmer until the artichokes are soft but still retain their shape. Taste for salt and pepper.

Place the toasted bread in individual soup bowls and pour the broth with the artichokes over the bread. Cover and let the *zuppa* rest for 10 minutes before serving. Grind some black pepper over each serving and sprinkle on the basil leaves. Do not serve with cheese.

Serves 8 to 10.

A flowering artichoke.

Rustic Soup from Maremma

Finely chop the celery, carrots, onion, parsley and garlic all together on a board. Heat the olive oil in a medium-sized stockpot over medium heat and when the oil is warm, add the chopped ingredients and sauté for 5 minutes, stirring with a wooden spoon.

Meanwhile, cut the spinach leaves into very thin strips and soak them in a bowl of cold water for 10 minutes. Drain the spinach, add it to the stockpot and sauté for 10 minutes more. Season with salt, pepper and the red pepper flakes. Add the cold water to the pot and simmer for ½ hour. By that time the water should be reduced by almost 2 cups. Taste for salt and pepper.

While the soup is still simmering, arrange one slice of the bread in each soup bowl. Sprinkle 1 tablespoon of *Parmigiano* over each slice of bread, then place an egg yolk on the slice of bread. Ladle enough broth into each bowl to cover the egg yolk completely so the egg yolk will be cooked. Sprinkle the parsley leaves over the broth and let the soup rest for 5 minutes before serving.

Serves 6.

2 celery stalks
3 medium-sized carrots, scraped
1 medium-sized red onion, cleaned
10 sprigs Italian parsley, leaves only
1 clove garlic, peeled
½ cup olive oil
8 ounces spinach, leaves only
Salt and freshly ground black pepper
A large pinch of hot red pepper flakes
2 quarts cold water

TO SERVE
6 (6-inch) slices crusty Tuscan bread, not more than 1½ inches thick, lightly toasted
6 tablespoons freshly grated *Parmigiano*
6 egg yolks
Italian parsley leaves

Z U P P A   A L L ' A R E T I N A

Antique Chicken "Zuppa"

Zuppa all'aretina from Arezzo is a very old recipe in which chicken is cooked in water with aromatic vegetables and then cut into strips and sautéed with additional vegetables in a casserole. The broth in which the chicken was originally cooked is then added to the casserole and reduced, and the whole mixture is served over bread slices. This dish is believed to be the precursor to the famous French chicken soup known as Petite marmite avec volaille.

Wash the chicken very well and dry it with paper towels. Place the whole bird, the water, carrot, celery and parsley in a medium-sized stockpot set over medium heat. When the water reaches a boil, add coarse salt to taste and simmer for 1 hour 45 minutes. Every so often skim the foam that forms on top.

When ready, transfer the bird to a board and pass the broth through a very fine strainer. Bone the chicken, discarding the bones and skin, and cut the meat into thin strips or medium-

1 chicken (about 3½ pounds), cleaned
4 quarts cold water
1 medium-sized carrot, scraped
1 large celery stalk
10 sprigs Italian parsley
Coarse-grained salt

FOR THE "ZUPPA"
2 medium-sized carrots, scraped
1 celery stalk
1 large red onion, cleaned
10 sprigs Italian parsley, leaves only

4 tablespoons (2 ounces) sweet butter
2 tablespoons olive oil
Salt and freshly ground black pepper

8 to 10 (6-inch) slices crusty
    Tuscan bread, several days old,
    not more than 1½ inches
    thick, lightly toasted
15 sage leaves, fresh or preserved
    in salt, coarsely chopped

sized pieces. Let the broth cool long enough to allow you to remove almost all the fat.

Meanwhile, prepare the *zuppa*: Finely chop the carrots, celery, onion and parsley together on a board. Place a medium-sized casserole with the butter and oil over medium heat and when the butter is melted, add the chopped ingredients and sauté for 15 minutes, stirring every so often with a wooden spoon. Add the chicken, season with salt and pepper and sauté for 10 minutes more. Add the strained and defatted broth, cover the casserole and simmer for 15 additional minutes. Taste for salt and pepper and reduce for 10 minutes more.

When ready, place the bread slices in individual soup bowls, ladle some of the broth with the chicken pieces over the *zuppa* and sprinkle with the chopped sage. Let the *zuppa* rest for 5 minutes before serving.

Serves 8 to 10.

ZUPPE DI FAGIOLI

*T*uscans are known to other Italians as bean eaters, and though they love borlotti, black-eyed peas and favas, closest to their hearts are the white cannellini beans (which are actually white kidney beans). Following are bean zuppe from Livorno, Monteriggioni and Montalcino.

The first two, Minestrone d'estate *from Livorno and* Minestrone di fagioli *from Monteriggioni, though called* minestroni, *are really* zuppe *because they are made with bread, not pasta. The* Minestrone d'estate *features late spring and early summer vegetables. In Italy, the spring asparagus and fresh fava beans are a little larger in early summer; and the tender cabbage called* lasagnino *appears in spring and summer as opposed to Savoy cabbage, which arrives in Italian markets in the winter.*

In Minestrone di fagioli, *kale, Savoy cabbage and tarragon, the favorite herb in the Siena area, are added to the full range of aromatic vegetables. Monteriggioni is a perfectly preserved walled village that was built by the Sienese in 1203 as an advance post of defense against Florence. In Dante's* Inferno, *Monteriggioni is described as all enclosed "nella sua cerchia tonda" (in its round circle of walls).*

Zuppa di fagioli is made with meat broth and spinach, and is served with red onion or, for the more delicate, scallions. This recipe comes from the walled hilltop town of Montalcino, the celebrated seat of Brunello di Montalcino, one of Italy's—and the world's—greatest wines.

MINESTRONE D'ESTATE O ALLA CONTADINA

Summer Minestrone or Country-Style Minestrone

Tall cypresses line the famous Viale di cipressi, Boulevard of Cypresses, which runs for four kilometers from S. Guido to Bolgheri and is surrounded by centuries-old olive trees. Many fine wines are produced in this area, including Sassicaia.

TO COOK THE BEANS
1 cup dried cannellini beans
1 tablespoon olive oil
1 large clove garlic, peeled and
    left whole
10 sprigs Italian parsley, leaves only
5 fresh basil leaves
Salt and freshly ground black pepper

FOR THE MINESTRONE
1 large red onion, cleaned
2 medium-sized carrots, scraped
3 celery stalks

10 sprigs Italian parsley, leaves only
5 fresh basil leaves
½ cup olive oil
1 pound tender cabbage (called
    lasagnino in Italy), cut into
    thin strips
4 ounces string beans, cleaned
4 ounces zucchini, cleaned and cut
    into ½-inch cubes
½ pound asparagus, white part
    discarded, cut into 2-inch
    pieces

½ pound fresh fava beans
1½ pounds very ripe fresh
   tomatoes or 1½ pounds
   drained canned tomatoes,
   preferably imported Italian
Salt and freshly ground black pepper

PLUS
10 (6-inch) slices crusty Tuscan
   bread, several days old, not
   more than 1½ inches thick

TO SERVE
Olive oil

Soak the beans in a bowl of cold water overnight.

The next morning, drain the beans and put them in a medium-sized stockpot, along with 3 quarts cold water, olive oil, garlic, parsley and basil. Place the pot over medium heat and when the water reaches a boil, lower the heat and let the beans simmer until very soft, about 50 minutes. Just before the beans are completely cooked, add salt and pepper to taste.

Meanwhile, coarsely chop the onion, carrots, celery, parsley and basil all together on a board. Heat the oil in a second stockpot over medium heat and when the oil is warm, add the chopped ingredients and sauté for 5 minutes.

Soak the cabbage, string beans, zucchini, asparagus, and fava beans in a bowl of cold water for ½ hour.

Pass the fresh or canned tomatoes through a food mill, using the disc with the smallest holes, into a crockery or glass bowl.

Add the tomatoes to the stockpot with the sautéed vegetables, lower the heat, season with salt and pepper and simmer for about 25 minutes, stirring every so often with a wooden spoon.

When ready, drain all the soaking vegetables and add them to the tomato mixture. Cover and cook for 5 minutes. By that time the vegetables should have given off a lot of liquid.

Pass the contents of the first stockpot with the beans through a food mill, using the disc with the smallest holes, directly into the other pot containing the vegetables. Let the soup simmer until the toughest vegetable is completely cooked; don't worry if softer vegetables dissolve because the broth is supposed to be quite thick and have the flavor of the different vegetables. Taste for salt and pepper.

Place the slices of bread in individual soup bowls, ladle the soup over the bread and let it rest for at least 10 minutes. Serve with a "C" of olive oil drizzled over each serving.

Serves 8 to 10.

MINESTRONE DI FAGIOLI DI MONTERIGGIONI

Bean Soup from Monteriggioni   MONTERIGGIONI

2 cups dried cannellini beans
3 quarts cold water
A large piece of prosciutto bone or
    3 ounces of prosciutto or
    pancetta, in one piece
Coarse-grained salt

FOR THE SOUP
1 pound kale, cleaned, large stalks
    removed
1 pound Savoy cabbage, cleaned
2 medium-sized carrots, scraped
2 large celery stalks
2 red onions, cleaned
10 sprigs Italian parsley, leaves only
5 large basil leaves, fresh or
    preserved in salt
½ cup olive oil
1 pound very ripe fresh tomatoes
    or 1 pound drained canned
    tomatoes, preferably
    imported Italian
Salt and freshly ground black pepper
Sprig of fresh tarragon

OPTIONAL
8 (5-inch) slices crusty Tuscan
    bread, about 3 inches thick

PLUS
Olive oil for serving

Minestrone di fagioli di
Monteriggioni *ladled into the traditional white-and-green glazed terra-cotta
bowls and placed in front of the head of a
pig stuffed with soprassata sausage. The
photograph was taken in front of one of
Monteriggioni's two main gates, which are
located at either end of this hilltop village's
one real street. The other gate still has its
Etruscan foundations, which indicates
that there was a village here before 1203
when the Sienese established Monteriggioni
as an advance post against Florence.
Historians believe that the orginal village
dates back to the sixth century* B.C.

Soak the beans in a bowl of cold water overnight.

The next morning, drain the beans and rinse them under cold running water. Set a stockpot with the 3 quarts cold water over medium heat. Add the beans and the prosciutto bone or prosciutto and cook for about 45 minutes. By that time the beans should be almost cooked. Add coarse salt to taste and simmer for 2 minutes more.

Drain the beans and the prosciutto or bone, saving the cooking water, and place in a crockery or glass bowl. Let the beans and prosciutto or bone rest, covered, until needed.

Cut the kale and cabbage into thin strips and soak in a bowl of cold water for 15 minutes. Finely chop the carrots, celery, onions, parsley and basil all together on a board. Heat the oil in a stockpot over medium heat and when the oil is warm, add the chopped ingredients and sauté for 2 minutes. Drain the kale and cabbage and add to the pot. Cook for 10 minutes. Pour all the cooking water from the beans into the pot, as well as two-thirds of the cooked beans and the prosciutto bone or the piece of prosciutto.

If fresh tomatoes are used, cut them into large pieces. Add the fresh or canned tomatoes to the stockpot and simmer for 1 hour. If necessary, add some of the bean water so that all the ingredients in the pot are covered.

Pass the contents of the stockpot through a food mill two times, using the disc with the medium-sized holes first and the disc with the smallest holes second, into a second stockpot. Place the new stockpot over medium heat, taste for salt and pepper and add the sprigs of tarragon. The minestrone is supposed to have a rather thick consistency. Add the remaining beans to the stockpot and cook for 2 minutes more.

If you are using the bread, place it in a large soup tureen, pour all the soup over it and let rest, covered, for at least 15 minutes before serving. Pour a few drops of olive oil over each serving.

Serves 8.

ZUPPA DI FAGIOLI DI MONTALCINO

Montalcino-Style Bean Zuppa

Soak the beans in a bowl of cold water overnight.

The next morning, rinse the beans very well and place them in a medium-sized stockpot with the pancetta and the 3 quarts cold water. Set the pot over medium heat and when the water reaches a boil, let the beans cook for about 45 minutes. By that time the beans should be cooked through but still retain their shape. Season with salt, stir and cook for 1 minute more.

Strain the beans, saving the cooking water, and place them in a crockery or glass bowl. Cover the beans with layers of wet paper towels.

Finely chop the onion, celery, carrots and garlic all together on a board. Pour the oil into a medium-sized stockpot and set the pot over medium heat. When the oil is warm, add the chopped ingredients and sauté for 10 minutes, stirring every so often with a wooden spoon.

Dissolve the tomato paste in 1 cup cold water, add to the stockpot and simmer for 15 minutes more. Coarsely chop the spinach on a board and add it to the stockpot along with the cooking broth from the beans. Simmer for 1 hour, adding the chicken or meat broth if the *zuppa* becomes too thick. Season with salt and pepper. After 1 hour, add the beans, discard the piece of pancetta, and simmer for 5 minutes more.

Arrange three slices of the bread in a large bowl, ladle half the soup over the bread, then the remaining three slices of bread and the remaining soup. Let the soup rest for at least 10 minutes before serving.

Serve the soup with slices of red onion or scallions and a few drops of olive oil.

Serves 6.

8 ounces dried cannellini beans	1 small clove garlic, peeled
2 ounces pancetta or prosciutto, in one piece	5 tablespoons olive oil
	2 tablespoons tomato paste
3 quarts cold water	1½ pounds spinach or Swiss chard, cleaned
Coarse-grained salt	
1 medium-sized red onion, cleaned	About 3 cups chicken or meat broth, preferably homemade
2 large celery stalks	
2 medium-sized carrots, scraped	Salt and freshly ground black pepper

PLUS
6 large slices crusty Tuscan bread, several days old

TO SERVE
Red onions or scallions
Olive oil

A view from the top of the castle of Montalcino. Notice the color of the roof-tops and the clouds in this nearly fantas-tical scene. We see before us Zuppa di fagioli di Montalcino (Montalcino-Style Bean Zuppa) with onion slices, a wonderful piece of Pecorino delle crete (the sheep's cheese that comes from the same area as the famous terra-cotta used for cooking), a plate of crostini topped with the rustic liver/spleen pâté, Tuscan salami and dried Sienese sausages, and, of course, the treasured bottle of Brunello wine. The Sienese sausages and salamis are celebrated because of the choice pork with which they are made and the beautiful way in which they are spiced.

ZUPPA CASALINGA ALLA LUCCHESE

Home-Style Bean Soup

In Zuppa casalinga alla lucchese, the beans are cooked in advance. Half of them are puréed and added to the bean broth, along with a variety of vegetables, including kale, cabbage, Swiss chard and butternut squash. The remaining whole beans are added during the final five minutes of cooking. This zuppa is flavored with wild fennel, basil and parsley.

Soak the beans in a bowl of cold water overnight.

The next morning, drain the beans and rinse them under cold running water. Place a stockpot with the 4 quarts water over medium heat. Add the beans and pancetta and simmer for 45 minutes. By that time the beans should be almost cooked. Add coarse salt to taste and simmer for 2 minutes more. Drain the beans, saving all the cooking water. Place half of the beans in a crockery or glass bowl and let rest, covered, until needed. Pour the saved water back into the stockpot.

Pass the second half of the beans through a food mill, using the disc with the smallest holes, directly into the stockpot with the bean broth. Place the pot over low heat and bring to a boil. Meanwhile, place the kale, cabbage, Swiss chard, carrots, celery, potatoes and squash in a large bowl of cold water for 15 minutes. Coarsely chop the parsley, basil and fennel all together on a board.

Drain the vegetables and add them to the stockpot, along with the chopped ingredients, tomato paste and olive oil. Season with salt and pepper and simmer for 1 hour. Add the reserved beans and cook for 5 minutes more. Taste for salt and pepper.

Place the bread in a large soup tureen, pour the contents of the stockpot over the bread and let rest for 15 minutes before serving.

Serve with fresh basil leaves and a little olive oil.

Serves 8 to 10.

1½ cups dried cannellini beans
4 quarts cold water
2 ounces pancetta or prosciutto, cut into tiny pieces
Coarse-grained salt

FOR THE SOUP
½ pound kale, cleaned, leaves cut into thin strips and large stalks discarded
½ pound Savoy cabbage, cleaned, large stems discarded, cut into thin strips
½ pound Swiss chard, cleaned, large stems discarded, cut into thin strips
2 medium-sized carrots, scraped and cut into 1-inch discs
2 celery stalks, cut into 1-inch pieces
2 medium-sized potatoes (about 8 ounces), peeled and cut into 1-inch cubes
½ pound butternut or acorn squash, peeled and cut into 2-inch cubes
10 sprigs Italian parsley, leaves only
10 basil leaves, fresh or preserved in salt
A few sprigs of wild fennel or leaves of fennel bulb
2 tablespoons tomato paste
½ cup olive oil
Salt and freshly ground black pepper

PLUS
8 to 10 (5-inch) slices crusty Tuscan bread, about 3 inches thick

TO SERVE
Fresh basil leaves
Olive oil

Zuppa casalinga alla lucchese (Home-style Bean Soup from Lucca) seen from the terrace of the palazzo occupied by Lucca's main branch of the Banca Commerciale Italiana, whose staff graciously allowed us to use the terrace for photography. The twelfth-century S. Michele in Foro church in the background is one of Lucca's greatest with its beautiful and elaborate rows of columns, each one different from the next. The remains of pagan temples and earlier churches may hide below this piazza, which was the site of the old Roman Forum and is today the center of the city.

ZUPPA DI BORLOTTI

Sienese Bean Soup with Borlotti

Siena's Zuppa di borlotti, which is cooked in the oven, calls for speckled red-and-white borlotti beans but if they are not available, lentils can be used instead. Whole scallions are traditionally served along with each portion.

Soak the beans in a bowl of cold water overnight. (The lentils do not need to be soaked.)

The next morning, preheat the oven to 375 degrees and drain and rinse the beans under cold running water. Place the beans (or lentils), the 1½ quarts water , the onion, garlic, basil and tarragon in a medium-sized (preferably terra-cotta) stockpot. Cover and cook in the oven for 20 minutes. (Alternatively, if the stockpot won't fit in the oven, simmer the beans on the stove for about 15 minutes.)

Meanwhile, coarsely chop the celery, onions and carrots all together on a board, and cut the pancetta into tiny pieces. Heat the oil in a medium-sized skillet over medium heat and when the oil is warm, add the pancetta and sauté for 10 minutes, stirring with a wooden spoon. Add the chopped ingredients and sauté for 10 minutes more.

Remove the stockpot from the oven (or stove) and add the contents of the skillet, along with the broth. Season with salt and pepper, re-cover and place the pot back in the oven for 1 hour. By that time the beans should be completely cooked. Borlotti beans generally cook more quickly than other dried legumes. Taste for salt and pepper.

Serve the soup as it is, being sure not more than about 10 cups of liquid remain, or pass all the contents of the stockpot through a food mill, using the disc with the smallest holes, into a clean stockpot and reduce the puréed ingredients over medium heat for 5 minutes. Place the toasted bread in individual soup bowls.

Pour the soup over the bread and season with pepper. Complete each serving with the whole scallions and a "C" of olive oil on top.

Serves 8 to 10.

---

2 cups dried borlotti beans or
    dried lentils
1½ quarts cold water
1 medium-sized red onion, cleaned
    and coarsely chopped
2 large cloves garlic, peeled
5 large basil leaves, fresh or
    preserved in salt
1 tablespoon tarragon leaves,
    fresh or preserved in salt, or
    ½ teaspoon dried tarragon

FOR THE SOUP
3 large celery stalks
2 medium-sized red onions, cleaned
4 medium-sized carrots, scraped
3 ounces pancetta or prosciutto,
    in one piece
6 tablespoons olive oil
1½ quarts chicken or meat broth,
    preferably homemade
Salt and freshly ground black pepper

PLUS
8 to 10 (6-inch) slices crusty Tuscan
    bread, not more than 1½ inches
    thick, toasted

TO SERVE
3 scallions per serving, cleaned
Olive oil

BREAD SOUP

Of the true bread soups, the most widely known is probably the one from Florence, which features tomatoes and garlic. I have included a lesser known but equally good bread soup that is flavored with sage and comes from Livorno. Like most bread soups, it is served with a little olive oil sprinkled over the top. Bread soups—probably descendants of ancient Roman grain porridges—and bread salads were developed by both the rich and the poor as ways of using precious leftover bread.

There are several versions of Ribollita from Florence, but all of them are made with the previous day's country vegetable soup layered with slices of bread. When the soup is ready to be served, the bread and soup are mixed together, creating a texture close to bread soup, or **pappa**. If you were to pour the soup over the bread instead of mixing the two together you would have an ordinary **zuppa**.

PAPPA AL POMODORO ALLA LIVORNESE

Livorno-Style Bread Soup   LIVORNO

1 pound crusty Tuscan bread,
   several days old
3 large cloves garlic, peeled
8 large sage leaves, fresh or
   preserved in salt
¾ cup olive oil
1½ pounds very ripe fresh
   tomatoes, cut into pieces, or
   1½ pounds drained canned
   tomatoes, preferably
   imported Italian
5½ cups boiling chicken or meat
   broth, preferably homemade
Salt and freshly ground black pepper

PLUS
6 to 8 teaspoons olive oil

Cut the bread into 1-inch cubes. Finely chop the garlic and sage together on a board. Heat the oil in a medium-sized casserole, preferably of terra-cotta, over medium heat. When the oil is warm, add the chopped ingredients and sauté for 5 minutes, or until very lightly golden.

Meanwhile, pass the fresh or canned tomatoes through a food mill, using the disc with the smallest holes.

When the chopped garlic and sage are ready, add the bread and sauté for 5 minutes, continuously mixing with a wooden spoon. Add the tomatoes, mix very well and when they are well incorporated into the bread, after about 2 minutes, add the boiling broth. Season with salt and pepper, mix very well with a wooden spoon and let the broth return to a boil. Mix, cover the casserole and transfer it to a trivet to rest for 1 hour.

When ready, mix the soup very well to remove any remaining lumps in the bread. Taste for salt and pepper and serve with a teaspoon of oil sprinkled over each serving.

Serves 6 to 8.

Twice-Cooked Country-Style "Zuppa"

Soak the beans in a bowl of cold water overnight.

The next morning, drain the beans and rinse under cold running water. Place the beans in a medium-sized stockpot with the 5 quarts cold water. Coarsely chop the celery, carrot and garlic all together on a board. Add the chopped ingredients to the pot, along with the olive oil and prosciutto. Set the pot over medium heat and when the water reaches a boil, cook for 45 minutes. By that time the beans should be cooked through but still retain their shape. Season with salt, mix well, cook for 1 minute more, then drain the beans, saving the cooking water. Place the beans in a crockery or glass bowl and cover with wet paper towels.

Start the soup: Coarsely chop the celery, onion, carrots and parsley all together on a board. Heat the olive oil in a large stockpot over medium heat and when the oil is warm, add the chopped ingredients and sauté for 10 minutes, stirring every so often with a wooden spoon. Add the tomato paste and cook for 5 minutes more.

Soak the cabbage, Swiss chard and potatoes in a large bowl of cold water.

Add the cooking water from the beans to the stockpot, season with salt, pepper and thyme, and simmer for 15 minutes. Drain all the vegetables in the bowl of cold water and add to the stockpot. Cook for 45 minutes, adding broth as needed. The soup should be rather thick. Add the beans 5 minutes before the soup is ready.

Arrange a layer of bread in a large crockery or glass bowl. Ladle the soup over the bread and repeat this layering of the bread and soup until all the bread and soup are used up, finishing with a layer of soup. Let cool for ½ hour, then cover and refrigerate overnight.

The following day, reheat the *ribollita* in a stockpot and serve hot with olive oil poured over each serving. In the Carmignano area, small portions of *ribollita* are reheated with some olive oil in a skillet so that the bread forms a thin crust. Additional olive oil is then sprinkled over each serving.

Serves 6 to 8.

8 ounces dried cannellini beans
5 quarts cold water
1 celery stalk
1 small carrot, scraped
2 medium-sized cloves garlic, peeled
1 tablespoon olive oil
2 ounces prosciutto or pancetta, in one piece
Coarse-grained salt

FOR THE SOUP
2 celery stalks
1 large red onion, cleaned
2 medium-sized carrots, scraped
15 sprigs Italian parsley, leaves only
6 tablespoons olive oil
2 tablespoons tomato paste
1 pound Savoy cabbage, cut into ½-inch strips
1 pound Swiss chard, cut into 1-inch strips, large stems discarded
2 all-purpose potatoes, peeled and cut into 2-inch cubes
Salt and freshly ground black pepper
A large pinch of dried thyme
3 cups chicken or meat broth, preferably homemade

PLUS
8 large slices Tuscan bread, several days old

TO SERVE
Olive oil

DRIED PASTA

The dried pasta shapes that are considered most characteristic of Tuscan cuisine are smooth or ridged penne (feathers), denti di cavallo (horse's teeth), which resemble small ridged rigatoni, and bavette, which look like flattened linguine and, in Tuscany, are used almost exclusively with seafood. (The people of Naples, so famous for their seafood and pasta dishes, instead use a thin spaghetti called vermicelli, and the flat linguine used for this purpose in Neapolitan seafood and pasta dishes overseas is not really popular there.)

Also popular in Tuscany (as in the rest of Italy) is spaghetti. The most popular pastine (little pasta shapes usually used in broths) include grandinina and orzo. In this section, I present dried pasta with vegetable, fish and meat sauces. Tuscan sauces, even when combined with sturdy dried pastas, retain their lightness.

Montalcino's splendid vineyards.

PASTA WITH TOMATOES

When sauces are made with fresh tomatoes, seasonings are kept
to a minimum in order to emphasize the flavor of the tomatoes.
The most classic of these sauces is seasoned only with basil, and
is served over the most delicate pastas. The recipe I have included
here, Chiocciole al pomodoro ed aglio, is made a little
more robust with the addition of garlic and a light pinch of hot
red pepper, and a more substantial pasta called chiocciole (a
short snail-shaped pasta). Because this dish is seasoned with hot
red pepper, it should not be sprinkled with cheese (as cheese and
hot red pepper are not a common combination in Tuscan cooking).
In Penne alla toscana, fresh or canned tomatoes are made into
a pommarola-type sauce with vegetables to which extra sautéed
onion is added. Spaghetti di San Giovanni, a dish to enjoy
after the fireworks on the celebration day for Florence's patron
saint, is made with tomato paste instead of fresh or canned
tomatoes, and is served with fresh mint instead of basil.

CHIOCCIOLE AL POMODORO ED AGLIO

Pasta with Garlic-Flavored Fresh Tomato Sauce ALL OVER TUSCANY

Clean the tomatoes, removing the tough part where the stem was
attached, then cut them in half and cut each half into slices about
½ inch thick. Do not peel the tomatoes or remove the seeds.

Place the tomatoes in a skillet. Coarsely chop the garlic,
then add the basil, olive oil and garlic to the skillet.

Place a medium-sized stockpot full of cold water over
medium heat. When the water reaches a boil, add salt to taste,
then the pasta and cook for 8 to 11 minutes, according to the
brand, that is, 1 minute less than for standard al dente. As you
add the pasta to the boiling water, place the skillet for the sauce
over high heat, season with salt, pepper and the hot red pepper
flakes, and stir as needed.

Drain the pasta, transfer it to the skillet, mix very well and
sauté for 1 minute. Add the basil, mix again and transfer to a
large serving platter. Serve hot.

Serves 4 to 6.

1 pound very ripe fresh tomatoes
3 large cloves garlic, peeled
5 large fresh basil leaves, torn
    into thirds
4 tablespoons olive oil
Salt and freshly ground black pepper
Pinch of hot red pepper flakes

PLUS
1 pound dried chiocciole (snail-
    shaped pasta) or short tubular
    pasta, preferably imported
    Italian

TO COOK THE PASTA
Coarse-grained salt

TO SERVE
10 fresh basil leaves

PENNE ALLA TOSCANA

Penne with Sautéed Onions

The ridged local tomatoes that are used to
make tomato sauce in Tuscany.

FOR THE SAUCE
2 pounds very ripe fresh tomatoes
    or 2 pounds drained canned
    tomatoes, preferably
    imported Italian
2 large red onions, cleaned
1 celery stalk
5 sprigs Italian parsley, leaves only
1 large carrot, scraped
5 large basil leaves, fresh or
    preserved in salt
10 tablespoons olive oil
Salt and freshly ground black pepper

PLUS
1 pound dried *penne*, preferably
    imported Italian

TO COOK THE PASTA
Coarse-grained salt

TO SERVE
Freshly grated *Parmigiano*

If fresh tomatoes are used, cut them into large pieces. Place the fresh or canned tomatoes in a medium-sized casserole.

Coarsely chop 1 of the onions, the celery, parsley, carrot and basil all together on a board. Transfer the chopped ingredients to the casserole and add 5 tablespoons of the oil. Set the casserole over medium heat and simmer, stirring every so often with a wooden spoon, for 30 minutes, or until the vegetables are soft. Season with salt and pepper.

Pass the contents of the saucepan through a food mill, using the disc with the smallest holes, into a crockery or glass bowl.

Finely chop the remaining onion on a board. Heat the remaining 5 tablespoons oil in a medium-sized skillet over medium heat. When the oil is warm, add the onion and sauté for 10 minutes, or until translucent, stirring with a wooden spoon. Add the strained tomato sauce to the sautéed onion, season with salt and pepper and simmer for 10 minutes more.

Bring a large pot of cold water to a boil over medium heat, add coarse salt to taste, then the pasta and cook for 9 to 12 minutes, according to the brand, until *al dente*.

Drain the pasta and transfer to a large serving bowl. Pour the sauce over the pasta, mix very well and serve hot with freshly grated *Parmigiano*.

Serves 4 to 6.

I FUOCHI DI SAN GIOVANNI ·
THE FIREWORKS FOR THE FEAST
OF SAN GIOVANNI

Florence has always expressed its civic pride extravagantly on June 24th, the celebration day of its patron saint, John the Baptist (San Giovanni). During Medieval times, huge fires were lit on the street and in front of the city's main palaces, but when this tradition proved too dangerous—a few too many buildings caught fire—the people chose, instead, to use a mass of oil lamps to illuminate the main piazzas and monuments. In the fifteenth century, after Marco Polo brought gunpowder back from China, the Florentines started to copy the Chinese tradition of using gunpowder to create fireworks. A fresco in the Palazzo Vecchio, Florence's city hall, portrays one of these Renaissance celebrations, complete with both the fireworks and the oil lamps.

In 1826, after the tower of the Palazzo Vecchio caught fire during the festivities, The Hapsburg-Lorraine Grand Duke Leopold II moved the fireworks display to the Carraia bridge over the Arno. Today, the fireworks are shot toward the Arno from the high hill of Piazzale Michelangelo and may be seen clearly from the banks of the river, where tens of thousands gather to watch on the evening of San Giovanni. While taking the photographs for this book, we enjoyed a grand buffet and a spectacular close-up view of the fireworks from the terrace of the Hotel Continental, which is located on the north bank of the river.

SPAGHETTI DI SAN GIOVANNI

Pasta for the Fireworks

FLORENCE

Cook the pasta and prepare the sauce at the same time: Bring a large pot of cold water to a boil over medium heat and place a large skillet with the oil over medium heat.

When the oil is warm, add the whole cloves of garlic and lightly sauté for 2 to 3 minutes, or until the garlic is very lightly golden; if the garlic is sautéed longer, the sauce will be very sour. Add the tomato paste to the skillet and season with salt, pepper and the hot red pepper flakes. Sauté for 2 minutes, then add 1 cup of the water boiling for the pasta.

Add coarse salt to the large pot of boiling water, then add the pasta and cook for 8 to 11 minutes, depending on the brand, that is 1 minute less than for standard *al dente*.

Meanwhile, while the sauce is simmering and the pasta is cooking, coarsely chop the parsley and finely chop the garlic.

FOR THE SAUCE
½ cup olive oil
6 medium-sized cloves garlic,
    peeled and left whole
6 tablespoons tomato paste
Salt and freshly ground black pepper
A large pinch of hot red pepper
    flakes

PLUS
1 pound dried spaghetti,
    preferably imported Italian

TO SERVE
20 large sprigs Italian parsley,
    leaves only
3 medium-sized cloves garlic, peeled
Several fresh mint leaves

When the pasta is ready, drain it and transfer to the skillet with the sauce. Raise the heat to high, mix very well, taste for salt and pepper and cook for 1 minute more. Sprinkle on the chopped parsley and garlic, mix very well and transfer to a large serving platter. Sprinkle the mint leaves all over and serve hot.

Serves 4 to 6.

GRANDININA O ORZO COI PISELLI

Grandinina or Orzo with Peas   LIVORNO

Although outside of Italy it has become popular in recent years to match orzo *with different vegetables and sauces and even fish and meats, in Italy this would never be done. In fact,* Grandinina o orzo coi piselli *is one of the rare instances where* pastine *are combined with sauce at all, as* pastine *are primarily reserved for use in broth. The match is made in this recipe because the peas require a pasta of their own size. Either* orzo, *which in Italian means both "barley" and this barley-shaped pasta, or* grandinina, *which means "a tiny drop of hail," can be used in this recipe.*

1 medium-sized red onion, cleaned
2 celery stalks
2 medium-sized carrots, scraped
20 sprigs Italian parsley, leaves only
6 large basil leaves, fresh or
    preserved in salt
4 ounces pancetta, in one piece
½ cup olive oil
Salt and freshly ground black pepper
1½ pounds shelled fresh peas, or
    frozen "tiny tender" peas

PLUS
3 quarts chicken or meat broth,
    preferably homemade
1 pound dried *grandinina* or other
    pastine, such as *orzo* or *stelline,*
    preferably imported Italian
15 sprigs Italian parsley, leaves only
10 fresh basil leaves

TO SERVE
Italian parsley, leaves only
Fresh basil leaves

Coarsely chop the onion, celery, carrots, parsley and basil all together on a board. Cut the pancetta into tiny pieces. Heat the oil in a medium-sized casserole over medium heat and when the oil is warm, add the pancetta and sauté for 2 minutes. Add the chopped ingredients and sauté for 15 minutes more, stirring every so often with a wooden spoon. Season with salt and pepper, then add 1 cup of the broth and let the sauce cook for 15 minutes more.

Meanwhile, bring the remaining broth to a boil over medium heat.

Add the peas to the casserole with the sauce and cook until heated through but still firm, adding lukewarm water if needed.

When the broth reaches a boil, add the pasta and cook 9 to 12 minutes, depending on the brand, until *al dente.* Drain the pasta, discarding the broth, and transfer it to the casserole with the peas. Add the parsley and basil leaves and mix very well. Serve with additional parsley and basil leaves sprinkled over each serving.

This dish is considered a soup and should be eaten with a spoon.

Serves 6 to 8.

SPAGHETTI AI FIORI DI ZUCCA

Pasta with Zucchini Blossoms

30 very large zucchini blossoms
3 ounces prosciutto or pancetta,
   in one piece
20 sprigs Italian parsley, leaves only
4 medium-sized cloves garlic, peeled
6 tablespoons olive oil
1 tablespoon (½ ounce) sweet
   butter
Salt and freshly ground black pepper
Pinch of ground saffron
1 cup chicken or meat broth,
   preferably homemade

PLUS
1 pound dried spaghetti,
   preferably imported Italian

TO COOK THE PASTA
Coarse-grained salt

TO SERVE
Italian parsley leaves

Chianti landscape.

Following pages: Spaghetti ai fiori di
zucca *(Pasta with Zucchini Blossoms)*
set against the famous sculpture of
Primavera (Spring) that decorates the
S. Trinita Bridge. This sculpture, along
with sculptures representing the other
three seasons, was moved from the Boboli
Gardens to the four corners of this bridge
in 1608 in order to decorate the bridge for
the marriage of Grand Duke Cosimo II
to an Austrian princess.

*Zucchini blossoms are eaten in many ways in Italy: fried, stuffed
or in risotti or pastas. In Spaghetti ai fiori di zucca, they are
flavored with prosciutto and saffron and are served over spaghetti.*

*In the photograph on pages 100–101, a serving platter of
Spaghetti ai fiori di zucca floats in front of the famous sculp-
ture of Primavera (Spring) that decorates the S. Trinita Bridge.
Architecturally, this bridge, designed by Ammanati with input
from Michelangelo, is preferred by the Florentines even to the Ponte
Vecchio. In the background is the white Palazzo dei Padre delle
Missioni and the bell tower of the church of S. Jacopo sopr'Arno.
This white palazzo was the seat of the Navy during the 1860s
when Florence was the capital of the newly united Italy.*

Remove the stems of the zucchini blossoms, being careful not to
break the blossoms, and detach the pistil from the inside. Wash
the cleaned blossoms under cold running water and lightly pat
them dry with paper towels.

Cut the prosciutto into tiny pieces and finely chop the parsley
and garlic on a board. Heat the oil and butter in a skillet over
medium heat and when the butter is melted, add the chopped
ingredients along with the cut-up prosciutto. Sauté for 2 minutes.

Meanwhile, place a large pot of cold water over medium heat.

Add the whole zucchini blossoms to the skillet and sauté for
3 minutes more.

When the water in the stockpot reaches a boil, add coarse
salt, then the pasta and cook for 9 to 12 minutes, depending on
the brand, until *al dente.*

Season the contents of the skillet with salt and pepper, then, in
a separate bowl, dissolve the saffron in the broth. Add the broth to
the skillet, raise the heat and cook until the pasta is ready.

Drain the pasta and transfer it to a large serving platter. Pour
the contents of the skillet over the spaghetti, mix very well,
then sprinkle the parsley leaves all over and serve hot.

Serves 4 to 6.

PASTA WITH SEAFOOD

Most Tuscan pasta sauces made with seafood include white wine.
They can be made with tomatoes or in bianco, without tomatoes.
In Spaghetti ai gamberi from Livorno, the tomato-wine sauce
for the shrimp or lobster is seasoned with hot red pepper, which is
typical of dishes from Livorno. In Pasta alla viareggina, a fish
wrapped in cheesecloth flavors the sauce while it is cooking but is
removed from the sauce before serving. Additional flavoring for this
dish comes from parsley, garlic and basil, an herb that is often used
with fish in the Viareggio area. In the seafood dish from Grosseto,
called Bavette all'ammiraglia in bianco, calamari, cuttlefish,
octopus, clams and peas are cooked in wine and olive oil, and it is
the liquid from the seafood that forms the base of the sauce.

S P A G H E T T I   A I   G A M B E R I

Spaghetti with Shrimp or Lobster

LIVORNO

Place the shrimp in a bowl of cold water with the coarse salt
and the lemon cut in half and squeezed, and soak for ½ hour.

Meanwhile, finely chop the carrot, onion, garlic and parsley
all together on a board. Heat the olive oil in a non-reactive skillet
over medium heat and when the oil is warm, add the chopped
ingredients and sauté for 10 minutes, stirring every so often with
a wooden spoon. Add the wine and simmer for 15 minutes.

If fresh tomatoes are used, blanch them, removing the skin
and seeds, and cut them into large pieces. If canned tomatoes
are used, pass them through a food mill, using the disc with the
smallest holes, into a crockery or glass bowl.

Add the tomatoes, season with salt, pepper and the hot red
pepper flakes, and cook for 30 minutes more, stirring every so
often with a wooden spoon.

Drain the shrimp and rinse under cold running water, then
shell and, if needed, devein them.

Bring a large pot of cold water to a boil over medium heat,
add coarse salt to taste, then the pasta and cook for 8 to 11
minutes, depending on the brand, that is 1 minute less than for
standard *al dente*.

As the pasta cooks, coarsely chop the parsley and garlic
all together.

Add the shrimp to the skillet with the sauce, mix very well
and cook, covered, for 2 minutes.

1 pound medium-sized shrimp or
    ¾ pound cooked lobster meat
    (see Note)
½ tablespoon coarse-grained salt
1 lemon
1 medium-sized carrot, scraped
1 small red onion, cleaned
1 large clove garlic, peeled
20 sprigs Italian parsley, leaves only
4 tablespoons olive oil
1 cup dry white wine
1½ pounds very ripe tomatoes or
    1½ pounds drained canned
    tomatoes, preferably
    imported Italian
Salt and freshly ground black pepper
A large pinch of hot red pepper
    flakes

PLUS
1 pound dried spaghetti,
    preferably imported Italian

TO COOK THE PASTA
Coarse-grained salt

TO SERVE
20 sprigs Italian parsley, leaves only
2 medium-sized cloves garlic, peeled

Drain the pasta, transfer to the skillet, mix very well and let the pasta cook for 2 minutes more. Sprinkle on the garlic-parsley mixture and mix very well. Transfer everything to a large serving platter and serve hot.

Note: If using lobster instead of shrimp, skip the directions for soaking and cooking the shrimp. Add the lobster to the skillet when you would have added the shrimp but sauté it for just 30 seconds; then add the pasta to the skillet and continue with the final steps of the recipe as directed.

Serves 4 to 6.

P A S T A   A L L A   V I A R E G G I N A

Viareggio-Style Pasta with Fish Sauce — VIAREGGIO

15 sprigs Italian parsley, leaves only
15 basil leaves, fresh or preserved
    in salt
4 large cloves garlic, peeled
6 tablespoons olive oil
1 cup dry white wine
1½ pounds very ripe fresh
    tomatoes, cut into pieces, or
    1½ pounds drained canned
    tomatoes, preferably
    imported Italian
Salt and freshly ground black pepper
A large pinch of freshly grated
    nutmeg
1 porgy or any other inexpensive,
    non-oily fish, with head and
    tail on, cleaned (about
    ¾ pound)
1 lemon

PLUS
1 pound dried short tubular pasta,
    such as *penne*, preferably
    imported Italian

TO COOK THE PASTA
Coarse-grained salt

TO SERVE
10 sprigs Italian parsley, leaves only

OPTIONAL
8 medium-sized shrimp, cleaned
    and parboiled in salted water,
    cut into thirds

Finely chop the parsley, basil and garlic all together on a board. Place a medium-sized skillet with the oil over medium heat and when the oil is warm, add the chopped ingredients and sauté for 5 minutes. Add the wine and cook for 10 minutes more.

Meanwhile, pass the fresh or canned tomatoes through a food mill, using the disc with the smallest holes, into a crockery or glass bowl.

Add the tomatoes to the skillet, season with salt, pepper and nutmeg, and simmer for 15 minutes more.

Place the fish in a bowl of cold water with the lemon cut in half and squeezed, and soak until the sauce is reduced. Rinse the fish in cold running water, then wrap it in cheesecloth and put it in the skillet with the sauce. Let cook for 25 minutes, turning it two or three times.

Meanwhile, place a large pot of cold water over medium heat. When the water reaches a boil, add coarse salt to taste, then the pasta and cook for 8 to 11 minutes, depending on the brand, that is 1 minute less than for standard *al dente.*

Drain the pasta, remove the fish from the sauce and add the pasta to the skillet. Raise the heat, mix the pasta very well, taste for salt and pepper and sprinkle the parsley all over. If using the shrimp, distribute them throughout. Mix again and transfer to a large serving platter. Serve hot.

Serves 4 to 6.

BAVETTE ALL'AMMIRAGLIA IN BIANCO

Bavette with Seafood and Peas

Cut the calamari and cuttlefish into ½-inch rings and the octopus into 2-inch pieces. Cut all the tentacles into small pieces. Place in a bowl of cold water with 1 lemon cut in half and squeezed and a little coarse salt, and soak for ½ hour. Place the clams in a second bowl of cold water. Add coarse salt and the other lemon (cut in half and squeezed), and soak for ½ hour.

Finely chop the garlic and parsley all together on a board. Heat the oil in a medium-sized skillet over medium heat. When the oil is warm, add the chopped ingredients and sauté for 2 minutes.

Drain the calamari, inksquid and octopus, rinse under cold running water and add to the skillet. Sauté for 10 minutes, stirring every so often with a wooden spoon. Add the wine and let it evaporate for 5 minutes. Season with salt and pepper. If the seafood is very small, by that time it should be very soft; otherwise add ½ cup lukewarm water and simmer, covered, for 15 minutes more. Add the peas, cook for 2 minutes and mix very well.

Drain the clams, rinse them under cold running water and add them to the skillet. Cover the skillet and cook for about 5 minutes or more, depending on the size of the clams. If the clams are small and very fresh, by that time they should all be cooked and open (discard the ones that do not open).

Meanwhile, place a large pot of cold water over medium heat. When the water reaches a boil, add coarse salt, then the pasta and cook for 9 to 12 minutes, depending on the brand, until *al dente*.

Add the parsley to the sauce, taste for salt and pepper and mix very well.

Drain the pasta and transfer it to a large serving platter. Pour the contents of the skillet over the pasta, mix very well and serve hot.

Serves 4 to 6.

½ pound calamari, cleaned
½ pound very small cuttlefish (inksquid), cleaned, or an additional ½ pound calamari
½ pound tiny octopus, cleaned, or an additional ½ pound calamari
2 lemons
1 pound of the smallest clams available, left in shell and scrubbed
Coarse-grained salt
4 large cloves garlic, peeled
35 sprigs Italian parsley, leaves only
½ cup olive oil
½ cup dry white wine
Salt and freshly ground black pepper
4 ounces shelled fresh peas, or frozen "tiny tender" peas

PLUS
1 pound dried *bavette* or linguine, preferably imported Italian

TO COOK THE PASTA
Coarse-grained salt

TO SERVE
15 sprigs Italian parsley, leaves only, coarsely chopped

Sautéed Penne with Meat Sauce

Dishes like this one, in which cooked penne is sautéed in a meat sauce, are very common in Tuscany. There are also various versions of meat sauce in this region (most of them feature red wine), and what makes Penne girate al sugo *unique is its use of beef only, ground rather than snipped, combined with prosciutto and, if desired, chicken livers.*

FOR THE MEAT SAUCE
2 celery stalks
1 large red onion, cleaned
2 medium-sized carrots
10 sprigs Italian parsley, leaves only
2 cloves garlic, peeled
4 tablespoons olive oil
4 tablespoons (2 ounces) sweet
    butter
4 ounces prosciutto or pancetta,
    in one piece
4 ounces ground beef
4 chicken livers (optional)
1 cup dry red wine
Salt and freshly ground black pepper
4 tablespoons tomato paste
1 cup chicken or meat broth,
    preferably homemade

PLUS
1 pound dried *penne*, preferably
    imported Italian

TO COOK THE PASTA
Coarse-grained salt

TO SERVE (OPTIONAL)
Freshly grated *Parmigiano*

Prepare the sauce: Finely chop the celery, onion, carrots, parsley and garlic all together on a board. Place a medium-sized saucepan with the oil and butter over medium heat and when the butter is melted, add the chopped ingredients and sauté for 10 minutes, stirring every so often with a wooden spoon.

Meanwhile, using a meat grinder, coarsely grind the prosciutto or pancetta, along with the ground beef (grinding the beef again) and the chicken livers (if using), into a crockery or glass bowl

Add the meat to the pan and sauté for 15 minutes, stirring every so often with a wooden spoon. Add the wine and season with salt and pepper. Let the wine evaporate for 15 minutes. Dissolve the tomato paste in ½ cup of the broth and add to the meat mixture. Lower the heat and simmer for 35 minutes, adding the remaining ½ cup broth as needed.

Place a large pot of cold water over medium heat. When the water reaches a boil, add coarse salt to taste, then the pasta and cook for 8 to 11 minutes, depending on the brand, that is 1 minute less than for standard *al dente.*

Drain the pasta, add it to the saucepan and *gira* (the word *gira* means to stir pasta with sauce) with a wooden spoon, until most of the sauce is absorbed by the pasta. Serve hot, with or without *Parmigiano.*

Serves 4 to 6.

F R E S H   P A S T A

There is no denying that the Florentine method of making basic yellow pasta with flour, whole eggs and a little oil and salt has been widely influential all over Tuscany, but it is still fascinating to consider the enormous variety of pastas that exist in this region. (This variety is not surprising when you consider that each Tuscan city and town was once an independent entity, and most hold on dearly to their own identities—and culinary traditions.) Just by altering the ingredients slightly a great variety of results can be achieved: The dough can be made with different flours, or it can include only egg yolks or whites; water, flavorings or vegetables (to change the pasta's color) can be added; or the oil can be eliminated. Additional variety is introduced by cutting the pasta into different shapes and varying its thickness.

The Tuscan aesthetic sense prompts the people of this region to shape their haystacks into small huts.

REGIONAL PASTAS: A CULINARY JOURNEY THROUGH TUSCANY

We *begin our tour in Florence with one of its great pasta dishes,* Toppe al sugo di cappone. Toppe *are three-inch pasta squares, affectionately referred to as "patches." The rich sauce that accompanies them draws its essence from a whole capon, which, once the sauce is ready, is removed and discarded, or saved for another use. Although this dish can be made with a chicken instead of a capon, this option should only be employed as a last resort—if you cannot find a capon—since capon has a much more full-bodied flavor than chicken, and will produce a more satisfying and authentic result.*

Next, we travel to the Chianti area, which begins right at the southern border of Florence and extends to the gates of Siena, for Pasta alle olive, *a dish that features this area's own ripe olives. We know that Chianti's olive oil is among the finest in the world, but it is its superb eating olives that are made into a paste and added to the pasta dough as well as the sauce in this dish. Also from Chianti are the fanciful* Pezze della nonna, *or grandmother's kerchiefs: pasta wrapped around a spinach stuffing, baked in a* balsamella *sauce and served with a* pommarola *sauce.*

Some of the castles of Chianti date back as far as 1000 A.D. and are built on Roman foundations. In the Middle Ages, though, when central authority had broken down, each Chianti castle became a fortress and its ruler a warrior knight of the Holy Roman Empire. (Their association, the League of Chianti, started as a group of warriors and was revived in later centuries as a league of wine producers.) As Florence became more powerful, one by one these feudal lords were forced to live inside the city walls. Once inside, each tried to outdo the others by building the highest tower—so that he could upset his rivals in a variety of ways, including pouring hot olive oil down on them (presumably the best extra-virgin). Finally, the city authorities had to intervene and pull down these towers.

"Patches" in Capon Sauce

Prepare the pasta with the ingredients and quantities listed at right (see Appendix, page 293). Stretch the layer of pasta to a thickness of less than $\frac{1}{16}$ of an inch; on the pasta machine take it to the last notch. Immediately cut the layer of pasta into 3-inch squares. Let the pasta rest on cotton dish towels until needed.

Prepare the sauce: Carefully wash the capon, then dry it with paper towels and place it in a crockery or glass bowl. Pour the wine over the capon and marinate for $\frac{1}{2}$ hour.

Meanwhile, finely chop the carrots, celery, onions, parsley, garlic and rosemary all together on a board.

Place a medium-sized heavy casserole with the oil over medium heat and when the oil is warm, add the chopped ingredients and sauté for 15 minutes, stirring every so often with a wooden spoon.

Add the whole clove to the wine with the capon and let sit for 10 more minutes.

Cut the pancetta into tiny pieces. When the sautéed vegetables are ready, add the pancetta and sauté for 5 minutes more.

Drain the capon, saving the wine, and add it to the casserole. Sauté until light gold all over, about 10 minutes. Discard the clove. Start adding the reserved wine to the casserole, $\frac{1}{2}$ cup at a time, letting each $\frac{1}{2}$ cup evaporate before adding the next, until it is all used up. Add the tomato paste, season with salt and pepper, then add 1 cup of the broth. Cover, lower the heat and cook for $1\frac{1}{2}$ hours, adding more broth as needed, stirring the sauce every so often and turning the capon over at least four times. By that time the capon should be cooked and soft.

Transfer the capon to a serving dish and pass the sauce through a food mill, first using the disc with the largest holes, then the disc with the medium-sized holes, into a casserole. Place the casserole over low heat, taste for salt and pepper and reduce for 10 minutes more, or until a fairly thick sauce forms.

Meanwhile, bring a large pot of cold water to a boil and melt the butter. When the water reaches a boil, add coarse salt to taste, then the pasta and cook for 1 to 3 minutes, depending on the dryness of the pasta.

FOR THE PASTA
3 ½ to 4 cups unbleached
    all-purpose flour
8 extra-large egg yolks
8 teaspoons olive oil or
    vegetable oil
½ cup cold water
Pinch of salt

FOR THE SAUCE
1 capon (about 3 ½ pounds),
    cleaned (see Note)
2 cups dry red wine
2 medium-sized carrots, scraped
3 celery stalks
2 medium-sized red onions, cleaned
20 sprigs Italian parsley, leaves only
1 medium-sized clove garlic, peeled
1 teaspoon rosemary leaves, fresh,
    preserved in salt or dried and
    blanched
½ cup olive oil
1 whole clove
4 ounces pancetta or prosciutto,
    in one piece
6 tablespoons tomato paste
Salt and freshly ground black pepper
3 cups lukewarm chicken or meat
    broth, preferably homemade

TO COOK THE PASTA
Coarse-grained salt

TO SERVE
4 tablespoons (2 ounces) sweet
    butter
½ cup freshly grated *Parmigiano*

Drain the pasta and transfer it to a large bowl. Add the melted butter, mix very well, then add all the sauce, mix again and transfer to a large serving platter. Serve hot with the *Parmigiano* sprinkled over each serving.

Note: The size of capons most often found is about 7 pounds. If you use a 7-pound capon, double the amounts of all the ingredients in sauce and either double the amount of pasta also or use only half of the sauce for this recipe, saving the other half for another time.

Serves 6 to 8.

P A S T A   A L L E   O L I V E

Olive Pasta

FOR THE PASTA
4 cups unbleached all-purpose flour
4 extra-large eggs
3 tablespoons olive paste,
    homemade from large black
    Greek olives, or commercial
    paste from a tube (made from
    black olives only, with no
    additional ingredients)
Pinch of salt

FOR THE SAUCE
6 tablespoons olive oil
4 large cloves garlic, peeled
2 pounds very ripe fresh tomatoes
    or 2 pounds drained canned
    tomatoes, preferably
    imported Italian
6 tablespoons olive paste (see
    above for description)
Salt and freshly ground black pepper

TO COOK THE PASTA
Coarse-grained salt

TO SERVE
20 sprigs Italian parsley, leaves only

Prepare the pasta with the ingredients and quantities listed at left (see Appendix, page 293), placing the olive paste in the well of the flour along with the eggs. Stretch the sheet of pasta to a thickness of about 1/16 of an inch; on the pasta machine take it to the next to the last notch. Cut the pasta into spaghetti, using the finer cutter on the pasta machine, and let rest on cotton towels until needed.

Prepare the sauce: Heat the oil in a medium-sized saucepan over medium heat. Meanwhile, coarsely chop the garlic on a board. When the oil is warm, add the chopped garlic and sauté for 2 minutes.

If fresh tomatoes are used, cut them into small pieces. Pass the fresh or canned tomatoes through a food mill, using the disc with the smallest holes, into a crockery or glass bowl.

Add the olive paste to the saucepan, mix very well, then add the tomatoes and simmer for 20 minutes, stirring every so often with a wooden spoon. Taste for salt and pepper. After 20 minutes the sauce should be quite thick and very smooth.

Meanwhile, bring a large pot of cold water to a boil, add coarse salt, then the pasta and cook for 3 to 5 minutes, depending on the dryness.

Coarsely chop the parsley on a board.

Drain the pasta and place it on a large warmed platter. Pour all the sauce over the pasta, toss very well and serve with the chopped parsley on top.

Serves 6.

Grandmothers' Kerchiefs (Stuffed Pasta Squares)

Prepare the *pommarola* sauce first: Very coarsely chop the onion, celery, garlic, carrot, parsley and basil all together on a board.

If fresh tomatoes are used, cut them into large pieces. Place the fresh or canned tomatoes in a medium-sized non-reactive casserole and add the chopped vegetables and oil. Do not mix. Cover the casserole, set over low heat and cook for 1½ hours, shaking (not mixing) the casserole every so often to prevent the tomatoes from sticking to the bottom.

Pass the contents of the casserole through a food mill, using the disc with the smallest holes, into a second casserole. Place the new casserole with the sauce over medium heat, add the butter and salt and pepper to taste. Mix very well and let reduce for 15 minutes, stirring every so often with a wooden spoon. When ready, transfer the sauce to a crockery or glass bowl and let stand until needed. The sauce can be prepared up to two days in advance and stored, covered, in the refrigerator.

Prepare the *balsamella:* Melt the butter over low heat in a heavy (preferably copper or enamel) saucepan. When the butter starts to froth, add all of the flour, in one addition, and stir with a wooden spoon. Continuing to stir, cook the mixture until the flour is completely incorporated, 1 to 3 minutes. If any lumps form, use the wooden spoon to crush them against the side of the pan. Remove the mixture from the heat and let stand for the time it takes for the milk to reach a boil.

While the butter-flour mixture is standing, pour the milk into another saucepan and heat until it comes close to the boiling point. Place the pan with the butter-flour mixture over low heat and, all at once, add the nearly boiling milk and stir until smooth. Continue to cook the sauce over low heat and when it starts to boil, add the salt and cook, stirring gently, for about 10 minutes. Transfer the *balsamella* to a crockery or glass bowl and press a piece of buttered waxed paper over it to prevent a skin from forming.

Prepare the stuffing: Soak the spinach in a bowl of cold water for ½ hour.

Place a large pot of cold water over medium heat and when the water reaches a boil, add coarse salt to taste, then drain the spinach, add it to the pot and boil for 5 minutes.

Drain the spinach and cool under cold running water. Squeeze the spinach (not absolutely dry) and finely chop it on a board.

Place the spinach, ricotta, egg, egg yolks and *Parmigiano* in a crockery or glass bowl and mix very well. Season with salt, pepper and nutmeg, mix again, cover and refrigerate until needed.

Prepare the pasta with the ingredients and quantities listed on the top of the following page (see Appendix, page 293). Stretch the layer of pasta to a thickness of a little less than ¹⁄₁₆ of an inch;

The round baking pan with all the pezze, or kerchiefs, in place. Next the balsamella will be added and the baking dish will be transferred to the oven. On the board you can see the technique for folding the "kerchiefs."

FOR THE *POMMAROLA* SAUCE
1 medium-sized red onion, cleaned
1 medium-sized celery stalk
1 large clove garlic, peeled
1 medium-sized carrot, scraped
10 sprigs Italian parsley, leaves only
8 large basil leaves, fresh or
    preserved in salt
2 pounds very ripe fresh tomatoes
    or 2 pounds drained canned
    tomatoes, preferably
    imported Italian
2 tablespoons olive oil
2 tablespoons (1 ounce) sweet
    butter
Salt and freshly ground black pepper

FOR THE *BALSAMELLA*
½ cup (4 ounces) sweet butter
4 tablespoons unbleached
    all-purpose flour
3 ½ cups whole milk
Salt and freshly ground black pepper

FOR THE STUFFING
2 ½ pounds spinach, cleaned,
    large stems removed
Coarse-grained salt
1 pound ricotta, drained very well
1 extra-large egg
3 extra-large egg yolks
1 cup freshly grated *Parmigiano*
Salt and freshly ground black pepper
Freshly grated nutmeg

FOR THE PASTA
2 ¼ cups unbleached all-purpose
  flour
4 extra-large egg yolks
¼ cup cold water
2 tablespoons olive oil or
  vegetable oil
Pinch of salt

TO COOK THE PASTA
Coarse-grained salt
2 tablespoons vegetable oil or
  olive oil

PLUS
2 tablespoons (1 ounce) sweet
  butter

TO SERVE
Large fresh basil leaves

A close-up of a single serving of the "kerchiefs." The pommarola *sauce is added at the table.*

on the pasta machine take it to the last notch. Cut the pasta sheet into 6-inch lasagne squares.

Precook the lasagne squares in salted water for a few seconds, then transfer them to a bowl of cold water to which the oil has been added. Remove the squares from the water and let rest on dampened cotton dish towels until needed.

Preheat the oven to 375 degrees. Use the 2 tablespoons of butter to grease an ovenproof 15-inch round baking dish or a 13½-by-8¾-inch glass baking pan.

Place 2 heaping tablespoons of the stuffing in the center of each pasta square. Fold it into a triangle, then take the two side ends and fold them to meet the lower end. Without pressing on them, gently transfer the stuffed *pezze* into the prepared dish, with the stuffed part of the *pezza* touching the side of the dish and the unstuffed part pointing towards the middle. Arrange the remaining *pezze* in the same way, forming two circles, one inside the other.

Pour the *balsamella* over the *pezze* and bake for 20 minutes.

Meanwhile, reheat the tomato sauce. When ready, place one or two *pezze* on each plate and pour some of the reheated tomato sauce over the unstuffed part of each *pezza*. Add a basil leaf to each plate.

Serves 8 or 16.

MUGELLO

Moving back through Florence to its northern side, we arrive at the valley of Mugello, an agricultural area whose towns include Borgo San Lorenzo and Vicchio, the birthplace of Fra Angelico. Unlike Chianti's majestic landscape, the Mugello is soft and rolling, and the gentle hillsides are covered with little country churches called pievi, many of which date back to about 1000 A.D. The people of the Mugello have always had to be frugal, and in recent centuries, the main stuffing for their pastas has been some form of puréed potatoes flavored with a little meat or sauce. The signature Tortelli di magro alla vicchiese *is enriched, however, with Parmigiano, egg and butter and a delicious vegetable sauce. Many a person has traveled to the Mugello just to eat this dish.*

TORTELLI DI MAGRO ALLA VICCHIESE

Tortelli with Vegetable Stuffing
VICCHIO

Prepare the stuffing first: Place water, coarse salt to taste and the unpeeled potatoes in a medium-sized saucepan. Set the saucepan over medium heat and cook the potatoes until soft, 30 to 40 minutes, depending on their size. Remove the potatoes, immediately peel them, then pass them through a potato ricer into a crockery or glass bowl.

Finely chop the parsley and garlic all together on a board, add to the potatoes and mix very well with a wooden spoon. When the potatoes are cool, add the egg, *Parmigiano,* and salt, pepper and nutmeg to taste. Mix very well and refrigerate, covered, until needed.

Prepare the pasta with the ingredients and quantities listed at right (see Appendix, page 293). Stretch the layer of pasta to a thickness of less than $\frac{1}{16}$ of an inch; on the pasta machine take it to the last notch. To make the *tortelli,* place ½ tablespoon dots of filling, 1½ inches apart, over half the layer of pasta and fold the other half of the layer of pasta on top. With the tips of your fingers, press down on the edges along the center of the two overlapped layers of pasta to remove the air. Using a pastry wheel with a scalloped edge, cut out 1½-inch filled squares. Let the *tortelli* rest on cotton towels until needed.

FOR THE STUFFING
Coarse-grained salt
12 ounces potatoes for boiling
   (not new potatoes)
15 sprigs Italian parsley, leaves only
1 medium-sized clove garlic, peeled
1 extra-large egg
½ cup freshly grated *Parmigiano*
Salt and freshly ground black pepper
Freshly grated nutmeg

FOR THE PASTA
4 cups unbleached all-purpose flour
4 extra-large eggs
4 teaspoons olive oil or
   vegetable oil
Pinch of salt

3 medium-sized celery stalks
3 medium-sized carrots, scraped
15 sprigs Italian parsley, leaves only
1 very small red onion, cleaned
1 small clove garlic, peeled
½ cup olive oil
4 tablespoons tomato paste
2 cups chicken or meat broth,
    preferably homemade
Salt and freshly ground black pepper

TO COOK THE PASTA
Coarse-grained salt

TO SERVE
6 tablespoons (3 ounces) sweet
    butter
½ cup freshly grated *Parmigiano*

Meanwhile, prepare the sauce: Finely chop the celery, carrots, parsley, onion and garlic all together on a board. Heat the oil in a medium-sized saucepan over medium heat and when the oil is warm, add the chopped ingredients and sauté for 5 minutes, stirring every so often with a wooden spoon. Dissolve the tomato paste in the broth and add it to the pan. Simmer over low heat for 20 minutes. Season with salt and pepper and simmer again until half the broth has evaporated. Taste for salt and pepper.

Bring a large pot of cold water to a boil over medium heat and add coarse salt to taste. Quickly but gently add the *tortelli* and cook for 30 seconds to 2 minutes, depending on the dryness of the pasta.

Meanwhile, melt the butter in a small saucepan over boiling water. When the pasta is ready, use a strainer-skimmer to transfer the *tortelli* to a large serving platter. Arrange half of the *tortelli* in a layer on the platter and spoon on half of the melted butter, the sauce and cheese. Make a second layer with the remaining *tortelli*, sauce and cheese.

Serves 8.

EMPOLI AND PISA

In the Arno Valley, from Florence toward the sea, wide handcut pappardelle *is used with a great range of sauces, such as the two presented here.* Pappardelle ai peperoni *from Empoli features the splendid yellow peppers for which this area is known. (Empoli is also famous for its wonderful large artichokes.) In the photograph on page 114, this dish is shown next to the central fountain of the Piazza Farinata degli Uberti, where the Collegiata, Empoli's cathedral, is located. The Collegiata, which was restored in 1093, probably dates back to the fifth century. Its green and white façade, made of marble from Prato and Carrara, is in the same style as Florence's oldest churches: the Baptistry and San Miniato al Monte.*

Continuing our journey southwest to the coast, we arrive in Pisa for Pappardelle alla pisana. *In this dish, the* pappardelle *is dressed with rich goose liver sauce embellished with sage. This dish is traditionally served during Pisa's famous regatta (see page 250), as a pair of geese is one of the prizes.*

Pappardelle with Sweet Peppers

Skin the peppers, remove the stems and pulp and cut the peppers into 1-inch-wide strips.

Finely chop the onions, celery, garlic and parsley all together on a board. Cut the pancetta into tiny pieces. Heat the olive oil in a medium-sized skillet over medium heat and when the oil is warm, add the chopped ingredients and the pancetta, and sauté for 10 minutes, stirring every so often with a wooden spoon.

Pappardelle ai peperoni (*Pappardelle with Sweet Peppers*) next to the central fountain in Empoli's cathedral square. This "young" fountain, which was designed by Pampoloni, dates back only to the early nineteenth century.

As the sauce cooks, prepare the pasta with the ingredients and quantities listed at right (see Appendix, page 293). Stretch the layer of pasta to a thickness of less than $\frac{1}{16}$ of an inch; on the pasta machine take it to the last notch. To make the *pappardelle*, cut the layer of pasta into 2-by-12-inch strips. Cut both sides of the *pappardelle* using a pastry wheel with a scalloped edge. Let the pasta rest on cotton towels until needed.

Season the sauce with salt and pepper, then add the peppers and cook for 5 minutes. Add 1 cup of the broth and keep cooking for 15 minutes more, adding more broth as needed. The sauce should be very creamy and not too thick.

Bring a large pot of cold water to a boil, add coarse salt to taste, then the pasta and cook for 1 to 3 minutes, depending on the dryness.

Drain the pasta and transfer it to the skillet holding the sauce. Sprinkle the parsley all over, mix very well, then transfer the pasta and sauce to a warmed serving platter and serve hot. No cheese should be added.

Serves 8.

FOR THE SAUCE
8 large yellow bell peppers
2 medium-sized red onions, cleaned
2 celery stalks
1 small clove garlic, peeled
10 sprigs Italian parsley, leaves only
4 ounces pancetta or prosciutto, in one piece
6 tablespoons olive oil
Salt and freshly ground black pepper
About 2 cups chicken broth, preferably homemade

PLUS
25 sprigs Italian parsley, leaves only

FOR THE PASTA
4 cups unbleached all-purpose flour
5 extra-large eggs
1 tablespoon cold water
Pinch of salt

TO COOK THE PASTA
Coarse-grained salt

PAPPARDELLE ALLA PISANA

Pappardelle with Goose or Duck Liver Sauce

FOR THE PASTA
4 cups unbleached all-purpose flour
5 extra-large eggs
4 teaspoons cold water
Pinch of salt

FOR THE SAUCE
1 large red onion, cleaned
4 ounces pancetta or prosciutto,
    in one piece
4 tablespoons olive oil
2 large goose or duck livers
    (see Note)
2 ounces dried porcini mushrooms
2 cups lukewarm water
1 cup dry red wine
1 pound very ripe fresh tomatoes,
    cut into pieces, or 1 pound
    drained canned tomatoes
4 large sage leaves, fresh or
    preserved in salt, wrapped in
    a piece of cheesecloth and
    secured with a string to create
    a bag
Salt and freshly ground black pepper

TO COOK THE PASTA
Coarse-grained salt

TO SERVE
Several fresh sage leaves

OPTIONAL
Freshly grated *Parmigiano*

Prepare the *pappardelle* with the quantities and ingredients listed at left (see Appendix, page 293). Stretch the layer of pasta to a thickness of less than $1/16$ of an inch (on the pasta machine take it to the last notch) and cut into 2-inch-by-12-inch strips. Cut both sides of the *pappardelle* using a pastry wheel with a scalloped edge. Let rest on cotton towels until needed.

Prepare the sauce: Finely chop the onion and cut the pancetta into tiny pieces. Place a medium-sized casserole with the oil over medium heat and when the oil is warm, add the onion and pancetta and sauté for about 10 minutes.

Be sure the livers are cleaned, then finely chop them on a board. Soak the mushrooms in the lukewarm water for 30 minutes, then drain them and clean them very well, making sure no sand remains attached to the stems. Save the soaking water, cleaning it by filtering it through paper towels several times.

Add the wine to the casserole, mix very well and let the wine evaporate for 15 minutes.

Pass the fresh or canned tomatoes through a food mill, using the disc with the smallest holes, into a crockery or glass bowl.

Add the mushrooms and tomatoes to the casserole, along with the bag of sage leaves. Cover the casserole and let the sauce simmer for 20 minutes, adding the soaking water from the mushrooms as needed, mixing every so often with a wooden spoon.

Bring a large pot of cold water to a boil over medium heat, add coarse salt to taste, then the pasta and cook for 1 to 3 minutes, depending on the dryness.

Meanwhile, discard the sage bag from the sauce, taste for salt and pepper and raise the heat to high. Add the liver, stir very well and cook for 30 seconds more.

Ladle half of the sauce onto a large serving platter. Drain the pasta and transfer it to the serving platter with the sauce. Pour the remaining sauce over the pasta, mix very well, sprinkle on the sage leaves and serve hot, with or without *Parmigiano*.

Note: For this sauce, use chicken livers only as a last resort.

Serves 8.

LUCCA

We now move inland from Pisa to Lucca, the first capital of Tuscany as created by the heirs of Charlemagne, and to the countryside around Lucca, known as the Lucchesia. This area retained some form of independence up until the unification of Italy, so it is not surprising that the people here jealously guard their culinary heritage.

Typical of this area is the square pasta called tacconi, which takes a rich sauce, whether of game, wild mushrooms or, as presented here, rabbit. Surely Puccini, a native of Lucca, must have eaten tacconi often while writing his beloved operas. Massaciuccoli, the lake on which Puccini's house sat, is today a unique repository of a rare wild duck called the folaghe.

The softness of the Lucchesia is seen in its rolling hills and its olive and chestnut trees, which protect one of Italy's most abundant sources of porcini mushrooms. The Serchio River winds through this area and enriches the soil while sea breezes from the nearby coast lend added humidity and fertility. Perhaps Lucchesia's softness may be grasped most easily by comparing its gentle olive oil to the lusty oil of the Chianti area.

TACCONI O MACCHERONI STIRATI ALLA LUCCHESE

Tacconi with Rabbit Sauce

1 rabbit, skinned, liver removed
  (about 2 pounds)

FOR THE MARINADE
2 medium-sized red onions, cleaned
2 medium-sized celery stalks
2 medium-sized carrots, scraped
5 large sprigs Italian parsley,
  leaves only
2 small cloves garlic, peeled
1½ teaspoons rosemary leaves,
  fresh, preserved in salt or dried
  and blanched
4 large sage leaves, fresh or
  preserved in salt
2 whole cloves
1 bay leaf
4 cups dry red wine

FOR THE SAUCE
4 ounces pancetta or prosciutto,
  in one piece
½ cup olive oil
2 pounds very ripe fresh tomatoes
  or 2 pounds drained canned
  tomatoes, preferably
  imported Italian
Salt and freshly ground black pepper

FOR THE PASTA
4 cups unbleached all-purpose flour
4 extra-large eggs
4 teaspoons olive oil or
  vegetable oil
2 teaspoons lukewarm water
Pinch of salt

TO COOK THE PASTA
Coarse-grained salt

TO SERVE
4 tablespoons (2 ounces) sweet
  butter, cut into small pieces
½ cup freshly grated *Parmigiano*

Clean and wash the rabbit well and place it, whole, in a medium-sized casserole over medium heat. Cover and cook for 5 minutes, turning the rabbit over once. Remove the rabbit, wash it again under cold running water and discard the white gamey juices left in the casserole. Dry the rabbit with paper towels and place it in a large crockery or glass bowl until needed.

Coarsely chop the onions, celery, carrots, parsley, garlic, rosemary and sage on a board. Sprinkle the chopped ingredients, the whole cloves and bay leaf over the rabbit in the bowl. Pour the wine on top. Refrigerate, covered, for at least 4 hours.

When ready, remove and discard the cloves and bay leaf. Lift out the rabbit and drain the vegetables, saving the wine.

Finely chop the coarsely chopped vegetables and cut the pancetta into tiny pieces.

Heat the oil in a medium-sized casserole over medium heat. When the oil is warm, add the pancetta and sauté for 5 minutes, stirring with a wooden spoon. Put in the whole rabbit and sauté for 5 minutes, then add the chopped ingredients and cook for 10 minutes more. Start adding the reserved wine marinade, ½ cup at a time, and do not add the following ½ cup until the previous one is completely evaporated.

If fresh tomatoes are used, cut them into pieces. Pass the fresh or canned tomatoes through a food mill, using the disc with the smallest holes, into a small bowl.

Add the tomatoes to the casserole, mix well, season with salt and pepper and let simmer until the rabbit is completely cooked, about 35 minutes or more (depending on the size of the rabbit), adding a little lukewarm water if more liquid is needed.

Transfer the rabbit to a board and remove all the meat from the bones. Coarsely chop the meat and place it back in the casserole. Mix well and let cook for 2 minutes more.

Prepare the pasta with the ingredients and quantities listed at left (see Appendix, page 293). Stretch the layer of pasta to a thickness of ¹⁄₁₆ of an inch; on the pasta machine take it to the next to last notch. Use a pastry wheel to cut the layer of pasta into 2-inch squares and let them rest on cotton towels until needed.

Bring a large pot of cold water to a boil, add coarse salt to taste, then the pasta and cook for 30 seconds to 1 minute, depending on the dryness.

Drain the pasta, transfer it to a large skillet with the butter and sauté for 30 seconds. Add the sauce, mix well and cook for 30 seconds more.

Transfer the pasta to a large serving platter, sprinkle on the *Parmigiano* and serve with a twist of black pepper over each portion.

Serves 8 to 10.

We now travel from Lucca to the Tuscan Riviera (or Versilia, as
it is also known), which stretches up from Pisa through Viareggio
and Forte dei marmi. The sandy beaches here have long been fashionable and through the years have attracted jet-setters and Arab
sheiks plus artists and writers, including Thomas Mann, Marino
Marini and Henry Moore. Though fancy and trendy restaurants
flourish here, there still remain hints of the quaint fishing villages
that once were. In Pasta alle zucchine con gamberi,
Versilia's especially sweet shrimp are combined with delicate
zucchini, another food native to the area.

PASTA ALLE ZUCCHINE CON GAMBERI

Pasta with Zucchini and Shrimp

NORTHERN COAST

Cut the zucchini into discs not more than ⅛ inch thick and let
them stand for 30 minutes in a bowl of cold water to which
coarse salt has been added.

Place the shrimp in a bowl of cold water with coarse salt and
the lemon cut in half and squeezed, and soak for 30 minutes.

Meanwhile, prepare the pasta with the ingredients and
quantities listed at right (see Appendix, page 293) and cut into
spaghetti, using the finer cutter on the pasta machine. Let the
pasta rest on cotton towels until needed. Place a pot of cold
water over medium heat.

Prepare the sauce: Drain the zucchini and rinse under cold
running water. Drain the shrimp and shell and devein them,
if needed.

Coarsely chop the garlic. Place a skillet with the oil over
low heat and when the oil is warm, add the garlic and sauté for
2 minutes. Dissolve the saffron in the broth.

Add the zucchini to the skillet and sauté for 30 seconds,
then raise the heat to high, season with salt and pepper and add
all the broth. Cover the skillet and cook for 2 minutes, stirring
every so often with a wooden spoon.

When the water in the pot reaches a boil, add coarse salt to
taste, then the pasta and cook it for 1 to 3 minutes, depending
on the dryness.

Put the shrimp and tomato in the skillet, mix well and cook
for 2 minutes more. Drain the pasta, add it to the skillet, sprinkle
on the parsley and mix gently. Serve hot.

Serves 6.

FOR THE SAUCE
2 small zucchini, cleaned (about
    10 ounces)
Coarse-grained salt
½ pound small shrimp, unshelled
    (if shrimp are not small,
    cut into halves)
1 lemon
1 large clove garlic, peeled
4 tablespoons olive oil
A large pinch of ground saffron
1 cup very warm chicken or meat
    broth, preferably homemade
Salt and freshly ground black pepper

FOR THE PASTA
3½ cups unbleached all-purpose
    flour
1 extra-large egg
2 extra-large egg yolks
½ cup cold water
Pinch of salt
1 tablespoon olive oil or
    vegetable oil

TO COOK THE PASTA
Coarse-grained salt

PLUS
1 very ripe large tomato,
    blanched, seeded and cut into
    ½-inch squares

TO SERVE
15 sprigs Italian parsley, leaves only

LUNIGIANA

Moving north on the Tuscan coast and passing Massa and Carrara, we arrive in an area called Lunigiana, located in the valley bordering the mountainous Garfagnana. A most interesting dish from Lunigiana is Falsi testaroli al ragù. *Whereas real testaroli, rarely prepared any more, are made from a batter that is cooked on a kind of waffle iron over coals and then cut into diamonds, these "mock" testaroli are cut from a layer of pasta dough. The method of making the ragù for this dish is unusual in that the ground meat is placed on top of a layer of chopped onions so that it is cooked by steam.*

Not surprisingly, Lunigiana borrows some of the culinary traditions of the nearby Garfagnana, and one example is the use of dried fava beans. Whereas fresh fava beans are popular all over Tuscany when they are in season in the spring, dried favas, such a staple in Southern Italy, are not really used in Tuscany except in the spartan mountain areas. In Maccheroni ai carciofi saporiti, *the dried favas are combined with artichokes, which come into season in the fall in Lunigiana, to make a sauce to coat maccheroni (wide strips of pasta).*

Lunigiana derives its name from the city of Luni, which was once a great center of the marble trade but no longer exists. Luni flourished until the early Middle Ages when it was continually attacked by invaders and pirates; it was not until 1200 that it succumbed, though, and that was to an epidemic of malaria. All that remains on the site, which is near the town of Massa, are the ruins of a Roman amphitheater and a church.

FALSI TESTAROLI AL RAGÙ

Mock Testaroli in Tuscan Ragù Sauce

FOR THE SAUCE
¾ pound beef sirloin, in one piece
½ pound pork, with some fat,
    in one piece
4 ounces prosciutto or pancetta,
    in one piece
2 sweet Italian sausages, without
    fennel seeds, or 6 ounces
    ground pork
1 large red onion, cleaned
5 tablespoons olive oil
2 medium-sized celery stalks
2 medium-sized carrots, scraped
1 cup dry red wine
1½ pounds very ripe fresh
    tomatoes or 1½ pounds
    drained canned tomatoes,
    preferably imported Italian
Salt and freshly ground black pepper
1 to 2 cups chicken or meat broth,
    preferably homemade
A large pinch of hot red pepper
    flakes (optional)

FOR THE PASTA
4 cups unbleached all-purpose flour
3 tablespoons chestnut flour
¼ cup cold water
5 extra-large egg whites, at room
    temperature
Pinch of salt

TO COOK THE PASTA
Coarse-grained salt
2 tablespoons olive oil or
    vegetable oil

PLUS
2 tablespoons plus several pats
    sweet butter
½ cup freshly grated *Parmigiano*

Prepare the sauce: Cut the beef, pork and prosciutto into 1-inch pieces, and remove the casing from the sausages. Grind all the meats together with a meat grinder, using the disc with the medium-sized holes, into a crockery or glass bowl.

Coarsely chop the onion on a board. Heat the oil in a medium-sized casserole over medium heat and when the oil is warm, place the onion, in one layer, over the oil. Reduce the heat to low, then place all the ground meat over the onion and cook, without stirring, for 10 minutes, or until the onion is translucent.

Meanwhile, coarsely chop the celery and carrots all together on a board. When the onion is ready, mix the onion and ground meat together very well with a wooden spoon, cook for 2 minutes more, then add the chopped vegetables and sauté over medium heat for 5 minutes. Add the wine and let evaporate for 5 minutes.

If fresh tomatoes are used, blanch and quarter them. If canned tomatoes are used, pass them through a food mill, using the disc with the smallest holes, into a crockery or glass bowl.

Add the fresh or canned tomatoes to the casserole and cook for 10 minutes, stirring every so often with a wooden spoon. Taste for salt and pepper, then start adding the broth, ½ cup at a time, until the sauce is homogeneous. It will take at least 1 hour from the moment the first ½ cup of broth is added. Taste for salt, pepper and the hot red pepper flakes, if using, before removing the sauce from the heat.

As the sauce cooks, prepare the pasta with the ingredients and quantities listed at left (see Appendix, page 293), placing the chestnut flour in the well of the flour along with the water, egg whites and salt. Stretch the layer of pasta to a thickness of less than 1/16 of an inch; on the pasta machine take it to the last notch. Cut the layer of pasta in half lengthwise and cut on the diagonal every 2 inches to create 2-by-4-inch diamonds.

Precook the diamonds in salted boiling water for a few seconds, a few at a time, then transfer them to a bowl of cold water to which the 2 tablespoons oil have been added. Arrange all the diamonds on dampened cotton dish towels and let rest until needed.

When the sauce is ready, preheat the oven to 375 degrees. Pour half the sauce into a large bowl, then all the pasta and the remaining sauce. Mix gently.

Heavily butter a baking dish with the 2 tablespoons butter and add all the pasta and sauce. Distribute the pats of butter all over, then bake, covered, for 15 minutes. Remove from the oven, mix very well and serve with the *Parmigiano*.

Serves 6 to 8.

MACCHERONI AI CARCIOFI SAPORITI

Maccheroni with Savory Artichoke Sauce

Prepare the pasta with the ingredients and quantities listed at right (see Appendix, page 293). Stretch the layer of pasta to a thickness of less than 1/16 of an inch; on the pasta machine take it to the last notch. Cut the layer of pasta into 6-inch pieces. Using a very sharp knife, cut each piece lengthwise into thirds, to make 2-inch-wide strips of pasta. Let the pasta rest on cotton towels until needed.

Prepare the sauce: Rinse the already prepared fava beans very well. Place them in a bowl of lukewarm water, season with a little salt and soak for ½ hour.

Place the artichokes in a bowl of cold water with the lemon cut in half and squeezed, and soak for ½ hour.

Cut the prosciutto into tiny pieces and remove the casing from the sausages. If using ground pork, cut the additional prosciutto into tiny pieces.

Clean the artichokes (see instructions on page 78), discarding the tough outer leaves and the choke, and cut them into 1-inch pieces. Mix the artichokes, prosciutto, sausages (or pork), garlic and parsley together, then coarsely grind everything with a meat grinder, into a crockery or glass bowl.

Heat the olive oil in a medium-sized casserole over medium heat and when the oil is warm, add the ground ingredients and sauté for 15 minutes, stirring every so often with a wooden spoon. Season with salt and pepper. Add the tomatoes, then drain and rinse the fava beans and add them to the casserole. Cook for 30 minutes or more, until the artichokes and fava beans are completely cooked and some of them seem puréed, adding the broth as needed. Taste for salt and pepper.

Set a large pot of cold water over medium heat and when the water reaches a boil, add coarse salt, then the pasta and cook for 1 to 3 minutes, depending on the dryness.

Drain the pasta, leaving a little water in it. Transfer the pasta to the casserole with the sauce, raise the heat to high and mix very well. Transfer everything to a large warmed serving platter, sprinkle on the cheese and serve hot.

Serves 8 to 10.

FOR THE PASTA
4 cups unbleached all-purpose flour
4 extra-large eggs
4 teaspoons olive oil or
  vegetable oil
4 teaspoons cold water
Pinch of salt

FOR THE SAUCE
½ pound dried fava beans, soaked
  overnight, boiled in salted
  water for 25 minutes and
  shelled
Coarse-grained salt
4 large artichokes
1 lemon
4 ounces prosciutto or pancetta,
  in one piece
3 sweet Italian sausages, without
  fennel seeds, or 7 ounces
  ground pork plus 2 ounces
  prosciutto
2 medium-sized cloves garlic, peeled
20 sprigs Italian parsley, leaves only
½ cup olive oil
Salt and freshly ground black pepper
1 pound very ripe fresh tomatoes,
  blanched and seeded, or
  1 pound drained canned
  tomatoes, preferably
  imported Italian, passed
  through a food mill
2 cups lukewarm chicken broth,
  preferably homemade

TO COOK THE PASTA
Coarse-grained salt

TO SERVE
Freshly grated aged *Pecorino* or
  Parmigiano

GARFAGNANA

Inland from Lunigiana, on the northern border of Tuscany, is the mountainous Garfagnana, an area that boasts a rich repertory of regional dishes. Pasta col pesto povero, literally "Pasta with Poor Pesto," takes its name from the scarceness of fresh basil in the winter, the season when this dish is prepared. The sauce, which covers squares of pasta made with unbleached flour and cornmeal, is prepared with different kinds of nuts combined with grated aged sheep's cheese, olive oil and tomatoes, if desired; if a few fresh basil leaves can be scavenged they are not added until the dish is served, in order to maximize their flavor. In earlier times, the only tomatoes available in the winter were the small cherry tomatoes—they could be stored on a layer of straw during the cold weather—and they were reserved for soups and, unusually, for this one pasta dish.

Another dish characteristic of Garfagnana is Tagliatelle di farro al sugo. The tagliatelle is made with farro flour, which is ground from the same kind of wheat that grew in Italy in Roman times, and still grows in both Garfagnana and Lucchesia. Ligurian in influence is the use of egg whites in the pasta. In this recipe, the whites are used instead of whole eggs.

PASTA COL PESTO POVERO

Pasta with Winter Pesto Sauce   GARFAGNANA

FOR THE SAUCE
6 large cloves garlic, peeled
4 ounces pine nuts (*pinoli*)
3 ounces shelled walnuts
1 ounce blanched almonds
4 ounces freshly grated aged
   Pecorino or *Parmigiano*
4 tablespoons olive oil
Salt and freshly ground black pepper

OPTIONAL
6 ounces cherry tomatoes

(continued on next page)

Prepare the sauce: Place the garlic, pine nuts, walnuts, almonds, cheese, olive oil and tomatoes (if using) in a food processor or blender, and blend until a very smooth sauce forms. Transfer the sauce to a crockery or glass bowl, add salt and pepper to taste, mix very well and refrigerate, covered, until needed.

Prepare the pasta with the ingredients and quantities listed on the following page (see Appendix, page 293), placing the cornmeal, eggs, egg whites, olive oil and salt in the well of the flour. Stretch the layer of pasta to a thickness of less than 1/16 of an inch; on the pasta machine take it to the last notch (see Note). Cut the layer of pasta into about 3-inch squares, using a pastry wheel with a scalloped edge. Let the pasta rest on cotton towels until needed.

Place a large pot of cold water over medium heat and when the water reaches a boil, add coarse salt to taste, then the

pasta, and cook from 30 seconds to 1½ minutes, depending on the dryness.

Meanwhile, remove the sauce from the refrigerator, add ¾ cup of the boiling water from the pot the pasta is cooking in and mix very well with a wooden spoon.

Ladle half the sauce onto a large serving platter. Drain the pasta, put it on the prepared serving dish, add the remaining sauce and mix gently but thoroughly. Sprinkle on the basil and serve hot. No extra cheese should be served with this dish.

Note: When making pasta with cornmeal (or chestnut flour) it is not always possible to take the dough to the last notch on the pasta machine without breakage. If necessary, only go to the next-to-last setting. If the cornmeal or chestnut flour is very fresh and moist, you may need to add extra white flour to the dough.

This dish may also be prepared with spaghetti.

Serves 8 to 10.

FOR THE PASTA
4 cups unbleached all-purpose flour
½ cup finely ground yellow
    cornmeal, preferably imported
    Italian
4 extra-large eggs
2 extra-large egg whites
4 teaspoons olive oil or vegetable
    oil
Pinch of salt

TO COOK THE PASTA
Coarse-grained salt

TO SERVE
16 medium-sized fresh basil leaves

TAGLIATELLE DI FARRO AL SUGO

Tagliatelle with Vegetable Sauce

FOR THE SAUCE
4 large leeks
4 medium-sized carrots, scraped
4 large celery stalks
1 ounce dried porcini mushrooms
4 cups lukewarm water
6 tablespoons olive oil
2 cups dry red wine
2 pounds fresh tomatoes, cut into
    pieces, or 2 pounds drained
    canned tomatoes, preferably
    imported Italian
4 heaping tablespoons tomato paste
2 whole cloves
Salt and freshly ground black pepper

FOR THE PASTA
2 cups farro flour or whole-wheat
    flour, sifted to remove large
    pieces of bran
2 cups unbleached all-purpose flour
6 extra-large egg whites
4 teaspoons olive oil or
    vegetable oil
4 teaspoons cold water
Pinch of salt

TO COOK THE PASTA
Coarse-grained salt

TO SERVE
Freshly grated aged *Pecorino* or
    Parmigiano

Clean the leeks very well, discarding the green parts. Cut the remaining white parts into 2-inch rings and soak them in a bowl of cold water for ½ hour.

Drain the leeks and rinse very well under cold running water. Finely chop the leeks, carrots and celery all together on a board.

Soak the mushrooms in the water for ½ hour.

Meanwhile, heat the olive oil in a medium-sized casserole over medium heat and when the oil is warm, add the chopped ingredients and sauté for 20 minutes, stirring constantly with a wooden spoon. Add the wine to the casserole and let cook for 20 minutes more.

Drain the mushrooms, then clean them very well, removing all the sand attached to the stems. Save the soaking water, cleaning it by filtering it through paper towels several times.

Pass the fresh or canned tomatoes through a food mill, using the disc with the smallest holes, into a crockery or glass bowl.

Add the tomatoes to the casserole and cook for 15 minutes more.

Coarsely chop the mushrooms and add them to the casserole. Dissolve the tomato paste in the mushroom water and start adding it to the casserole, 1 cup at a time, until all the liquid is used up. After adding the second cup of mushroom water, add the cloves and season with salt and pepper. Cook the sauce for at least 1 hour.

As the sauce cooks, prepare the pasta with the ingredients and quantities listed at left (see Appendix, page 293), placing the egg whites, olive oil, water and salt in the well of the two flours mixed together. Stretch the layer of pasta to a thickness of less than ¹⁄₁₆ of an inch; on the pasta machine take it to the last notch. To make *tagliatelle*, cut the layer of pasta using the wider cutter on the pasta machine. Let the pasta rest on cotton towels until needed.

When the sauce is almost ready, discard the cloves and set a large pot of cold water over medium heat.

Pour 1 cup of the sauce onto a large serving dish and place the dish over the pot of water as a lid. When the water reaches a boil, add coarse salt to taste, then the pasta and cook it for 30 seconds or more, depending on the dryness.

Drain the pasta, transfer it to the prepared serving dish, pour on all the remaining sauce, gently mix all together and serve hot, along with the grated cheese.

Serves 8.

Maccheroni stirati from Pontremoli in Lunigiana combines many elements characteristic of Tuscan cooking as well as elements characteristic of the cooking of regions nearby. The pasta is made with chestnut and unbleached flour and egg whites; it is then cut into small squares like the tacconi *from Lucchesia. But a Ligurian touch is added when the pasta is cooked together with thinly sliced potatoes.*

Pontremoli is known for a particularly interesting custom. When its small river dries up each summer, the residents plant vegetable gardens in the riverbed and surround them with fences. After the harvest, when the rains come and the river swells, it is the custom to watch the gardens being swept away without any emotion. There are no property rights here, and the next season the gardens are planted again by the first arrivals.

MACCHERONI STIRATI DI PONTREMOLI

Pontremoli-Style Pasta and Beans with Pesto

PONTREMOLI

Soak the beans in a bowl of cold water overnight.

The next morning, drain the beans and rinse them under cold running water. Place the beans in a medium-sized stockpot with the 2 quarts water, 2 cloves of the garlic (left whole), the sage, pancetta and clove. Place the pot over medium heat and simmer for 45 minutes. By that time the beans should be cooked through but should still retain their shape. Add coarse salt to taste and simmer for 2 minutes more.

Drain the beans, saving the cooking water, place them in a crockery or glass bowl and cover them with a wet cotton dish towel.

Place the basil in a medium-sized crockery or glass bowl, then finely chop the remaining 3 cloves of garlic, the parsley and walnuts all together on a board. Transfer the chopped ingredients to the bowl with the basil, add the cheese and enough oil to make a smooth sauce and season with salt and pepper. Mix very well and refrigerate until needed.

Prepare the pasta with the ingredients and quantities listed on the top of the following page (see Appendix, page 293), placing

FOR THE SAUCE
1 cup dried cannellini beans
2 quarts cold water
5 cloves garlic, peeled
3 sage leaves, fresh or preserved
   in salt
2 ounces pancetta or prosciutto,
   in one piece
1 whole clove
Coarse-grained salt
15 fresh basil leaves, torn into thirds
20 sprigs Italian parsley, leaves only
10 shelled walnuts
¾ cup aged *Pecorino* or *Parmigiano*
¾ to 1 cup olive oil
Salt and freshly ground black pepper

FOR THE PASTA
2 cups unbleached all-purpose flour
1 cup chestnut flour
1 extra-large egg
3 extra-large egg whites
3 teaspoons olive oil or
    vegetable oil
3 teaspoons cold water
Pinch of salt

TO COOK THE PASTA
1 potato (about 4 ounces)
Coarse-grained salt

TO SERVE
Fresh basil leaves

the chestnut flour in the well of the flour, along with the egg, egg whites, olive oil, water and salt. Stretch the layer of pasta to a thickness of less than 1/16 of an inch; on the pasta machine take it to the last notch. Cut the layer of pasta into 2-inch squares and place them on cotton towels until needed.

Place a large pot of cold water and the reserved bean cooking water over medium heat. Peel the potato and slice it very thin. When the water reaches a boil, add coarse salt to taste, then the potato and cook for 5 minutes. Add the pasta and cook it for 2 to 4 minutes, depending on the dryness.

One minute before the pasta is ready, discard the garlic, sage and clove from the beans and add the beans to the pot with the pasta. Mix very well, finish cooking, then drain everything, reserving the pasta cooking water, and transfer to a large serving platter.

Pour the sauce all over the pasta and beans, mix very well, sprinkle on the basil and serve hot. If the sauce has become too thick in the refrigerator, stir in about 1 cup of the pasta water before combining it with the pasta.

Serves 6 to 8.

AREZZO

Arezzo, in the center of Tuscany's north-south axis but close to the region's eastern border, was founded by the Etruscans, was already famed as an artistic center in Roman times, and flourished as an independent city-state until 1289, when it fell to the rising might of Florence. Still, Arezzo has stubbornly maintained its individual character through the centuries.

The heart of Arezzo, the Piazza Grande, is sometimes called Piazza Vasari because Grand Duke Cosimo I sent Vasari, the artist who was responsible for so much of the urban design of Renaissance Florence, back to his hometown to beautify it and to update it to Renaissance style.

In the photograph on page 129, on the balustrade of Vasari's palazzo, we see a plate of Gnocchi verdi, a dish that comes from nearby Casentino and resembles the famous Florentine ravioli nudi; it is the small amount of flour in the gnocchi that differentiates them from the ravioli. On the other side of the piazza are buildings with wooden terraces that make this square unique.

GNOCCHI VERDI DEL CASENTINO

Gnocchi of the Casentino

Rinse the spinach very well and discard the large stems. Soak the spinach in a bowl of cold water for ½ hour. Place a pot of cold water over medium heat and when the water reaches a boil, add coarse salt to taste, then drain the spinach and add it to the pot to cook for about 5 minutes. Drain the spinach and cool it under cold running water.

Lightly squeeze the spinach and finely chop it. Finely chop the onion on a board, then heat the olive oil in a sauté pan over low heat and when the oil is warm, add the onion and sauté until translucent. Add the spinach, season with salt and pepper and cook for 5 minutes, mixing continuously with a wooden spoon.

Transfer the spinach to a crockery or glass bowl and let rest until cool, about ½ hour.

Add the ricotta to the bowl of spinach, along with the egg yolks, *Parmigiano* and flour. Mix very well with a wooden spoon, season with salt, pepper and nutmeg to taste and mix again. Refrigerate, covered, until needed.

Prepare the sauce, a flavored *balsamella*, with the ingredients and quantities listed at right, adding the *Mascarpone* once the heavy cream is completely incorporated (see instructions on page 110). Transfer the sauce to a crockery or glass bowl, press a piece of buttered waxed paper over it and let rest until needed.

Bring a large pot of cold water to a boil over medium heat.

Meanwhile, spread the 2 cups flour out on a large piece of aluminum foil on the table. Take 1 heaping tablespoon of the ricotta mixture from the bowl and roll it on the floured surface to form a little ball. Be sure the ball is uniformly compact, with no empty spaces inside; the outside should be uniformly floured.

When the water reaches a boil, add coarse salt to taste, then drop the first ball in to test. It should retain its shape and rise to the top, cooked, after a minute or two. If the ball falls apart, add a little more flour to the mixture (if this is necessary, your *gnocchi* will be tougher than desired).

Continue to make the *gnocchi*, rolling them in flour, until all the contents of the bowl have been used up.

Melt the tablespoon of butter in a baking dish by placing the dish like a lid over the pot of boiling water.

When the butter is melted, drop the *gnocchi* into the boiling water, five or six at a time, and as they rise to the surface, remove them with a strainer-skimmer, transferring them directly onto the baking dish in one layer, not one on top of another.

Preheat the oven to 375 degrees. When all the *gnocchi* are in the baking dish, sprinkle them with the *Parmigiano*, then arrange the *balsamella* all over the *gnocchi*. Bake, covered, for 15 minutes and serve hot with no extra cheese.

Serves 8 to 10.

Gnocchi verdi del Casentino (*Gnocchi of the Casentino*) set on the balustrade of Vasari's Palazzo in Arezzo's central Piazza Grande. This piazza is the site of a monthly antiques fair and Arezzo's main festival, the Giostra del Saracino, at which a famous joust in the city's history is reenacted.

FOR THE GNOCCHI
3 pounds fresh spinach
Coarse-grained salt
1 very small red onion, cleaned
2 tablespoons olive oil
Salt and freshly ground black pepper
15 ounces ricotta, well drained
4 extra-large egg yolks
2 cups freshly grated *Parmigiano*
2 tablespoons unbleached
   all-purpose flour

Freshly ground nutmeg

PLUS
2 cups unbleached all-purpose flour

TO COOK THE GNOCCHI
Coarse-grained salt

FOR THE SAUCE
½ cup (4 ounces) sweet butter
3 tablespoons unbleached
   all-purpose flour

2 cups heavy cream
1 cup milk
4 ounces *Mascarpone*

TO BAKE THE GNOCCHI
1 tablespoon (½ ounce) sweet
   butter
½ cup freshly grated *Parmigiano*

MONTEPULCIANO

Southeast of Siena, a little below Sinalunga in the Valdichiana, we come to the home of one of Tuscany's most celebrated wines, Vino Nobile. Interestingly, Montepulciano and its great wine rival, Montalcino (where Brunello is produced) share the same signature pasta, pici or pinci, individual cubes of dough made of flour and water and laboriously rolled out by hand into strands. This method of rolling produces a lusty pasta that acts as a perfect foil for a robust meat sauce, and it is the sauce that marks the difference between the towns. The sauce from Montepulciano is made with

Pinci di Montepulciano
(*Montepulciano-Style Fresh Pasta*)
set against the hilltop town where the recipe originated. The hand-rolled strands of pasta are dressed with a full-bodied sauce featuring Vino Nobile di Montepulciano, the great red wine of the area.

three different meats and the proportion of meat to vegetables is higher than in Montalcino's. It is, of course, each town's remarkable wine that creates the most significant differences in taste. In all Tuscan meat sauces, the use of a full-bodied red wine—either Chianti or one from Montepulciano or Montalcino—is crucial; in addition, the flavor of the meat must be strong enough to complement the wine.

PINCI DI MONTEPULCIANO

Montepulciano-Style Fresh Pasta   MONTEPULCIANO

FOR THE SAUCE
2 medium-sized red onions, cleaned
2 celery stalks
1 clove garlic, peeled
8 ounces beef, in one piece
4 ounces chicken breast,
    in one piece
4 ounces prosciutto or pancetta,
    in one piece
6 tablespoons olive oil
¼ cup dry red wine
3 tablespoons tomato paste
Salt and freshly ground black pepper
A large pinch of hot red pepper
    flakes
2 cups chicken or meat broth,
    preferably homemade

FOR THE PASTA
4 cups unbleached all-purpose flour
1½ to 1¾ cups cold water
Pinch of salt

TO COOK THE PASTA
Coarse-grained salt

TO SERVE
Freshly grated aged *Pecorino* or
    Parmigiano

Prepare the sauce: Finely chop the onions, celery and garlic all together on a board. Cut the beef, chicken breast and prosciutto into 2-inch pieces. Grind the meats together with a meat grinder, using the disc with the medium-sized holes, into a bowl.

Heat the oil in a casserole over medium heat and when the oil is warm, add the chopped ingredients and sauté for 5 minutes. Add the ground meats, mix very well and sauté for 10 minutes more. Add the wine and cook for 2 minutes more. Add the tomato paste and season with salt, pepper and the hot red pepper flakes. Add ½ cup broth, mix very well and keep cooking the sauce, adding more broth as needed, until all of it is used up. Taste for salt and pepper.

Meanwhile, prepare the pasta dough with the ingredients and quantities listed at left (see Appendix, page 293), without stretching it or feeding it through the pasta machine. Flatten the ball of dough with both hands to a thickness of less than ½ of an inch. Cut the layer of dough into strips less than ½-inch wide. Cut across the pasta, making the strips into small cubes. Take an individual cube, and, holding it between the thumbs and first fingers of both hands, pinch the cube so that it extends sideways only, into a non-rounded strip about 3 inches long. With the four fingers of both hands, lightly roll the strip of dough, moving both hands gradually apart from the center and to the sides. Keep repeating this motion until the strip is rounded and about 9 inches long. Let the pasta rest on cotton towels until needed.

Bring a large pot of cold water to a boil, add coarse salt to taste, then the pasta and cook for 1 to 3 minutes, depending on the dryness.

Drain the pasta and transfer it to a large serving platter. Pour the sauce over the pasta and mix very well. Sprinkle with the cheese and serve hot.

Serves 6 to 8.

RISOTTI AND RICE TIMBALE

I *present here a selection of four Tuscan* risotti. *The technique for making the* risotto *is the same in each recipe but the kind of liquid used is varied— from chicken or meat broth to mushroom-soaking water to bean broth. The broth for the* Risotto al basilico *is quite unusual in that it is made by simmering fresh basil leaves in chicken broth.* Risotto ai fagioli, *the Tuscan version of rice and beans, employs the bean broth. Its sauce is flavored with parsley and basil.*

In Risotto al pesce *from Maremma, the* risotto *is made in a combination of chicken broth and tomato sauce in which squid and shrimp have been cooked. Typical of the cooking of this area, the finished dish is sprinkled with chopped raw parsley and garlic before serving. Maremma, a wild, undeveloped area on the southwestern coast, still teems with game, including wild boar. The rivers are filled with eels and there are even some water buffalo, so valued for making mozzarella cheese.*

Risotto ai funghi con piccione *combines the wonderful mushrooms from Garfagnana with the subtle flavor of squab.*

RISOTTO AL BASILICO

Fresh Basil Risotto

7 cups homemade light chicken
    broth
30 fresh basil leaves
1 large white onion
6 tablespoons (3 ounces) sweet
    butter
1 tablespoon olive oil
3 cups raw rice, preferably Italian
    Arborio
Salt and freshly ground black pepper

PLUS
30 fresh basil leaves
2 tablespoons (1 ounce) sweet
    butter
4 tablespoons freshly grated
    Parmigiano

TO SERVE
Freshly grated *Parmigiano*

Bring the broth with the basil leaves to a boil over medium heat, lower the heat and let simmer for 15 minutes. The broth will reduce to about 6 cups.

Meanwhile, finely chop the onion on a board. Place a medium-sized casserole with the butter and oil over medium heat and when the butter is melted, add the onion and sauté for 5 minutes, or until the onion is translucent. Add the rice and sauté for 4 minutes, stirring constantly with a wooden spoon. When the rice is ready, discard the basil leaves from the broth and start adding 6 cups of the boiling broth to the rice, ½ cup at a time, stirring constantly with a wooden spoon, without adding any additional broth until the previous ½ cup has been completely absorbed. Season with salt and pepper. When 6 cups of the broth are used up, the risotto should be ready and cooked *al dente*.

Immediately, finely chop the basil (or have somebody else do it for you because the basil must be chopped at the very last moment, while you are busy stirring the risotto).

Remove the casserole from the heat, add the basil, butter and *Parmigiano*, and mix very well with a wooden spoon. Serve hot with additional freshly grated *Parmigiano*.

Serves 6 to 8.

RISOTTO AI FAGIOLI

Risotto with Cannellini Beans

Soak the beans in a bowl of cold water overnight.

The next morning, drain the beans and place them in a medium-sized stockpot along with the 5 cups cold water, the garlic and sage. Set the pot over medium heat and when the water reaches a boil, lower the heat and simmer for about 45 minutes. By that time the beans should be cooked but still firm. Drain the beans, saving the water, and place the beans in a crockery or glass bowl. Sprinkle salt and pepper over them and cover the bowl until needed.

Prepare the sauce: Coarsely chop the onions, carrots, garlic, celery, parsley and basil all together on a board. Cut the pancetta into tiny pieces. Place a large casserole with the oil over low heat and when the oil is warm, add all the chopped vegetables and the herbs and pancetta. Sauté for 20 minutes, stirring every so often with a wooden spoon. Season with salt, pepper and the hot red pepper flakes.

If using fresh tomatoes, blanch them, remove the skin and seeds and add them to the casserole; if using canned tomatoes, pass them through a food mill, using the disc with the smallest holes, directly into the casserole. Stir very well and simmer for 30 minutes more. When the sauce is ready, take 2 cups of it and pour it over the beans.

With the remaining sauce in the casserole, start making the risotto: Bring to a boil the water from the beans and enough cold water to yield about 4 cups liquid.

Add the rice to the sauce and sauté over medium heat for 4 minutes, mixing constantly with a wooden spoon. When the rice is ready, start adding the boiling liquid, ½ cup at a time, mixing constantly with the spoon, without adding any additional liquid until the previous ½ cup is completely absorbed.

After adding the last ½ cup of liquid to the risotto, quickly mix the beans, add them to the casserole, stirring the risotto constantly. Taste for salt and pepper while continuing to stir.

When all the liquid is incorporated and the rice is cooked (but still has a "bite," as risotto should), transfer the risotto to a warmed serving platter and serve immediately, with the basil leaves. For a minestrone using this sauce, see *Minestrone ai fagioli,* page 76.

Serves 8 to 10.

1 cup dried cannellini beans
5 cups cold water
1 large clove garlic, peeled
2 sage leaves, fresh or preserved
    in salt
Salt and freshly ground black pepper

FOR THE SAUCE
2 medium-sized red onions, cleaned
2 medium-sized carrots, scraped
1 large clove garlic, peeled
1 celery stalk
10 sprigs Italian parsley, leaves only
10 basil leaves, fresh or preserved
    in salt
4 ounces pancetta or prosciutto,
    in one piece
5 tablespoons olive oil
Salt and freshly ground black pepper
A large pinch of hot red pepper
    flakes
1½ pounds very ripe fresh
    tomatoes or 1½ pounds
    drained canned tomatoes,
    preferably imported Italian

FOR THE RISOTTO
2 cups raw rice, preferably Italian
    Arborio
All the broth from the beans

TO SERVE
Several fresh basil leaves

Maremma-Style Seafood Risotto

FOR THE SAUCE

1 medium-sized red onion, cleaned
2 large cloves garlic, peeled
1 large carrot, scraped
1 large celery stalk
10 sprigs Italian parsley, leaves only
5 basil leaves, fresh or preserved
     in salt
6 tablespoons olive oil
1 pound very ripe fresh tomatoes,
     cut into pieces, or 1 pound
     drained canned tomatoes,
     preferably imported Italian
Salt and freshly ground black pepper
A large pinch of hot red pepper
     flakes
¼ pound medium-sized shrimp,
     shelled and deveined
¼ pound cleaned calamari, cut
     into ⅓-inch rings (tentacles
     cut into small pieces), or an
     additional ¼ pound shelled
     and deveined shrimp
1 lemon
Coarse-grained salt

PLUS

2 cups raw rice, preferably Italian
     Arborio
About 4 cups chicken broth,
     preferably homemade

TO SERVE

15 sprigs Italian parsley, leaves only
2 medium-sized cloves garlic, peeled

Finely chop the onion, garlic, carrot, celery, parsley and basil all together on a board. Heat the oil in a large heavy casserole over medium heat and when the oil is warm, add the chopped ingredients and sauté for 15 minutes, or until the onion is translucent.

Meanwhile, pass the fresh or canned tomatoes through a food mill, using the disc with the smallest holes, into a crockery or glass bowl. Add the tomatoes to the casserole, lower the heat and simmer for 30 minutes. Season with salt, pepper and the hot red pepper flakes.

Meanwhile, place the seafood in a bowl of cold water with the lemon cut in half and squeezed, and a little coarse salt, and soak for 15 minutes.

When the tomato sauce is ready, drain and rinse the seafood under cold running water and add it to the casserole. If using shrimp and calamari, first add the calamari and cook until soft, 5 to 20 minutes, depending on the size; then add the shrimp (adding water if needed) and cook for 2 minutes. Use a slotted spoon to transfer the seafood to a board. Remove the casserole from the heat until you are ready to prepare the risotto.

Coarsely chop the seafood, place it in a crockery bowl and cover. Coarsely chop the parsley and finely chop the garlic for serving and put it in a small bowl.

Place the casserole back over medium heat. Bring the broth to a boil in a medium-sized saucepan. When the sauce in the casserole reaches a boil, add the rice and sauté for 3 minutes, then start incorporating the boiling broth, ½ cup at a time, constantly mixing with a wooden spoon, without adding additional broth until the previous ½ cup is completely absorbed by the rice. When the risotto is almost ready and all the broth but the last ½ cup is incorporated, add the chopped seafood, then add the last ½ cup broth and taste for salt, pepper and hot red pepper flakes.

Remove the casserole from the heat, add the chopped parsley and garlic and mix very well. Transfer the mixture to a large serving platter and serve hot. Do not serve cheese with this dish.

Serves 6 to 8.

BOMBA DI RISO ALLA LUNIGIANESE

Rice Timbale with Squab

Lunigiana is not only on the border with Liguria but is also very close to Emilia-Romagna; its rice timbale, Bomba di riso alla lunigianese, shares some characteristics with the famous bomba of Parma. The rice crust in the Tuscan version is much more aromatic, as it is flavored with nutmeg, cinnamon and clove, and the squab stuffing is covered with Swiss chard or spinach and an additional layer of the fragrant rice.

FOR THE CRUST
1 tablespoon coarse-grained salt
1 whole clove
3 cups raw rice, preferably Italian
    Arborio
Juice of 1 medium-sized lemon
5 extra-large eggs
½ cup freshly grated *Parmigiano*
Salt and freshly ground black pepper
Pinch of freshly grated nutmeg
Pinch of ground cinnamon
5 heaping tablespoons capers,
    preserved in wine vinegar,
    drained

PLUS
1 tablespoon (½ ounce) sweet
    butter
¼ cup unseasoned bread crumbs,
    preferably homemade

FOR THE STUFFING
4 pounds Swiss chard or spinach,
    large stems removed
Coarse-grained salt
3 squabs
4 medium-sized carrots, scraped
3 celery stalks
2 medium-sized red onions, cleaned
1 medium-sized clove garlic, peeled
10 sprigs Italian parsley, leaves only
5 basil leaves, fresh or preserved
    in salt
6 tablespoons olive oil
1 pound very ripe fresh tomatoes,
    skinned and seeded, or
        1 pound drained and seeded
        canned tomatoes, preferably
        imported Italian
2 cups lukewarm beef or chicken
    broth, preferably homemade
Salt and freshly ground black pepper

TO SERVE
Fresh basil leaves

Prepare the crust: Bring a large pot of cold water to a boil. When the water reaches a boil, add the salt and clove, then the rice. Stir very well and cook the rice for 8 minutes.

Drain and cool the rice under cold running water and transfer it to a crockery or glass bowl. Discard the clove. Add the lemon juice to the rice and mix very well. Cover the bowl and let the rice stand until needed.

Begin preparing the stuffing: Soak the Swiss chard in a bowl of cold water for ½ hour.

Bring a large pot of cold water to a boil, add coarse-grained salt to taste, then the chard and cook for 5 minutes. Drain and cool the chard under cold running water. Lightly squeeze it, then coarsely chop it on a board.

Meanwhile, clean the squabs very well and dry with paper towels. Finely chop the carrots, celery, onions, garlic, parsley and basil on a board.

Heat the oil in a large heavy casserole over medium heat. When the oil is warm, add the chopped ingredients and sauté for 10 minutes. Add the whole squabs and sauté on all sides for 15 minutes more. Add the tomatoes, cover and let cook for · 40 minutes, turning the squabs several times and adding the broth as needed. The squab should be completely cooked and a thick sauce should be formed. Remove the casserole from the heat and transfer the squabs onto a board.

Using a paring knife, remove the meat from the bones and discard the bones. Do not cut up the pieces of meat. Return the meat to the casserole. Place the casserole over medium heat for 10 minutes more. Taste for salt and pepper. Transfer the contents of the casserole to a crockery or glass bowl and let stand until cool, about ½ hour.

Finish the crust: Remove 1 cup of the liquid from the squab sauce and pour it onto the cold rice. Add the eggs and *Parmigiano*

The unmolded Bomba di riso alla lunigianese *and a* Bomba di riso *with a wedge removed to reveal the layers of stuffing inside.*

and season with salt, pepper, nutmeg and cinnamon. Add the capers and mix all the ingredients very well with a wooden spoon.

Heavily butter a 3-quart, 10-inch glass casserole and line it with the bread crumbs. Save the leftover bread crumbs.

Preheat the oven to 400 degrees.

Line the casserole with two-thirds of the rice mixture. Cover the rice with two-thirds of the boiled Swiss chard and pour the squab pieces and sauce into the center. Over the sauce, make a layer of the remaining Swiss chard, then a layer of the remaining rice. Sprinkle the leftover bread crumbs over the rice. Bake for 35 minutes.

Remove the *bomba* from the oven, let cool for a few minutes, then unmold onto a large round serving dish. Slice the *bomba* like a cake and serve immediately with the basil leaves.

Serves 8 to 10.

RISOTTO AI FUNGHI CON PICCIONE

Risotto with Mushroom-Squab Sauce

Soak the mushrooms in 2 cups lukewarm water for ½ hour.

Meanwhile, clean the squabs very well, then remove all the bones from one of the squabs and grind its meat with a meat grinder, using the disc with the medium-sized holes, into a crockery or glass bowl. Combine the bones and 5 cups broth in a saucepan and let simmer for 20 minutes.

Finely chop the celery, carrot, onion and parsley all together on a board. Heat the oil in a large, heavy casserole over medium heat and when the oil is warm, add the chopped ingredients and sauté for 5 minutes. Add the ground meat and the whole squab and sauté for 5 minutes more.

Drain the mushrooms, then clean them very well, being careful to remove all the sand attached to the stems. Save the soaking water, cleaning it by filtering it through paper towels several times. Coarsely chop the mushrooms and add to the casserole. Add ½ cup of the wine and simmer for 15 minutes more. By that time the whole squab should be cooked and tender; if not, add a little of the remaining broth and cook until soft. Remove the squab and let rest on a serving platter, covered, until needed.

Add the rice to the sauce in the casserole and sauté for 3 minutes, mixing continuously with a wooden spoon. Add the remaining ½ cup wine and keep mixing, adding more liquid as needed, ½ cup at a time, first of the mushroom soaking water, then the broth. You will need a total of about 6 cups. Taste for salt and pepper.

When the risotto is almost ready, reheat the whole squab in the oven. Sprinkle the sage leaves over the risotto and serve with small pieces of the squab.

Serves 6 to 8.

1 ounce dried porcini mushrooms
2 squabs
5 to 6 cups chicken or beef broth, preferably homemade
1 celery stalk
1 small carrot, scraped
1 medium-sized red onion, cleaned
10 sprigs Italian parsley, leaves only
½ cup olive oil
1 cup dry white wine
3 cups raw rice, preferably Italian Arborio
Salt and freshly ground black pepper

TO SERVE
Fresh sage leaves

TUSCANY'S SHEEP'S MILK CHEESES: PECORINO MAKING

A flock of sheep graze on the grass peeping up among the wheat stubble in one of the valleys stretching between Montepulciano and Pienza. The gentle rolling hills lead up to a farmhouse.

The milk from the night before is combined with the early morning milk and animal rennet, which is added to curdle the milk. All the mixing is done mechanically; when the curd forms, it is left in small pieces rather than being pressed together as it is with most cheeses. Shepherds used to make their own vegetable rennet by gathering wild artichokes and soaking them in cold water for twelve hours, and they did all the mixing by hand with a stick called a chiurla.

The contents of the mixer are poured into a large tray that is separated into individual molds called cascini.

The pure sheep's milk cheeses of Tuscany were first made in ancient times in the Chianti area and, over the centuries, became known for their creamy delicacy and sweetness. By the sixteenth century, a Pecorino called Marzolino (because it was made in March) had been introduced to France by Caterina de' Medici and was already prized as far away as Antwerp.

Today, an especially prized Pecorino is produced in the valleys that stretch from Montepulciano to Pienza in the province of Siena. The grass in this area derives an aromatic savor from the native clay (called crete) from which it springs. The grass, in turn, flavors the milk of the sheep that graze on it and, ultimately, produces the unique bouquet and flavor of the local Pecorino. In some other areas in Tuscany, cow's milk is added to the sheep's milk used to make Pecorino.

Unlike Parmigiano and Pecorino Romano, Pecorino Toscano is not formed into large wheels but is made into smaller convex shapes called caciotte. Today, some commercially-produced Tuscan cow's milk cheeses are made in the form of the Tuscan Pecorino and are called caciotte.

As the perforated molds are filled, the whey drains off into a strainer that separates the whey from the curd that has overflowed the molds. The whey is saved and used to make ricotta.

After the molds are drained from the bottom, they are turned over and drained from the top.

Unlike many cheeses, Pecorino is not soaked in brine: When the curd in the molds is cold, it is sprinkled with fine salt and left for eight hours; the process is then repeated on the second side. After the second eight-hour period, the cheese is left to rest in the molds for an additional twenty-four hours.

The cheeses are removed from the molds and are placed on wooden shelves to dry. They are turned quite frequently until they are ready. The drying process takes about ten days in the summer and a month in the winter.

After the drying period, during which a thin crust forms, the cheeses are washed. They are either eaten immediately or allowed to age for several more months. Generally, Pecorino Toscano is eaten while still quite young.

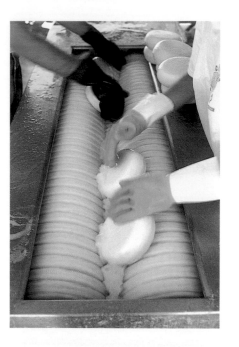

Shelves of Pecorino at different ages. The cheese that has been aged longest acquires the strongest flavor, of course, but Pecorino never loses its sweetness.

The whey that was drained off and saved is transferred to a large kettle. More rennet is added and the mixture is heated. The second curd, which forms on top, is used to make the famous ricotta. Because ricotta does not come from the first curd, it is not considered a real cheese.

The ricotta is placed in perforated molds to drain.

The molded ricotta shrinks from the sides of the mold and assumes a somewhat dry consistency, which allows it to hold its shape when unmolded. This is the way ricotta is sold in Italy.

A display of Pecorino at varying ages, ranging from about three weeks to six months. The color of the cheese does not change during aging; notice the wedge that has been cut. As a dessert cheese, Pecorino Toscano is perfectly matched with pears.

This photograph was taken in the main piazza in Pienza. Pope Pius II, who wanted his native village transformed, commissioned sixteenth-century architect Leone Battista Alberti to re-create his most famous buildings on this central square. The palace in the background, named Palazzo Piccolomini, is a copy of Alberti's Palazzo Rucellai in Florence, one of the landmark buildings of the Renaissance.

MAIN COURSES

In The Fine Art of Italian Cooking, *I included many of Tuscany's most well-known poultry, game and meat dishes. Here, I have chosen a sampling of different recipes that, while well known in the towns and provinces where they originated, have not yet become popular elsewhere. I have tried to choose specialties from as many of the provinces as possible, but concede that in the interest of space this could not be an exhaustive selection. These recipes feature not only Tuscany's distinguished chicken, lamb, beef, pork and veal, but also pheasant, guinea hen and rooster.*

A statue in the gardens of the Villa Garzoni.

POULTRY

In Tuscan cooking, strong distinctions are made among the different kinds of chickens: The common barnyard fowl, the free-range chicken, or pollo ruspante, the capon and the hen all retain their own repertoire of dishes. Furthermore, Tuscans do not reserve the boned whole chicken for gourmet dining; it is found in many family dishes, several of which are included here.

I begin with the Pollo al mattone, in which a whole chicken is cooked between two pieces of heated terra-cotta. The cooked chicken emerges from this unique cooking vessel not only flattened but crusty on the outside and juicy and delicious on the inside. For Gallo alla salvia ed aglio, a large rooster is cut into pieces, marinated in wine flavored with an abundance of sage and garlic, and then sautéed with still more sage and garlic. This dish should be made with a large rooster as only a bird of such strong texture and taste can support this intense flavoring.

Preceding pages: Gallo alla salvia ed aglio (Rooster with Sage-Garlic Sauce) serves as a main course for a dinner in the magnificent gardens of Villa Garzoni located in Collodi, hometown of Carlo Lorenzini (also known as Carlo Collodi), the author of Pinocchio.

The Manneristic/Baroque gardens are filled with sculptures, playful fountains, bushes shaped like giant animals, and an overwhelming stairway that leads all the way up a hill, past waterfalls, to the great villa on top. There is also a marvelous Pinocchio fantasy park. In the seventeenth and eighteenth centuries, these gardens served as a backdrop for the outdoor balls and other festivities of the European nobility. They are still among the most celebrated gardens in Europe.

Left: As you leave the gardens of the Villa Garzoni, you are faced with hundreds of Pinocchios at the entrance to Pinocchioland.

Right: Chicken cooking between two pieces of terra-cotta for Pollo al mattone. The bottom vessel remains over the burner; the heavier top piece is preheated and used as a weight to flatten the chicken.

POLLO AL MATTONE

Chicken Cooked Between Terra-Cotta

1 chicken (about 3½ pounds)
1 teaspoon olive oil
Coarse-grained salt
Freshly ground black pepper
1 large sprig rosemary or
    1 tablespoon rosemary leaves,
    fresh, preserved in salt or dried
    and blanched

TO SERVE (OPTIONAL)
1 tablespoon olive oil

Place the top (heavy) part of a terra-cotta *mattone* ("vessel," see photograph) over a burner, using a flame tamer. Lightly oil the bottom part and place it over a second burner, also with a flame tamer. Heat the two parts of the terra-cotta for at least 15 minutes; they must be very hot.

Meanwhile, cut the chicken through the breast all the way down. Pound the chicken so it will be flat when placed between the two pieces of terra-cotta. Sprinkle a large pinch of coarse salt over the bottom part of the terra-cotta, then place the chicken on it. Sprinkle a little more coarse salt, a little pepper and the rosemary over the chicken and cover with the top part of the terra-cotta. Cook for about 40 minutes, turning the chicken over four times. The chicken will be crisp and very juicy. If desired, drip a little oil over the chicken before serving.

Serves 4.

GALLO ALLA SALVIA ED AGLIO

Rooster with Sage-Garlic Sauce

Cut the chicken into 8 pieces. Place the chicken in a crockery or glass bowl, add the wine, 5 whole sage leaves and 5 whole garlic cloves. Let the chicken marinate for 1 hour in a cool place or in the bottom part of your refrigerator.

Finely chop the remaining sage and garlic all together on a board.

Add the whole clove to the marinade just a few minutes before removing the chicken, and heat the olive oil and butter in a medium-sized casserole over medium heat. When the butter is melted, transfer the chicken from the marinade to the casserole and sauté for 4 to 5 minutes, or until lightly golden all over. Add the chopped ingredients and sauté for 2 minutes more. Discard the clove from the marinade, add 1 cup of the marinade to the casserole and cook for 10 minutes more. Season with salt and pepper.

Dissolve the tomato paste in the broth.

The cooking time will vary depending on the size and firmness of the chicken (if you use a rooster the cooking time will be longer). The meat is supposed to be half-cooked at this point so, if this is the case, go ahead and add the broth with the dissolved tomato paste and finish cooking. If the meat is still very firm, add more marinade and continue cooking for a while longer before adding the broth. Taste for salt and pepper.

When ready, transfer the chicken and its sauce to a large serving platter and serve with a lot of sage leaves. The flavor and the smell of the fresh sage leaves will be absorbed by the cooked meat.

Serves 4 to 6.

1 rooster or large chicken (about
   4 ½ pounds), cleaned
3 cups dry red wine
15 sage leaves, fresh or preserved
   in salt
15 cloves garlic, peeled
1 whole clove
6 tablespoons olive oil
2 tablespoons (1 ounce) sweet
   butter
Salt and freshly ground black pepper
5 tablespoons tomato paste
About 1 cup chicken broth

TO SERVE
Fresh sage leaves

FRIED AND GRILLED CHICKEN

Pollo fritto al ramerino is one of several fried chicken dishes that are popular in Tuscany. The use of arugula in Pollo alla ruchetta reflects the influence of the Lazio region around Rome, where arugula is very popular. In this recipe, the hot grilled chicken is served with a cold herb sauce, not an uncommon practice in Italy. In Pollo affinocchiato allo spiedo, the chicken is boned, stuffed with pancetta and fennel seeds and wrapped up like a salami. It is cooked either on a spit over a wood fire or in the oven.

POLLO FRITTO AL RAMERINO

Fried Marinated Chicken

CHIANTI AREA

1 chicken (about 3½ pounds),
    cut into 18 pieces
2 tablespoons olive oil
Juice of 1 large lemon
1 tablespoon rosemary leaves,
    fresh, preserved in salt or dried
    and blanched
Salt and freshly ground black pepper

PLUS
2 extra-large eggs
Pinch of salt
About 1 cup unbleached
    all-purpose flour
1 quart vegetable oil (⅔ corn oil,
    ⅓ sunflower oil)
½ cup olive oil

TO SERVE
1 lemon, cut in wedges

Place the chicken pieces in a crockery or glass bowl. Pour the oil and lemon juice over them. Finely chop the rosemary on a board and sprinkle it over the chicken. Season with salt and pepper and mix very well. Cover and refrigerate for at least 1 hour, mixing the chicken pieces with the marinade twice.

Lightly beat the eggs with a pinch of salt in a medium-sized bowl, and put the flour on a plate.

Heat the vegetable oil and olive oil in a deep-fryer over medium heat. When the oil is hot (about 375 degrees), lightly flour the chicken pieces and dip each piece in the eggs. Fry about six pieces of chicken at a time, until light golden all over.

Using a slotted spoon, transfer the cooked pieces of chicken to a serving dish lined with paper towels. When all the pieces are cooked, remove the paper and serve the chicken with lemon wedges.

Serves 4.

POLLO ALLA RUCHETTA

Grilled Whole Chicken with Arugula Sauce

Clean the chicken very well, then dry it with paper towels. Open the chicken from the breast and flatten it. Place the chicken in a crockery or glass serving dish.

Squeeze the lemons and pour the juice into a small glass bowl. Finely chop the garlic and add it to the lemon juice, along with the oil and salt and pepper to taste. Mix very well with a wooden spoon, then pour the mixture over the chicken. Cover the dish and refrigerate for at least 1 hour.

Prepare the sauce: Cut the arugula into thin strips and place in a glass bowl. In a small glass bowl, combine the lemon juice, olive oil and salt and pepper to taste, then toss with the arugula. Add the chopped garlic and mix again, then cover the bowl and refrigerate the sauce until needed.

Prepare the grill or preheat the oven to 400 degrees. When ready, grill the chicken for about 40 minutes, turning the chicken four times. Or, place the chicken in the oven on a lightly oiled baking dish and bake for about 40 minutes, turning and basting the chicken with leftover marinade four times.

Transfer the cooked chicken to a large serving platter, discarding the juices if oven-baked. Pour the arugula sauce all over and serve hot with the tomato and lemon slices.

Serves 4.

1 chicken (about 3 ½ pounds)
2 medium-sized lemons
1 medium-sized clove garlic, peeled
4 tablespoons cup olive oil
Salt and freshly ground black pepper

FOR THE SAUCE
About 3 bunches arugula, large
   stems removed, washed and
   dried (to yield about 6 ounces)
1 ½ tablespoons lemon juice
½ cup olive oil
Salt and freshly ground black pepper
2 medium-sized cloves garlic,
   peeled and finely chopped

TO SERVE
2 large, very ripe fresh tomatoes,
   sliced
1 lemon, thinly sliced

POLLO AFFINOCCHIATO ALLO SPIEDO

Fenneled Chicken Cooked on a Spit

If cooking the chicken on a spit, prepare the ashes. If cooking the chicken in the oven, preheat it to 400 degrees.

Bone the chicken as for a galantine, except leave all the meat attached to the skin (see Appendix, page 295). Tuck in the legs and wings and place the chicken, skin-side down, on a board.

Coarsely grind the prosciutto, pancetta, garlic and sage all together. Transfer the ground ingredients to a bowl and add the fennel seeds and salt and pepper to taste. Arrange the ground ingredients on the chicken.

1 chicken (about 3 ½ pounds)
3 ounces prosciutto, in one piece
3 ounces pancetta, in one piece
3 medium-sized cloves garlic, peeled
10 large fresh sage leaves
1 teaspoon fennel seeds
Salt and freshly ground black pepper

TO COOK THE CHICKEN
3 medium-sized cloves garlic,
   peeled and left whole
15 thin slices pancetta

In the center of this large spit threaded with different meats is Pollo affinocchiato allo spiedo *(Fenneled Chicken Cooked on a Spit). Below the skewer is a long pan, called a ghiotta. The beans in the ghiotta will be flavored with the drippings from the meat.*

Roll up the chicken, from one of the shorter sides, and tie it like a salami (see Appendix, page 294). Rub the 3 cloves of garlic all over the chicken, then place the pancetta slices all over the chicken roll and tie the chicken roll again to keep the pancetta firmly attached.

Place the meat in a roasting pan and bake for 1 hour, turning the chicken four times. Or, thread the meat on a skewer and fit it onto a spit. When the ashes are hot, start turning the spit and cook the chicken for about 1 hour.

After an hour the chicken should be cooked and still very juicy. Remove the chicken from the spit or the roasting pan and let rest for 10 minutes before untying it and discarding the pancetta. Serve immediately.

Serves 6 to 8.

BONED CHICKEN

In "Pane" di pollo, *the bird is boned from the cavity but not cut open. It is then stuffed with a meat mixture unusually flavored with chives, along with sage, formed into the shape of a round loaf of bread and poached in a broth that includes additional chives. This dish is served with its own aspic and is accompanied by boiled vegetables with a green sauce. In both* Pollo disossato ai carciofi *and* Galantina involtata, *the chicken is cut open from the back, the bones are removed and the meat is left attached to the skin. Whereas the former is stuffed with artichokes, the latter is filled only with seasonings (not a true stuffing).*

" P A N E "   D I   P O L L O

Chicken "Bread"

LIVORNO

Bone the chicken from the bottom cavity, leaving the chicken whole with all the meat attached to the skin. Sew up the large cavity and tuck the legs inside, leaving the top cavity open.

Prepare the stuffing: Coarsely chop the chives and sage on a board. Transfer the herbs to a large crockery or glass bowl and add the veal, beef, eggs and *Parmigiano*. Mix very well with a wooden spoon. Season with salt, pepper and nutmeg to taste.

Soak the bread in the milk for a few minutes, then squeeze out the milk and add the bread to the bowl. Mix again and be sure the bread is well amalgamated with the other ingredients.

Stuff the chicken, then sew up the open cavity, including the holes from the wings. Spread out a large cotton towel. Place the pancetta all over the stuffed chicken and, using your hands, shape the chicken into a round loaf (like a round bread loaf). Place the chicken in the center of the towel and tie the towel to make a closed bag. Refrigerate the chicken as you prepare the poaching broth.

Bring the broth to a boil over medium heat. Add the carrot, celery, onion, parsley, garlic, cloves, chives and white wine. Let the broth simmer for 1 hour.

After 1 hour of simmering, let the broth cool for ½ hour, then add the chicken. Place the pot back over medium heat and when the broth reaches a boil, lower the heat and let the *"pane"* simmer for 1 hour 45 minutes.

Let the chicken rest in the poaching broth for ½ hour before transferring it to a serving dish to cool completely, then strain the broth, discard all the vegetables and aromatic herbs and pour the broth into a large crockery or glass jar. Refrigerate the jar of broth until all the fat comes to the top, then defat the broth completely.

Bring 2 cups of the defatted broth to a boil in a small saucepan. Meanwhile, place the gelatin in a large bowl and when the broth is ready, pour it into the gelatin. Mix well with a

1 chicken (about 3 ½ pounds)
20 chives
3 sage leaves, fresh or preserved in salt
1 pound ground veal shoulder
1 pound ground beef, preferably sirloin
2 extra-large eggs
4 tablespoons freshly grated *Parmigiano*
Salt and freshly ground black pepper
Freshly ground nutmeg
4 slices white bread, crusts removed
1 cup whole milk
4 ounces pancetta or prosciutto, sliced

TO COOK THE CHICKEN
4 quarts chicken or beef broth, preferably homemade
1 carrot, scraped
1 celery stalk
1 medium-sized red onion, cleaned
10 sprigs Italian parsley
1 clove garlic, peeled
2 whole cloves
10 chives
1 cup dry white wine
Salt
3 tablespoons (3 envelopes) unflavored gelatin

A serving of "Pane" di pollo (Chicken "Bread") before the aspic and vegetables are added. This photograph was taken on the roof terrace of the Hotel Continental overlooking the Ponte Vecchio and the shops that are built into it The upper part of the bridge, the so-called Vasari corridor, connects the Uffizi Gallery on one side of the Arno with the Pitti Palace on the other. Once a secret passageway, this corridor now serves as a public gallery that exhibits self-portraits by such artists as Raphael, Titian, Rubens, Bernini, Rembrandt, Del Sarto and Velasquez.

TO SERVE
Boiled carrots and string beans
   with a green sauce, such as
   the one included in recipe for
   Trippa alla pisana prepared
   without the nuts (see page 23),
   or dressed with salt, pepper,
   olive oil and fresh basil

wooden spoon to dissolve the gelatin very well. Add 6 more cups cold broth to the bowl with the gelatin and mix again. Open the bag of chicken, discard all the pancetta and wipe off the bird with paper towels.

Place the chicken in a glass bowl for serving. Pour the gelatin over it, cover the bowl and refrigerate at least overnight before serving.

When ready, arrange the carrots and string beans all around the bowl on top of the gelatin, leaving a space between the "pane" and the vegetables, so you are able to see the "chicken bread" sticking out.

Each serving should consist of a slice of the chicken, some of the gelatin, the vegetables and some of the green sauce you have selected to prepare along with the vegetables.

Serves 8 to 10.

Boned Chicken Stuffed with Artichokes

Prepare the stuffing: Place the artichokes in a bowl of cold water with the lemon cut in half and squeezed, and let soak for ½ hour.

Meanwhile, clean the chicken very well, removing the extra fat from the cavity. Bone the chicken as for a galantine, except leave all the meat attached to the skin (see Appendix, page 295).

Clean the artichokes, removing all the tough outer leaves and the choke (see instructions on page 78). Cut the tender part remaining into pieces not larger than an almond and put the pieces back into the acidulated water until needed.

Finely chop the garlic and coarsely chop the parsley on a board, then mix them together. Heat the oil in a medium-sized casserole over low heat and when the oil is warm, add the chopped ingredients and sauté for 2 minutes. Drain the artichokes, add them to the casserole and sauté for 5 minutes more, stirring every so often with a wooden spoon. Season with salt and pepper, then add the wine, raise the heat and let the wine evaporate for 2 minutes. If the artichokes are tough and woody, add ½ cup cold water, cover and let cook until tender, adding more cold water if needed. Transfer the cooked artichokes to a platter and let rest until cool, about ½ hour.

Preheat the oven to 400 degrees.

Spread out the boned chicken on a board, skin-side down, like a large *braciola*. Butterfly the meaty parts in order to make one even layer of meat. Cut the single 4-ounce piece of pancetta into tiny pieces and arrange them all over the opened chicken. Season with salt, pepper and 1 heaping teaspoon of the tarragon. Arrange the cooled artichokes all over the pancetta, then roll up the chicken from one of the shorter sides, being careful to keep all the stuffing inside the chicken. Tie the chicken like a salami (see Appendix, page 294).

Spread out a large sheet of aluminum foil, shiny-side up, grease it with the olive oil, sprinkle on the remaining tarragon and place all the pancetta slices in the center of the foil, forming a rectangle close to the size of the chicken. Place the chicken on the pancetta, wrap it up tightly with the foil and close the open ends very well.

Place the package in a jelly-roll pan and bake for about 1 hour. Then turn the chicken over and bake for 25 minutes

FOR THE STUFFING
3 large artichokes (to yield
     1 pound after cleaning)
1 lemon
2 medium-sized cloves garlic, peeled
15 sprigs Italian parsley, leaves only
5 tablespoons olive oil
Salt and freshly ground black pepper
1 cup dry white wine

1 large chicken (about 6 pounds)

PLUS
4 ounces pancetta or prosciutto,
     in one piece, plus 10 slices
     (about 4 ounces more)
Salt and freshly ground black pepper
2 teaspoons dried tarragon
1 teaspoon olive oil

TO SERVE (OPTIONAL)
Salsa d'agresto (see page 290)

more. Remove the chicken from the oven and let rest for a few minutes before removing the foil. Untie the chicken, discard the pancetta and slice the chicken like a salami. If desired, strain the juices from the chicken and reserve for serving with the chicken.

Transfer the slices of chicken to a serving dish and serve with the strained juices or the Salsa d'agresto on the side.

Serves 8.

G A L A N T I N A   I N V O L T A T A

Rolled Chicken Galantine

1 chicken (about 3 ½ pounds)
4 ounces pancetta or prosciutto, in one piece
12 large fresh sage leaves
1 tablespoon fresh rosemary leaves
2 cloves garlic, peeled
Salt and freshly ground black pepper
1 tablespoon olive oil

FOR THE PEPPER SAUCE
1 large bell pepper, preferably yellow
1 clove garlic, peeled
10 sprigs Italian parsley, leaves only
4 tablespoons olive oil
1 tablespoons unbleached all-purpose flour
2 tablespoons (1 ounce) sweet butter
1 cup chicken or meat broth, preferably homemade
Salt and freshly ground black pepper

Clean and wash the chicken very well, then dry it with paper towels. Bone the chicken as for a galantine, except leave all the meat attached to the skin (see Appendix, page 295). Spread out the chicken skin-side down.

Cut the pancetta into tiny pieces and coarsely chop the sage and rosemary together. Finely chop the garlic.

Arrange the pancetta all over the chicken, then sprinkle on the chopped herbs and garlic. Season with salt and pepper.

Preheat the oven to 375 degrees.

Roll up the chicken from one of the shorter sides, tucking in the legs and wings. Tie the rolled-up chicken like a salami (see Appendix, page 294). Season with salt and pepper and place it in a baking dish with the tablespoon of oil. Bake for 1 hour, turning the chicken three or four times.

Remove the chicken from the oven and cool for 15 minutes, then untie the chicken and cut it into ½-inch-thick slices.

To prepare the sauce, cut the pepper into small pieces, discarding the seeds and all the filaments, and soak in a bowl of cold water for 30 minutes.

Finely chop the garlic and parsley together on a board.

Set a medium-sized saucepan with the oil over medium heat and when the oil is warm, drain the pepper pieces and add them to the pan. Sauté for 5 minutes, stirring every so often with a wooden spoon.

Incorporate the flour and chopped parsley and garlic into the butter, add the mixture to the sautéed peppers and mix very well. Add the broth, mix again, lower the heat and simmer for 5 minutes.

Pass the contents of the pan through a food mill, using the disc with the smallest holes, into a clean saucepan. Season with salt and pepper and reduce for at least 5 minutes more, until a smooth sauce forms.

Serve the chicken slices (hot or at room temperature) with sauce on the side.

Serves 6 to 8.

SWEET-AND-SPICY POULTRY

The matching of fruit with meat, a cooking method that dates back to Medieval times, has become a popular device of today's *nouvelle* or *nuova* cooking in France and Italy. To the modern-day palate, the resulting flavors seem new and often intriguing.

In *Pollo alle melograne*, a dish that originated during the Renaissance but is newly popular in Italy, pomegranate seeds are cooked with chicken. Although today it is more common to make this dish with only the juice of the pomegranate, I prefer to use the seeds (as was done originally) because it retains more of the flavor of the pomegranate. This is one of the few dishes in modern Italian cooking that call for the combination of cinnamon, nutmeg and ginger, among the so-called sweet-and-hot spices of the Renaissance. Interestingly, ginger all but disappeared from Italian cooking in the early sixteenth century, around the time that hot red pepper was introduced from the Americas, and the word for ginger, *zenzero*, was transferred to hot red pepper.

Both the sauce for *Crostini di lepre* (page 15) and the sauce for *Anitra o pollo in dolce e forte* call for the sweet-and-sour combination of chocolate and wine vinegar; interestingly, in neither case is the chocolate flavor revealed or the result overly sweet. The term "dolce e forte" really means sweet and spicy, which suggests to me that this dish, like the Sienese dessert *panforte*, which also dates back to Medieval times, once used black pepper more abundantly.

A private dining room for the Medici family in the Palazzo Vecchio, where they lived before moving to the Pitti Palace. It was recently restored to its sixteenth-century splendor, but it isn't open to the public. On the table are the ingredients for Pollo alle melograne (Chicken with Pomegranates), an appropriate dish for this Renaissance setting.

POLLO ALLE MELOGRANE

Chicken with Pomegranates   OLD TUSCAN RENAISSANCE DISH

Cut the chicken into quarters. Rub the quarters with the table-spoon of butter and sprinkle them with salt and pepper.

Heat the oil in a medium-sized casserole over medium heat and, when the oil is warm, place the chicken in a single layer in the bottom of the casserole. Sauté for 2 minutes, then turn the chicken over and sauté for 2 minutes more. Add the wine and let it evaporate for 10 minutes. Season with salt and pepper, then add the cinnamon and a large pinch of nutmeg. Start adding the broth a little at a time, turning the chicken two or three times and adding more broth as needed.

1 chicken (about 3½ pounds)
1 tablespoon (½ ounce) sweet
   butter
Salt and freshly ground black pepper
5 tablespoons olive oil
1 cup dry white wine
A large pinch of ground cinnamon
Freshly grated nutmeg
1 to 2 cups chicken broth,
   preferably homemade

PLUS
2 large pomegranates

TO SERVE
A large pinch of ground ginger

Meanwhile, peel the pomegranates, removing all the seeds and discarding the skins.

When the chicken is almost cooked, about 25 minutes from the moment you started adding the broth, add the pomegranate seeds to the casserole, mix very well, cover and cook for 5 minutes more, stirring occasionally to be sure the seeds do not stick to the bottom. Taste for salt and pepper.

Just before serving, sprinkle the ginger all over the chicken and pomegranates, mix very well and transfer to a large serving platter. Serve hot.

Serves 4.

ANITRA O POLLO IN DOLCE E FORTE

Duck or Chicken in Sweet-and-Spicy Sauce

Place the water and vinegar along with the onion and celery in a large crockery or glass bowl. Add the chicken (or duck) and let stand, covered, in a cool place or on the bottom shelf of your refrigerator for 1 hour.

Meanwhile, start to prepare the sauce: Finely chop the celery, carrots and onion all together on a board. Heat the oil in a skillet over medium heat and when the oil is warm, add the chopped ingredients and sauté for 15 minutes, mixing every so often with a wooden spoon.

Drain the chicken, discarding the liquid and vegetables, and add it to the skillet. Sauté for 15 minutes or until golden all over. Season with salt and pepper, add the wine and let evaporate for 15 minutes more. By that time the chicken should be cooked; if not, add a little broth.

Prepare the sweet-and-spicy seasoning. Place the raisins, pine nuts, chocolate, sugar and vinegar in a small bowl.

When the chicken is ready, use a slotted spoon to transfer it to a serving platter.

Remove almost all the fat from the skillet, add the prepared sweet-and-spicy mixture and use a wooden spoon to deglaze the skillet. (Over low heat, scrape the bits of chicken and vegetables stuck to the skillet and stir them together with the sweet-and-spicy mixture in order to make a sauce.) Pour the sauce over the chicken and serve hot.

Serves 4 to 6.

5 cups cold water
½ cup red wine vinegar
1 medium-sized red onion, cleaned and cut into large pieces
1 large celery stalk, cut into large pieces
1 chicken or duck, cleaned and cut into 8 pieces

FOR THE SAUCE
2 celery stalks
2 medium-sized carrots, scraped
1 small red onion, cleaned
½ cup olive oil
Salt and freshly ground black pepper
½ cup dry white wine
½ cup lukewarm chicken or meat broth, preferably homemade (if needed)

FOR THE SWEET-AND-SPICY SEASONING
3 tablespoons raisins
2 tablespoons pine nuts (*pinoli*)
1 tablespoon grated bittersweet chocolate or cocoa powder
1 tablespoon granulated sugar
½ cup strong red wine vinegar

FAGIANO O POLLO ALLA "CRETA"

Pheasant or Chicken Baked in a Crust

Around Siena one can obtain the marvelous pure and nontoxic clay from which terra-cotta cooking vessels are made. As a result, a cooking tradition has arisen of baking chicken or other fowl wrapped in this clay; when the chicken is done the clay is broken with a hammer and the bird emerges succulent and full of juices. Because away from Siena it is very difficult to be sure that the clay is nontoxic, I have chosen a different but related method for Fagiano o pollo alla "creta." In this case, a pheasant or chicken is wrapped in a simple dough that, like the clay, becomes quite hard and must be cracked with a hammer; the dough, of course, is inedible and should be discarded. Fagiano o pollo alla "creta" is a simple and delicious dish that needs no sauce.

Wash the pheasant or chicken very well and dry it with paper towels. Place the rosemary, sage and sausage in the cavity of the bird. Place the pancetta slices all over the breast of the pheasant. Very lightly season the inside and outside of the pheasant with salt and pepper.

Preheat the oven to 375 degrees.

Prepare the crust: Place the flour in a mound on a board and make a large well in the center. Place the salt in the well of the flour, then add the water and start mixing the water with the salt. Start adding the flour from the edges of the well, a little at a time. When a rather thick dough is formed, start working with your hands, incorporating the remaining flour.

Roll out the dough, with a rolling pin, into a disc that is wide enough to wrap around the bird.

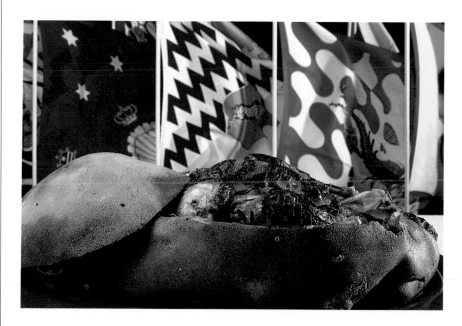

Fagiano alla creta (*Pheasant Baked in a Crust*) *with the bottom crust still attached. Waving in the background are the flags of many of the clubs that compete in Siena's famous Palio horse race.*

1 pheasant or free-range chicken
    (about 3 pounds), cleaned
    (see Note)
1 sprig fresh rosemary or
    1 tablespoon rosemary leaves,
    fresh, preserved in salt or dried
    and blanched
4 large sage leaves, fresh or
    preserved in salt
1 sweet Italian sausage, without
    fennel seeds, skinned
About 20 slices pancetta or
    prosciutto
Salt and freshly ground black pepper

FOR THE CRUST
3 cups unbleached all-purpose flour
1½ cups salt
1 cup plus 2 tablespoons cold water

Wrap the bird in a large piece of parchment paper. Be sure the bird is securely enclosed, and the paper has no holes; this is to prevent any salt from being absorbed by the bird. Place the wrapped bird on the dough, breast-side up and wrap completely with the dough.

Transfer the bird to a jelly-roll pan and bake for 2 hours. (If using a chicken, the baking time will be much shorter, about 1 hour 15 minutes.) If the bird is well protected by the parchment paper, it will be very juicy and not salty at all because the crust becomes an extremely tough covering, holding in all the flavor and juice of the bird.

When ready, remove the bird from the oven, cut off the top part of the crust and lift out the bird. Unwrap the bird (the crust should not be eaten) and transfer it to a serving platter. Serve hot.

Note: If the fowl is larger than 3 pounds, the ingredients for the crust must be increased proportionately.

Serves 4 to 6.

LA MAREMMA

Strange as it may seem, there actually is such a thing as an Italian cowboy. Even more remarkable, these home-grown cowboys live in southern Tuscany in an area known as the Maremma. They rope cows like any cowboy would, and they hunt wild boar. The landscape of the Maremma stretches 100 miles along the coastline from near Siena in the north to Viterbo in the south, and includes flat beaches and dunes, which give way first to woods thick with umbrella pines and then to a wilderness, really, an area so dense it is called the "bush," or macchia in Italian.

The name "Maremma" originally came from marittima, "land along the sea." Later, because of the character this land had acquired, maremma came to mean "marsh." But it was not always marshland. The Maremma was once a prosperous center of Etruscan civilization. Ancient art shows that the Etruscans loved to hunt there, and pictures them playing the double flute to attract curious boars and wild hare into their nets. The Etruscans also appreciated both the thermal waters of what is present-day Saturnia and the wine that they produced and consumed with great pleasure.

The region in those pre-Roman days was a small paradise and retained much of its prosperous character and rich farmland long after the Roman conquest. It was only after the collapse of the Roman Empire that the region fell on hard times. Its distinctive aqueducts in ruins, its farms and fields abandoned, it became more and more isolated and overgrown. By the Middle Ages, the sea and nearby rivers had invaded much of the long coastline, turning it into swampland, and it soon acquired its "marsh" name and the capital letter that marked it as a distinct region—the Maremma. Over the centuries, the Maremma became a natural breeding ground for mosquitoes, and also became known for its unwholesome, poisonous air. In fact, it wasn't until the 1950s that, with the use of pesticides, the malaria-carrying mosquitoes that had overtaken the area were wiped out and people began to return in significant numbers.

The wilderness and wildlife returned, too; people rediscovered farming and, most of all, the hunt. With cows and wild boars again abundant, the world of the Italian cowboy was restored. Interestingly, today it not only is home to the Italian cowboys but is one of the most fashionable vacation spots in Italy. Wealthy tourists and Italians gather to show themselves on the splendid beaches of Porto Ercole and Santo Stefano.

The cooking of the Maremma has always centered on game and, in particular, wild boar, which is the symbol for the region. Almost as characteristic of the Maremma is wild hare. With much of the game, the pasta of choice is pappardelle, a broad noodle made in bands at least two inches wide. The story is that the

An Italian cowboy, or buttero.

woodsmen, charcoal makers and shepherds who spent the winter season working in Maremma introduced these robust dishes to the region. They lived like pioneers in the cold and isolated winter environment and needed hearty foods to keep them going. It is said that the first pappardelle was used with duck because duck was so abundant and easy to come by. Two other popular foods, dating back to the Maremma's less prosperous days, are panzanella, or bread salad, and acquacotta, a soup specialty—actually boiled water, prepared without meat, with a variety of vegetables and aromatic spices—of which there are at least 25 varieties. The home of one of Italy's most distinguished wines, Brunello di Montalcino, is in Sant'Angelo in Colle, in the north of this area.

FARAONE ALL'UVA ED OLIVE

Guinea Hens or Squabs with Grapes and Olives

Sweet-and-savory dishes that utilize grapes have had a continuous history in the wine-producing areas of Italy. And since Tuscany is equally celebrated for the quality of its olive oil and its wine, what could be more natural than the combination of grapes and olives in this dish? The result is, of course, wonderful.

This preparation is much more appropriate to rich-tasting game hens than chicken. Both wine and olive oil are used in the cooking and they integrate the two fruits beautifully. All that is needed is onion, for a hint of sweetness (not garlic, which would be inappropriate here) and some chicken broth; guinea hen or squab broth would be even better, but chicken broth works just fine. This hearty dish provides an exemplary demonstration of how to use disparate elements in a truly integrated way.

Pour the wine in a large bowl and place the birds in it. Refrigerate for 1 hour.

Meanwhile, coarsely chop the onions on a board. Heat the oil in a medium-sized casserole over medium heat and when the oil is warm, add the onions and sauté for 5 minutes.

Remove the birds from the wine, add 1 cup of the wine to the casserole and cook until the wine evaporates. Add the hens and sauté all over for 15 minutes. Add the butter to the casserole and cook for 10 minutes longer. Season with salt and pepper. Add the remaining wine and cook for 20 minutes more, adding broth as needed, until the birds are almost ready, about 15 minutes more. Add the olives and grapes, cover the casserole and cook until the guinea hens or squabs are ready, adding more broth as needed.

Transfer the birds to a large serving platter, pour the sauce, including the olives and grapes, all over the birds and arrange the slices of boiled potato all around the platter. Add two lemon slices per serving, if desired.

Serves 6.

2 cups dry white wine
3 guinea hens or squabs, cleaned
2 large red onions, cleaned
½ cup olive oil
1 tablespoon (½ ounce) sweet butter
Salt and freshly ground black pepper
1 to 2 cups chicken broth, preferably homemade
½ pound black Greek olives, preserved in brine, drained
1 pound seedless red grapes, carefully cleaned and washed

TO SERVE
2 pounds unseasoned boiled potatoes, cut into slices
12 lemon slices (optional)

Faraone all'uva ed olive (*Guinea Hens with Grapes and Olives*) in front of the Palazzo dei Priori in the main piazza in Volterra. The palace was built in 1208 to be the seat of government of the independent commune. By the fifteenth century, Volterra had come under Florentine rule and, indeed, on the façade of the palace are the coats of arms of the Florentine governors of the fifteenth and sixteenth centuries.

Volterra is the capital of the Maremma, an area famous for its alabaster, cowboys and game. This area was once a large source of buffalo-milk mozzarella, but the water buffalo population has decreased over the years and the availability of the cheese has become limited.

CONIGLIO ED INSALATA

Rabbit Salad

Rabbit was once the most affordable of meats and was employed as often as chicken. Although its popularity among Tuscans has remained steady, its availability has diminished and it has become relatively expensive. The techniques for cooking rabbit are as varied as those for chicken; indeed, many of the methods are identical. Cold Coniglio ed insalata, which has always been popular, is traditionally made with pieces of freshly cooked rabbit and radicchio verde, the very bitter green radicchio with delicate leaves. Do not consider the radicchio a bed for the meat: It is an integral part of the dish. In fact, it would not occur to Tuscans to adopt the trendy method of presenting meat on a "bed of lettuce," as then the greens would not be a true part of the dish, but just a visual setting, something nonfunctional and ornamental.

Rabbit is combined with leaves of fragile green radicchio in Coniglio ed insalata (Rabbit Salad). Rabbit is all lean white meat and fits well into today's health-conscious diet.

1 medium-sized rabbit, skinned,
    liver removed (about 3 pounds)
4 tablespoons red wine vinegar
2 tablespoons coarse-grained salt
1 tablespoon rosemary leaves,
    fresh, preserved in salt or dried
    and blanched
2 medium-sized cloves garlic, peeled
Salt and freshly ground black pepper
3 ounces pancetta or very fatty
    prosciutto, cut into thin strips
4 tablespoons olive oil
1 cup dry white wine
About ½ cup chicken or meat
    broth, preferably homemade

PLUS
Several bunches of green radicchio
    or 1 small head Boston
    lettuce and 1 very small head
    Romaine lettuce
1 large clove garlic, peeled and
    left whole
Salt to taste
2 tablespoons red wine vinegar
3 tablespoons olive oil

Place the rabbit in a bowl of cold water with the vinegar and salt and soak for 1 hour. Drain the rabbit, clean it and rinse thoroughly under cold running water, then dry it with paper towels.

Coarsely chop the rosemary and finely chop the garlic on a board, mix them together, and add salt and pepper to taste.

Use a sharp knife to make several holes in the rabbit and insert some of the rosemary-garlic mixture into each hole. Use a larding needle to lard the leg and shoulder meat with the pancetta.

Heat the oil in a medium-sized casserole over medium heat and when the oil is warm, add the rabbit and sauté for 2 minutes on each side. Add ½ cup of the wine, cover the casserole and cook for 10 minutes. Add the remaining wine, turn the rabbit over, re-cover and cook for 5 minutes more. Season with salt and pepper, then start adding the broth, a small amount at a time, waiting to add more broth until the previously added broth is completely absorbed. If the rabbit is young and fresh, by the time all the broth is used up, the rabbit should be cooked and soft. When ready, transfer the whole rabbit to a serving platter, cover and let cool completely.

Meanwhile, clean the lettuces and cut them into thin strips.

When the rabbit is ready and cooled, cut it into 2-inch pieces, leaving the meat on the bone.

Use the whole clove of garlic to rub the inside part of a crockery or glass bowl, then discard the garlic.

Dissolve the salt in the vinegar. Put the lettuce in the bowl, pour in the vinegar, then the oil. Mix well, then arrange the salad on a large serving platter. Place the rabbit pieces over the salad and serve.

Serves 6.

VEAL DISHES

In Polpettone di vitella con le patate, *ground veal held together with eggs and grated cheese is formed into a large meat loaf and baked together with potatoes. When a veal scallop is rolled up and stuffed it is called* involtini *in Tuscany. In the* Involtini di carciofi, *the scallop is stuffed with artichokes. In* Stracotto di vitella alla fornarina, *cubed veal shank is sautéed in oil infused with sage and garlic and then baked. Fornarina means "the baker's wife," and this is how she would prepare this dish. The special* Crocchette al forno al limone *are first fried, then baked in lemon juice, which adds flavor and removes any heaviness caused by the frying.*

POLPETTONE DI VITELLA CON LE PATATE

Veal Meat Loaf

ALL OVER TUSCANY

Coarsely grind the pancetta, garlic and rosemary all together with a meat grinder.

Place the veal, eggs, *Parmigiano* and the ground pancetta mixture in a crockery or glass bowl and mix very well with a wooden spoon. Season with salt and pepper and mix again.

Peel the potatoes and cut them into about 1½-inch cubes. Boil the potatoes in salted water for 5 minutes. Drain them and cool under cold running water.

Mix the cooked potatoes with the rosemary leaves and salt and pepper to taste.

Pour the oil in a baking pan and preheat the oven to 375 degrees.

Transfer the veal mixture to the prepared pan, forming an 8-inch-long loaf. (If desired, the carrots can be inserted lengthwise into the meat loaf while forming it, so when it is sliced, there will be bits of bright orange.) Arrange the potatoes all around the meat loaf and bake for 50 minutes, stirring the potatoes once or twice.

Remove the meat loaf from the oven and serve directly from the baking pan or transfer the meat and potatoes onto an oval serving platter before serving.

Serves 6.

4 ounces pancetta or (quite fatty) prosciutto, in one piece
2 large cloves garlic, peeled
1 tablespoon rosemary leaves, fresh, preserved in salt or dried and blanched
2 pounds ground veal shoulder
3 extra-large eggs
4 tablespoons freshly grated *Parmigiano*
Salt and freshly ground black pepper

PLUS
3 pounds potatoes (not new potatoes)
Coarse-grained salt
1 tablespoon rosemary leaves, fresh, preserved in salt or dried and blanched
Salt and freshly ground black pepper
4 tablespoons olive oil
3 thin boiled carrots (optional)

INVOLTINI DI CARCIOFI

Veal Bundles Stuffed with Artichokes

12 veal scallopini
4 large artichokes
1 lemon
20 sprigs Italian parsley, leaves only
2 large cloves garlic, peeled
10 tablespoons olive oil
Salt and freshly ground black pepper
1 cup cold water
4 tablespoons freshly grated
　Parmigiano
2 extra-large eggs
About 1 cup unbleached
　all-purpose flour
2 tablespoons (1 ounce) sweet
　butter
1 to 2 cups chicken or meat broth,
　preferably homemade

TO SERVE
15 sprigs Italian parsley, leaves only
1 lemon, very thinly sliced

If the butcher has not done so, pound the veal between two pieces of waxed paper dampened with cold water (so the meat does not stick to the paper).

Place the artichokes in a bowl of cold water with the lemon cut in half and squeezed and soak for ½ hour.

Clean the artichokes, removing the tough green leaves and the choke (see instructions on page 78), then cut them into small pieces and return the pieces to the acidulated water until ready to be cooked.

Finely chop the parsley and garlic together on a board. Heat 6 tablespoons of the oil in a medium-sized skillet over medium heat and when the oil is warm, add the chopped ingredients and sauté for 1 minute. Drain the artichokes, rinse under cold running water and add them to the skillet. Sauté for 5 minutes, stirring every so often with a wooden spoon, and season with salt and pepper. Add the water and cook, covered, until the artichokes are tender, adding more cold water if needed.

Using a slotted spoon, transfer 12 heaping tablespoons of the artichokes, leaving the liquid, to a crockery or glass bowl, and let cool completely. Remove the skillet from the heat. Transfer the remaining artichokes and all the juices to a second crockery or glass bowl and let stand until needed.

When the artichokes in the first bowl are cooled, add the Parmigiano and eggs and mix the stuffing very well. Taste for salt and pepper.

Divide the stuffing among the 12 scallopini, then roll them up, tucking in the ends. Tie each bundle like a small salami (see Appendix, page 294).

Lightly flour all the involtini, then melt the butter with the remaining olive oil in a medium-sized casserole, and when the butter is melted, add the meat and lightly sauté on all sides for 2 minutes. Add the contents of the second bowl, cover the casserole and cook for 10 minutes, or until the meat is cooked but still very juicy, adding some of the broth if more liquid is needed. Transfer the meat to a serving dish and cover to keep warm. Raise the heat under the sauce and reduce the sauce for 5 minutes. Taste for salt and pepper.

Meanwhile, coarsely shop the parsley.

When the sauce is ready, remove the threads from the involtini and place one on each plate. Pour on the sauce and add a sprinkling of parsley and a slice of lemon to each serving.

Serves 12.

STRACOTTO DI VITELLA ALLA FORNARINA

Roasted Veal Shank

2 tablespoons unbleached
   all-purpose flour
3 pounds veal shank, cut into
   2-inch cubes
6 tablespoons olive oil
3 large cloves garlic, peeled and
   left whole
5 large sage leaves, fresh or
   preserved in salt
1 tablespoon rosemary leaves,
   fresh, preserved in salt or dried
   and blanched
2 pounds very ripe fresh tomatoes,
   cut into pieces, or 2 pounds
   drained canned tomatoes,
   preferably imported Italian
2 tablespoons tomato paste
1 cup dry red wine
Salt and freshly ground black pepper
A large pinch of hot red pepper
   flakes
1 to 2 cups chicken or beef broth,
   preferably homemade

TO SERVE
5 tablespoons olive oil
2 medium-sized cloves garlic,
   peeled and finely chopped
4 pounds spinach, boiled in salted
   water, squeezed and coarsely
   chopped
Salt and freshly ground black pepper
A large pinch of hot red pepper
   flakes

PLUS
6 (5-inch) slices crusty Tuscan
   bread, ½ inch thick, lightly
   toasted and rubbed with garlic

A serving of Stracotto di vitella alla
fornarina *(Roasted Veal Shank) and a
plate of Tuscan bread rubbed with garlic
in front of an abandoned church in the
tiny village of Bugialla. My family has
always believed that our ancestors lived
here many centuries ago as we are the only
family with this name.*

Lightly flour the meat by placing it in a colander, sprinkling the flour over it and shaking the colander to remove the excess flour.

Heat the oil in a medium-sized casserole over medium heat and when the oil is warm, add the whole cloves of garlic, the sage and rosemary. Sauté for 5 minutes, stirring with a wooden spoon, or until the garlic is golden.

Strain the oil, discarding the sautéed garlic and aromatic herbs. Pour the oil back into the casserole, set it over low heat and add the veal. Sauté for 5 minutes, stirring every so often with a wooden spoon.

Meanwhile, pass the fresh or canned tomatoes through a food mill, using the disc with the smallest holes, into a crockery or glass bowl. Dissolve the tomato paste in the strained tomatoes.

Add the wine to the casserole and let it evaporate for 10 minutes.

Preheat the oven to 375 degrees.

Season the meat with salt, pepper and the hot red pepper flakes. Add the tomatoes to the casserole, cover and bake for 1½ hours, adding broth as needed. (It is possible that the meat will give off enough liquid and no broth will be needed.) After 1½ hours, the meat should be soft and very juicy.

Meanwhile, heat the oil in a skillet. Add the garlic and sauté for 20 seconds. Add the spinach, season with salt, pepper and hot red pepper flakes, and sauté for 5 minutes.

When the meat is ready, use a slotted spoon to transfer it to a large serving platter.

Reduce the leftover sauce in the casserole over medium heat. Taste for salt and pepper.

When the sauce is rather thick, pour it over the meat. Arrange the warm spinach all around the meat and serve hot, along with the toasted bread.

Serves 6.

Croquettes Baked with Lemon

Sunflowers grow in fields throughout Tuscany and are the source of the oil most commonly used in lightly fried dishes like this one.

Place the bread in a bowl with the milk and soak for 30 minutes.

Meanwhile, cut the meat into 1-inch cubes.

When ready, squeeze the bread very dry, mix it with the meat and, using a meat grinder, grind everything into a crockery or glass bowl. Add the eggs, the juice of 1 of the lemons, the *Parmigiano* and salt and pepper to taste. Mix very well with a wooden spoon. The mixture will be quite loose.

Heat the vegetable oil in a deep-fat fryer over medium heat and when the oil is hot (about 375 degrees), shape the croquettes into 2-inch-thick ovals, using 4 tablespoons of the mixture each. Lightly flour each croquette and fry until lightly golden all over.

Transfer the cooked croquettes to a baking dish and preheat the oven to 300 degrees. When all the croquettes are in the dish, sprinkle them with the olive oil, place pats of butter all over and pour in the juice of the remaining 3 lemons. Bake for 10 minutes. Remove from the oven and serve hot with some of the juices from the baking pan.

Serves 4 to 6.

10 slices white bread, crusts removed
2 cups whole milk
¾ pound veal shoulder, in one piece
4 extra-large eggs
4 large lemons
4 ounces freshly grated *Parmigiano*
Salt and freshly ground black pepper

TO COOK THE CROQUETTES
1 quart vegetable oil (⅔ corn oil, ⅓ sunflower oil)
About 1½ cups unbleached all-purpose flour
2 tablespoons olive oil
4 tablespoons (2 ounces) sweet butter

CUSCUSSÙ ALLA LIVORNESE CON FAGIOLI

Couscous with Beans

In Cuscussù alla livornese con fagioli, *one of the many couscous dishes that are made in Livorno, the steamed grain is served with small poached meatballs, vegetables and a good amount of cannellini beans, not the token quantity of chick-peas that one sees in most couscous dishes. Though this particular dish is of Livornese origin and may reflect the influence of the area's once large Sephardic Jewish population, couscous itself is used all over Italy, and many people feel that it has been used there since ancient Roman times. This is one of the most complex couscous dishes I know.*

Beside this platter of Cuscussù alla livornese con fagioli *(Livornese-Style Couscous with Beans) is the insert of the couscous pot, which holds the grain during steaming. This couscous pot differs from the North African receptacle in two ways: It has a cover, and the holes in the insert are much larger and must be covered with basil or bay leaves in order to hold in the grain.*

Place the couscous on a large serving platter. Combine the eggs, olive oil, water and salt to taste in a crockery or glass bowl. Pour this mixture all over the couscous, then use the palms of your hands to rub the couscous with the liquid, until all the liquid has been absorbed by the grain. Let rest for 1 hour.

Meanwhile, prepare the broth for steaming the couscous: Finely chop the carrots, onions, celery and parsley all together on a board. Place a medium-sized stockpot with the olive oil over medium heat and when the oil is warm, add the chopped ingredients and sauté for 5 minutes. Add the water and simmer for 45 minutes.

Prepare the vegetables: Cut the carrots and celery into 3-inch pieces and soak in a bowl of cold water until needed. Slice the cabbage leaves into thin strips and soak them in a different bowl of cold water. Cut the zucchini into two pieces and soak in a third bowl of cold water to which a little coarse salt has been added. Pass the fresh or canned tomatoes through a food mill, using the disc with the smallest holes, into a crockery or glass bowl, and let rest until needed.

Prepare the beans: Drain and rinse the beans and place them in a medium-sized casserole with enough cold water to come 2 inches above the beans. Set the casserole over medium heat and simmer for about 45 minutes. By that time the beans should be cooked through but still retain their shape. Season with salt and pepper. Drain the beans, saving the cooking water. Transfer the beans to a crockery or glass bowl, place a towel dampened in cold water over them and let rest until needed.

By this time (after 1 hour of resting) the couscous should be ready to be steamed. Use the stockpot with the simmering vegetable broth as the bottom part of an improvised double boiler for steaming the couscous. Line the top part of a *cuscussiera* or a large colander with the basil leaves, then place a large piece of cheesecloth over the leaves. Transfer the couscous to the prepared colander and place the colander over the boiling water. Cover the colander with a piece of aluminum foil and if the colander does not fit very well in the pot, seal it by preparing a quite tough dough made with flour and water and filling in the space all around the colander. Let the couscous steam for 1 hour.

As the couscous cooks, prepare the *polpettine*: Bring a small pot of cold water to a boil over medium heat.

Meanwhile, mix the ground meat with the bread. When the water reaches a boil, add salt and the potato and cook until the potato is very soft, about 25 minutes. When ready, drain the potato and peel it. In a meat grinder, using the disc with the

FOR THE COUSCOUS
2 pounds couscous (not instant)
3 extra-large eggs
½ cup olive oil
4 tablespoons cold water
Salt
Basil leaves, fresh or preserved
   in salt

FOR THE STEAMER
4 medium-sized carrots, scraped
2 large red onions, cleaned
3 celery stalks
10 sprigs Italian parsley, leaves only
6 tablespoons olive oil
4 quarts cold water

FOR THE VEGETABLES
4 medium-sized carrots, scraped
6 celery stalks
1 pound Savoy cabbage, cleaned
4 medium-sized zucchini
Coarse-grained salt
1 pound very ripe fresh tomatoes,
   cut into pieces, or 1 pound
   drained canned tomatoes,
   preferably imported Italian
Salt and freshly ground black pepper

FOR THE BEANS

1 pound dried cannellini beans (soaked overnight in cold water)
Coarse-grained salt
2 medium-sized red onions, cleaned
3 large cloves garlic, peeled
6 tablespoons olive oil
2 pounds very ripe fresh tomatoes, cut into pieces, or 2 pounds drained canned tomatoes, preferably imported Italian
Salt and freshly ground black pepper

FOR THE *POLPETTINE* (MEATBALLS)

1 pound ground beef, preferably sirloin
3 slices white bread, crusts removed
Coarse-grained salt
1 all-purpose potato (about 8 ounces)
1 medium-sized red onion, cleaned and cut into medium-sized pieces
15 sprigs Italian parsley, leaves only
4 tablespoons freshly grated *Parmigiano*
3 extra-large eggs
Salt and freshly ground black pepper
A large pinch of hot red pepper flakes

TO SERVE

Fresh basil leaves

smallest holes, grind the beef, bread, potato, onion and parsley all together into a crockery or glass bowl. Add the *Parmigiano*, eggs, salt and pepper to taste and the hot red pepper flakes, and mix very well with a wooden spoon.

Place the leftover water from the beans over medium heat. When the water reaches a boil, start forming the *polpettine*, using about 2 tablespoons of the mixture for each one. A few at a time, cook the *polpettine* in the boiling broth for 2 minutes, then transfer them to a large serving dish. When all the *polpettine* are cooked, cover the dish to prevent them from drying out.

When the couscous is ready (after 1 hour of steaming), remove the cheesecloth with the couscous and transfer it to a large serving platter. While still very hot, start rubbing the half-cooked couscous between the palms of your hands, to dissolve big lumps that might have formed. A little broth will help you to do this. Let the couscous rest until cool, about ½ hour.

When ready, detach the top part (the colander) from the stockpot. Drain and rinse all the vegetables that have been soaking and add them to the pot. Bring the broth with all the vegetables to a boil, add the 1 pound of tomatoes that you already passed through the food mill, and season with salt and pepper.

Place the cheesecloth with the cooled couscous back on top of the boiling water. Cover the colander and let steam for 1 hour more. By that time the grain will be ready and some of the vegetables will be cooked perfectly, while others will be overcooked: The overcooked vegetables will melt into the thick sauce created with the reduced broth.

As the couscous steams and the vegetables are cooking in the stockpot, finish the preparation of the beans. Finely chop the onion and garlic all together on a board, then heat the 6 tablespoons of olive oil in a large skillet over medium heat. When the oil is warm, add the chopped ingredients and sauté for 15 minutes, stirring every so often with a wooden spoon.

Pass the 2 pounds of fresh or canned tomatoes through a food mill, using the disc with the smallest holes, into a crockery or glass bowl.

When ready, add the tomatoes to the skillet, season with salt and pepper and cook for 15 minutes. Add the cooled *polpettine* and the beans and gently mix all the ingredients together. Taste for salt and pepper.

Prepare for serving: Drain the vegetables, reserving the broth, then arrange all the couscous in a ring on a large serving platter and place the vegetables in the center of the ring. Transfer the contents of the skillet to a large bowl.

Each serving should consist of couscous with vegetables and, on the side, the *polpettine* mixed with beans, and some of the sauce. If the couscous is too dry, add some of the reserved broth. Discard the basil leaves in the colander and sprinkle fresh basil leaves over each serving.

Serves 12.

BISTECCA ALLA FIORENTINA

Florentine Beefsteak

No *Tuscan coobook can omit* Bistecca alla fiorentina, *the signature meat dish of all Italy, even though it can be made authentically only with the beef from the Vadichiana, which is a remarkable combination of leanness and tenderness and is full of rare flavor. The meat is cooked over real charcoal or wood ash and is removed from the heat when still extremely rare. The meat is not marinated and no butter or oil is used.*

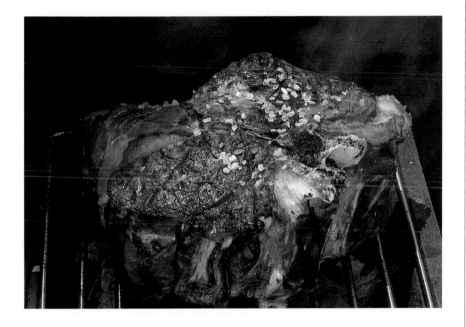

Preheat the grill until there is no longer any flame, just wood or charcoal ash.

Using your hands or a spatula (not a fork), place the steaks on the grill and cook on one side for 4 to 5 minutes, or until a brown crust forms. Salt the side facing up, then turn the steaks with a spatula, allowing some salt to fall off. Cook the second side of the steak for 4 to 5 minutes, then flip back to the first side and cook for another 4 to 5 minutes; the steaks should still be quite rare inside, in the true Florentine style.

Quickly transfer the steaks to a serving platter and sprinkle lightly with pepper. Cut the fillet and contrafillet sections of each steak in two so that each of the 4 servings has some of both.

Serve with lemon wedges, to be squeezed over the steaks.

Note: Ask the butcher to cut the steaks three inches thick and to include a section of fillet and contrafillet in each one. Each 1¾-pound steak should serve two people. Do not have the steaks cut into smaller individual portions.

Serves 4.

2 (1¾-pound) steaks, cut 3 inches thick (see Note)
Coarse-grained salt
Freshly ground black pepper
Lemon wedges

Chianti-Style Fricassea

In Fricassea alla chiantigiana, *lamb shoulder is boned and cubed and then sautéed in olive oil with garlic and bay leaves in order to remove any gamey flavor. The lamb is then cooked in butter (perhaps in former times it was cooked in lard), together with vegetables. Wine and broth are added, and as with most Italian lamb dishes, even those from Chianti, white rather than red wine is used. Like all Italian* fricassee, *this one is served with an egg-lemon sauce.*

6 large cloves garlic, peeled
6 bay leaves
8 tablespoons olive oil
2 pounds boneless lamb shoulder, trimmed and cut into 2-inch cubes
4 tablespoons (2 ounces) sweet butter
2 medium-sized red onions
2 celery stalks
Salt and freshly ground black pepper
Freshly grated nutmeg
1 cup dry white wine
1 cup chicken or meat broth, preferably homemade

PLUS
3 extra-large egg yolks
3 tablespoons lemon juice

TO SERVE
10 sprigs Italian parsley, leaves only

Place 3 cloves of the garlic, the bay leaves and 4 tablespoons of the olive oil in a skillet over medium heat and when the oil is warm, add the meat and sauté until lightly golden all over, about 15 minutes.

Place the butter in a large casserole over low heat. Meanwhile, coarsely chop the remaining 3 cloves of garlic, the onions and celery all together on a board.

When the butter is melted, add the remaining 4 tablespoons olive oil, then add the chopped vegetables and sauté for 2 minutes.

Use a slotted spoon to transfer the lamb cubes from the skillet to the casserole, discarding the juices along with the garlic and bay leaves. Sauté for 5 minutes more, stirring with a wooden spoon, then season with salt, pepper and nutmeg. Add the wine and let it evaporate for 15 minutes. Add ½ cup of the broth, cover the casserole and cook until the meat is soft, adding more broth as needed, about 20 to 45 minutes, depending on the tenderness of the meat.

Mix the egg yolks and lemon juice in a small bowl.

When ready, transfer the meat, leaving all the juices in the casserole, to a large serving platter, and cover the meat to keep warm.

Taste the juices in the casserole for salt and pepper, mix very well and reduce for 10 minutes. Incorporate ½ cup of the boiling sauce, little by little, into the egg-lemon mixture (tempering it), constantly stirring with a wooden spoon so the eggs do not separate. Lower the heat under the sauce to a simmer, then, little by little, add the "tempered" egg-lemon mixture to the sauce, again stirring continuously until the eggs are incorporated. (This tempering technique is used to assure that the eggs are completely cooked, but do not separate.)

Pour the sauce over the meat, sprinkle on the parsley and serve hot.

Serves 6.

SALSICCE E FAGIOLI ALLA SENESE

Sienese-Style Beans and Sausages

The celebrated Sienese pork is at its best when stuffed into the city's famous sausages. To achieve a near-authentic result when preparing Salsicce e fagioli alla senese, be sure to use sausages that have no fennel seeds or hot pepper in them; the sausages you buy should be made of pork, salt and pepper only. In this recipe, after the sausages are cooked with garlic and sage, boiled cannellini beans are warmed in their juices.

Soak the beans in a bowl of cold water overnight. The next morning, drain the beans and rinse them under cold running water.

Place a medium-sized pot of cold water over medium heat and, when the water reaches a boil, add the beans along with the garlic and sage and simmer for about 45 minutes. By that time the beans should be cooked through but still quite firm. Add the oil and salt and pepper to taste, mix very well and simmer for 1 minute more. Drain the beans and transfer them to a crockery or glass bowl, placing a wet towel over the beans to keep them from drying out.

Puncture the sausages with a fork in three or four places. Heat the oil in a flameproof casserole over medium heat. When the oil is hot, add the sausages and sauté over low heat for 15 minutes, turning them over several times. Add the garlic and sage and sauté for 2 to 3 minutes more. Add the water, tomato paste (if using) and salt and pepper to taste. Cook over low heat until the sausages are cooked through, about 10 minutes.

Remove the sausages to a crockery or glass bowl and add the beans to the skillet. Season with salt and pepper, mix very well and cook for 2 minutes more. Place the sausages back in the casserole, mix very well and cook for 5 minutes more.

Transfer the contents of the skillet to a large serving platter and serve with additional sage leaves.

Serves 6.

2 cups dried cannellini beans
1 large clove garlic, peeled and left whole
4 large sage leaves, fresh or preserved in salt
2 tablespoons olive oil
Salt and freshly ground black pepper

FOR THE SAUSAGES
12 sweet Italian sausages, without fennel seeds
4 tablespoons olive oil
4 large cloves garlic, unpeeled
12 large sage leaves, fresh or preserved in salt
½ cup cold water
1 tablespoon tomato paste (optional)
Salt and freshly ground black pepper

TO SERVE
Fresh sage leaves

A platter of Salsicce e fagioli alla senese *(Sienese-Style Beans and Sausages) in front of Siena's cathedral, which the Sienese tried to expand throughout the Renaissance in order to outdo the efforts of their Florentine rivals. The large extension was only partially completed, as is evidenced by the unfinished wall standing in the open air today. What was completed is magnificent, though: a façade by Giovanni Pisano, a pulpit by Nicola Pisano and the unique inlaid floors.*

If you have ever been to the Palio—the horse race held every July 2 and August 16 between competing Sienese neighborhoods, or con-trade, as they are called—you begin to understand the extra-ordinary role neighborhoods play in the life of the Sienese. While the horse race is only 450 years old, the seventeen contrade—which boast such names as Drago (Dragon), Oca (Goose) and Istrice (Porcupine)—are much older than that. They date back to the early Renaissance, when strong local neighborhoods were the trademark of democracy in action.

No people anywhere can match this intense identification with neighborhood. And no "outsiders," including other Italians, can completely comprehend the degree of feeling that accompanies the Palio. The races are exciting for anyone who attends, but the tourist need only appear for the occasion, get caught up in the excitement and go home; for the Sienese, the Palio is a year-long ritual.

"Palio fever" is, of course, at its most intense in the few weeks before, during and after the horse races. It is of major importance to the contrada what horse and rider will represent them and both of these factors are determined by lottery; the good or bad fortune of the whole neighborhood "rides" on the outcome of the race.

But the Palio season affects Siena in even more personal ways. It is obligatory for the Sienese to return to their old neighborhood for each Palio—to visit their ancestral home, the contrada feast-

The Palio horse race takes place in Siena's huge, shell-shaped central piazza called the Piazza del campo. It is the rehearsals for the race rather than the race itself that arouse the greatest excitement, rivalries and animosities among the Sienese.

This former church is typical of the build-ings where the contrade have their head-quarters and keep their precious horses.

After the ceremony in the church, the flag throwers put on a display outside.

The evening before the race, the members of each contrada gather for a huge dinner, called il braciere, at which many types of meat are cooked on a large grill.

ing hall and the local church. But since a husband and wife can easily belong to two different contrade, whole families can break up during the week or so of festivities. Drama can occur in even the most tranquil household if the spouses come from not only rival, but age-old, arch-enemy contrade. Saddest of all are situations where child loyalties are fought over, though more than likely, passions cool long enough to find a resolution. And just as history has provided the Sienese with enemy contrade, there are fortunately "ally" contrade as well.

For the most part, the Palio is an extraordinarily festive time, regardless of contrada, when the people engage in a degree of feasting, drinking, parading and championing that is the envy of all other Italian cities. "Outsiders" can never truly appreciate the full impact of the occasion and the ancient spirit that sustains it. Nonetheless, they can enthusiastically join in the excitement and fun, enjoy the marvelous parades, banners and ceremonies, and passionately cheer for their favorite contrada in the horse race.

While working on this book, for the first time I decided to take advantage of the fact that my grandmother was Sienese and I am, therefore, a legitimate member of the Chiocciola (Snail) contrada. I got our little group invited to all of this contrada's Palio events, including the huge dinner that takes place the night before the race.

FISH AND SEAFOOD

There are many rivers in Tuscany—and a coastline for its entire length—so both freshwater and ocean fish are plentiful. The fish is so good, in fact, that most of the time it is cooked very simply: grilled over a wood fire or on a spit; deep-fried with the lightest of coatings; or poached and served with an uncooked herb sauce. But, of course, there are also dishes that are more complex and I present some of those here.

Although it is difficult to match some varieties of fish, sweet shrimp or tiny clams that come from the Mediterranean, substitutions can be made and satisfying results can be achieved.

A view of the side of Prato's cathedral and its famous outdoor pulpit. Made with white marble from Carrara and Prato's own famous green marble, this Romanesque cathedral is considered to be one of Tuscany's finest. The bronze top of the pulpit was executed by Michelozzo and the stone-relief is the work of Donatello.

Preceding pages: For the Luminaria, Pisa's entire waterfront is illuminated with thousands of tiny candles, each in its own little glass. If you look closely at the table setting you can see the platter of Polpo in guazzetto (Octopus in Sauce) that we prepared for the occasion.

Above: Frittura del Bisenzio set on a terrace overlooking the side of the cathedral.

The Bisenzio River, at its widest at Prato, flows south past Campi Bisenzio and empties into the Arno a little west of Florence. Once famous for its purity and abundance of fish, it is now mainly known for the delicious little fish that the people of Prato like to fry and eat whole.

Place the fish in a bowl of cold water with the vinegar, and soak for ½ hour. Drain the fish and rinse it under cold running water.

Place the flour in a colander, place the fish on top of the flour, then shake the colander vigorously; in this way the fish will be uniformly coated with the flour and the excess flour will fall through the holes of the colander.

Heat the oil in a large skillet over high heat and when the oil reaches about 375 degrees, add the fish (the whole amount or half depending on the size of the skillet). After 30 seconds, start moving the fish with a slotted spoon to be sure they do not stick together. When they are golden and very crisp all over, transfer them to a serving dish lined with paper towels.

Transfer the fish to another serving dish or remove the paper towels, sprinkle some salt all over and serve hot with lemon wedges.

Serves 6 as an appetizer.

1 pound tiny freshwater fish or
    1 pound whitebait or smelts
2 tablespoons red wine vinegar

TO FRY
1 cup unbleached all-purpose flour
1 quart vegetable oil (⅔ corn oil,
    ⅓ sunflower oil)
Salt

TO SERVE
Lemon wedges

TROTA ALLE ERBE

Poached Trout in Herb Sauce

Because of the high number of freshwater streams in Tuscany, good-quality trout is plentiful. It is often poached and served with a mayonnaise or, as in this recipe, with a fresh herb sauce.

Place the trout and vinegar in a bowl of cold water, and soak for ½ hour.

Meanwhile, prepare the poaching broth: Set a medium-sized stockpot with the water, wine, lemon juice, parsley, basil, garlic, scallions and salt over medium heat and simmer for 35 minutes. Strain the broth and transfer it to a fish poacher. Let the broth cool for ½ hour. Drain the trout and dry it with paper towels.

As the broth cools, prepare the sauce: Finely chop the parsley, garlic and scallions all together on a board. Transfer to a crockery or glass bowl, season with salt and pepper, then add the lemon juice and oil. Mix well with a wooden spoon and let rest until needed.

When the broth is ready, place the trout in the fish poacher in one layer. Bring to a boil over medium heat and poach it for 5 minutes or more, until perfectly soft but still firm. Lift the trout with the slotted insert of the poacher, being sure to remove the excess broth. Arrange the trout on a large serving platter.

Mix the sauce again, taste for salt and pepper and arrange it all over the trout. Sprinkle the basil all over and serve, or cover the dish and let it sit at room temperature for a few hours before serving.

Serves 4.

4 medium-sized brook trout, cleaned
2 tablespoons red wine vinegar

TO POACH THE TROUT
2 quarts water
1 cup dry white wine
1 tablespoon lemon juice
10 sprigs Italian parsley, leaves only
5 fresh basil leaves
1 medium-sized clove garlic, peeled
2 scallions, green part removed
Coarse-grained salt

FOR THE SAUCE
25 sprigs Italian parsley, leaves only
1 very small clove garlic, peeled
5 scallions, green part removed
Salt and freshly ground black pepper
1 tablespoon lemon juice
½ cup olive oil

TO SERVE
Several fresh basil leaves

CLAMS AND MUSSELS

I *have chosen two clam dishes and one mussel and clam dish from the seacoast. In* Telline alla livornese, *tiny clams are cooked with tomato and mixed, in the last minutes of cooking, with beaten eggs. This dish comes from Livorno, sometimes called Leghorn in English. From the coast south of Livorno, I present* Zuppa di telline, *tiny clams and puréed tomatoes served with country bread rubbed with garlic, or with garlic* focaccia. *In* Cozze e vongole stufate in guazzetto, *the mussels and clams are flavored with vegetables and herbs but are cooked in wine and in their own juice (called* in guazzetto *in Italian). All three of these dishes are spiced with hot red pepper.*

Telline *is the Tuscan name for the smallest clams. The slightly larger clams are often referred to as* arselle *or* vongole, *words of Ligurian and Neapolitan origin, respectively. The largest clams used along this coast, named* vongole veraci, *are still much smaller than the clams of the Western Hemisphere.*

TELLINE ALLA LIVORNESE

Leghorn-Style Baby Clams

LIVORNO

2 pounds tiny clams, the smallest you can find
1 lemon
Coarse-grained salt
1 small red onion, cleaned
1 large clove garlic, peeled
½ cup olive oil
1 pound very ripe fresh tomatoes, blanched, seeded and cut into large pieces, or 1 pound drained canned tomatoes, preferably imported Italian, seeded and cut into large pieces
Salt and freshly ground black pepper
A large pinch of hot red pepper flakes
2 extra-large eggs
15 sprigs Italian parsley, leaves only, coarsely chopped

Leave the clams in their shells and wash them well. Place the clams in a bowl of cold water with the lemon cut in half and squeezed and a little coarse salt, and soak for ½ hour.

Finely chop the onion and garlic on a board. Heat the olive oil in a skillet over medium heat and when the oil is warm, add the chopped ingredients and sauté for 2 to 3 minutes, stirring every so often with a wooden spoon. Add the tomatoes, lower the heat and cook for 5 minutes more. Season with salt and pepper and the hot red pepper flakes.

Drain the clams, rinse them under cold running water, add them to the skillet, cover and cook. The really tiny Mediterranean clams, called *telline,* cook in 2 to 3 minutes, whereas even small Atlantic clams can take much longer, as long as 10 minutes, depending on their size. Quickly remove and discard those that don't open.

Meanwhile, mix the eggs with a pinch of salt in a small bowl. Remove the skillet from the heat, sprinkle the parsley all over, pour in the eggs, mix very well so the eggs are incorporated, and serve very hot.

Serves 6.

ZUPPA DI TELLINE

Clam "Zuppa"

2 pounds tiny clams, the smallest
    you can find
1 lemon
Coarse-grained salt
3 large cloves garlic, peeled
4 tablespoons olive oil
Salt and freshly ground black pepper
A large pinch of hot red pepper
    flakes
¾ cup dry red wine
1 pound very ripe fresh tomatoes,
    cut into pieces, or 1 pound
    drained canned tomatoes,
    preferably imported Italian

TO SERVE
Italian parsley, leaves only
Slices of crusty Tuscan bread,
    toasted and rubbed with garlic,
    or garlic focaccia pieces

Leave the clams in their shells and wash them very well. Place them in a bowl of cold water with the lemon cut in half and squeezed and a little coarse salt, and soak for ½ hour.

Finely chop the garlic on a board. Heat the olive oil in a skillet over medium heat and when the oil is warm, add the chopped garlic and sauté for 1 minute. Season with salt, pepper and the hot red paper flakes, and add the wine. Cook until the wine is reduced by half.

Meanwhile, pass the fresh or canned tomatoes through a food mill, using the disc with the smallest holes, into a crockery or glass bowl.

Drain and rinse the clams, then add them to the skillet along with the tomatoes. Raise the heat to medium, taste for salt and pepper, and cook for 3 to 4 minutes more, depending on the size of the clams. Remove and discard the clams that don't open.

Transfer to a serving dish, sprinkle with the parsley and serve hot, with the bread or the garlic focaccia.

Serves 6.

Zuppa di telline, *tiny sautéed clams served over country bread, photographed from the medieval hill town of Populonia. In the distance is the bay of Baratti, where one can see the remains of an important Etruscan and Roman port.*

COZZE E VONGOLE STUFATE IN GUAZZETTO

Mussels and Clams Stewed Livorno Style

Leave the clams and mussels in their shells and wash them very well. Place them in a bowl of cold water with the lemon cut in half and squeezed and a little coarse salt, and soak for ½ hour.

Finely chop the carrot, onion, garlic and parsley all together on a board. Heat the oil in a medium-sized casserole over low heat and when the oil is warm add the chopped vegetables and sauté for 10 minutes, stirring every so often with a wooden spoon. Add the bay leaves and season with salt, pepper and the hot red pepper flakes. Add the wine and reduce it by half. Raise the heat, drain and rinse the mussels and clams, and add them to the casserole. Mix very well, cover and cook for 4 to 5 minutes, depending on the size of the mussels and clams. Taste for salt and pepper and remove and discard the bay leaves as well as mussels and clams that don't open.

Use a slotted spoon to transfer the shellfish to a serving platter. Reduce the sauce for 1 minute more, stirring constantly.

Prepare six dinner plates with a slice of bread on each. Ladle some of the reduced sauce over each slice of bread and serve immediately with a sprinkling of parsley on each serving. Pass the shellfish at the table.

Serves 6.

1½ pounds mussels
1½ pounds clams
1 lemon
Coarse-grained salt

FOR THE SAUCE
1 medium-sized carrot, scraped
1 medium-sized red onion, cleaned
1 large clove garlic, peeled
25 sprigs Italian parsley, leaves only
½ cup olive oil
3 bay leaves
Salt and freshly ground black pepper
A large pinch of hot red pepper flakes
1 cup dry white wine

TO SERVE
6 large slices crusty Tuscan bread, toasted
15 sprigs Italian parsley, leaves only

SHRIMP

*S*hrimp *is a great favorite in Tuscany, and each area along the coast perfumes its shrimp with different herbs and spices.* Gamberi alla rucola con sedano *is flavored with lemon verbena, an herb characteristic of Sicilian cooking but sometimes found in Tuscan dishes like this one. Lemon verbena can occasionally be found in old Tuscan gardens, along with jasmine bushes and lemon trees. The Shrimp on Skewers from Livorno, a port of entry for exotic ingredients, features rosemary branches as skewers; it is surprising how much of the flavor of the herb is imparted from the branches. The sauce is flavored with nutmeg, cinnamon, cloves and thyme.* Gamberi e patate alla maremmana *features the wild fennel that one finds in the marshlands of the southern coast. The aromatic wine sauce includes a generous helping of rosemary leaves and hot red pepper.*

GAMBERI ALLA RUCOLA CON SEDANO

Shrimp Marinated with Arugula and Celery Hearts   ALL OVER TUSCANY

A branch of fresh lemon verbena.

32 medium-sized shrimp, unshelled
Coarse-grained salt
1 lemon
1 very large ripe tomato (about
    8 ounces)
2 very fresh celery hearts, cleaned
3 bunches arugula

THE SEASONING
4 tablespoons lemon juice
6 tablespoons olive oil
Salt and freshly ground black pepper

TO SERVE
Fresh basil leaves
Fresh lemon verbena leaves
    (optional)

Place the shrimp in a bowl of cold water with coarse salt and the lemon cut in half and squeezed, and soak for ½ hour.

Bring a medium-sized casserole of cold water to a boil over medium heat. When the water reaches a boil, add coarse salt to taste, then drain and rinse the shrimp under cold running water and add them to the boiling water. Cook for 2 to 3 minutes depending on their size. Cool the shrimp under cold running water, then shell and devein them and place them in a large crockery or glass bowl.

Cut the tomato into large pieces and pass them through a food mill, first using the disc with the largest holes, then using the disc with the smallest holes, into a crockery or glass bowl.

Cut the celery into very thin, 2-inch-long strips and add to the bowl with the tomato. Clean the arugula very well, discarding all the stems, and cut into thin strips. Add the arugula to the bowl with the other vegetables and season with the lemon juice, olive oil and salt and pepper. Mix very well, then cover the shrimp with this marinade. Let rest, in a cool place or in the refrigerator, covered, for at least ½ hour before serving.

When ready, remove the shrimp mixture from the refrigerator, mix very well and serve with the basil and lemon verbena leaves, if desired.

Serves 8.

"SPIEDINI" DI GAMBERI IN SALSA

Shrimp on Skewers with Thyme Sauce

Place the shrimp in a bowl of cold water with coarse salt and the lemon cut in half and squeezed, and soak for ½ hour.

Meanwhile, prepare the sauce: Finely chop the celery, onion, parsley and carrot all together on a board. Place a saucepan with 2 tablespoons of the butter and the olive oil over medium heat and when the butter is melted, add the chopped ingredients. Lower the heat to the minimum and sauté as long as possible without burning, stirring every so often with a wooden spoon. Season with salt, pepper, nutmeg and cinnamon, and add the whole clove along with the thyme. When ready, add the wine and, still over low heat, let not only the alcohol of the wine evaporate, but all the liquid; the result should look like a vegetable paste.

Melt the remaining 3 tablespoons butter in a medium-sized saucepan over medium heat and when the butter is melted, add the flour, mix very well and sauté for 2 minutes. Bring the broth to a boil, add it to the flour mixture and stir very well with a wooden spoon. When the sauce starts simmering, lower the heat to the minimum, discard the whole clove from the vegetable sauce, and add the vegetable sauce to the pan of white sauce. Simmer for 20 minutes, stirring every so often with a wooden spoon. When ready, remove the sauce from the heat and let rest, covered, until needed.

Prepare the shrimp: Shell and devein the shrimp. Remove all but the top leaves from the sprigs of rosemary. Thread the shrimp onto the rosemary sprigs by bending the shrimp in half to make the letter "C" and passing the rosemary sprig through both halves.

Preheat the oven to 400 degrees.

Place a large skillet with the oil over low heat. When the oil is warm, add the *spiedini*, raise the heat to medium, season the shrimp with salt and pepper, and sauté for 30 seconds on each side. Season again with salt and pepper.

Spread the bread crumbs on a board, transfer the *spiedini* onto the board and coat them with the crumbs. Place the shrimp, still on the rosemary stems, in a baking dish and bake for 10 minutes (if jumbo shrimp are used, the baking time will be at least 5 minutes longer).

Reheat the sauce, transfer the *spiedini* onto individual plates, ladle some of the sauce and some of the tomato pieces on the side and serve with fresh rosemary sprigs.

Serves 6 to 8.

FOR THE SHRIMP
18 large or 12 jumbo shrimp
Coarse-grained salt
1 large lemon
6 to 8 large sprigs of fresh rosemary
4 tablespoons olive oil
Salt and freshly ground black pepper
About 1 cup unseasoned bread
    crumbs, preferably homemade

FOR THE SAUCE
1 celery stalk
1 medium-sized red onion, cleaned
10 sprigs Italian parsley, leaves only
1 medium-sized carrot, scraped
5 tablespoons (2 ½ ounces) sweet
    butter
4 tablespoons olive oil
Salt and freshly ground black pepper
A large pinch of freshly ground
    nutmeg
A large pinch of ground cinnamon
1 whole clove
½ teaspoon dried thyme
½ cup dry white wine
3 tablespoons unbleached
    all-purpose flour
2 ½ cups chicken or meat broth,
    preferably homemade

TO SERVE
2 large very ripe tomatoes, seeded
    and cut into very small pieces
Sprigs of fresh rosemary

Shrimp and Potatoes Baked with Fennel

MAREMMA

Wild fennel grows abundantly in Tuscan fields.

Place the shrimp in a bowl of cold water with the lemon cut in half and squeezed and coarse salt, and soak for ½ hour.

Meanwhile, bring to a boil a medium-sized pot of cold water over medium heat. Peel the potatoes and cut them into 2-inch cubes. When the water reaches a boil, add salt to taste, one stalk of the wild fennel and the potatoes, and boil until almost completely cooked but still firm, about 15 minutes.

As the potatoes are cooking, brush the shiny side of a large piece of aluminum foil with 1 tablespoon of the oil. Shell and devein the shrimp and rinse them under cold running water.

Preheat the oven to 400 degrees.

Drain the potatoes and arrange them on the oiled side of the prepared foil. Place the shrimp over the potatoes and sprinkle with salt and pepper. Add the remaining stalk of fennel, drip the remaining olive oil all over and wrap everything in the foil. If the foil bag is only one layer, bake for 15 minutes on the lower shelf of the oven; if you wrap the foil in two layers or if you place the bag on a cookie sheet or jelly-roll pan, the cooking time will be longer.

Prepare the sauce: Heat the olive oil in a medium-sized casserole over low heat. Coarsely chop the garlic. When the oil is warm, add the garlic and rosemary, and season with the hot red pepper flakes and salt and pepper. Raise the heat to medium, and when the garlic is very lightly golden, add the water, vinegar and wine. Let the sauce reduce vigorously while the shrimp and potatoes are baking.

When ready, transfer the contents of the foil bag to a large serving platter, then immediately strain the sauce (by that time the sauce should be reduced by more than half).

Pour half of the sauce over the shrimp and potatoes and mix well. Prepare individual servings, each consisting of a slice of bread with some of the remaining sauce dripped over it, shrimp, potatoes and a few basil leaves on top.

Serves 4 to 6.

1½ pounds medium-sized shrimp, unshelled
1 lemon
Coarse-grained salt
2 pounds all-purpose potatoes (not new potatoes)
2 stalks fresh or dried wild fennel
3 tablespoons olive oil
Salt and freshly ground black pepper

FOR THE SAUCE
5 tablespoons olive oil
2 medium-sized cloves garlic, peeled
2 tablespoons rosemary leaves, fresh, preserved in salt or dried and blanched
A large pinch of hot red pepper flakes
Salt and freshly ground black pepper
1 cup cold water
½ cup red wine vinegar
1 cup dry white wine

TO SERVE
4 to 6 slices crusty Tuscan bread, toasted and rubbed with garlic.
16 to 20 fresh basil leaves, torn into thirds

LE "FEMMINNELLE" DI MAREMMA

She-Crabs Marinara

In Orbetello on the Argentario coast, there are several dishes made with small she-crabs, including a she-crab zuppa *thickened with the crab's roe that is traditionally prepared on Christmas Eve. In addition, there is this recipe, in which the crabs are combined with tomatoes. Though she-crabs are preferred, this dish can be made with any hard- or soft-shell crabs.*

The Argentario is a peninsula south of Grosseto and across from the island of Giglio. Though once a fishing village, its most fashionable town, Porto Santo Stefano, has become a resort.

12 crabs (about 3 pounds), cleaned
1 lemon
Coarse-grained salt
3 cloves garlic, peeled
20 sprigs Italian parsley, leaves only
1½ pounds very ripe fresh
    tomatoes, cut into pieces,
    or 1½ pounds drained
    canned tomatoes, preferably
    imported Italian
5 tablespoons olive oil
Salt and freshly ground black pepper

TO SERVE
Italian parsley leaves

Place the crabs in a bowl of cold water with the lemon cut in half and squeezed and a little salt, and soak for ½ hour.

Meanwhile, finely chop the garlic and parsley on a board, then pass the fresh or canned tomatoes through a food mill, using the disc with the smallest holes, into a crockery or glass bowl.

Heat the oil in a medium-sized skillet over medium heat, and when the oil is warm, add the chopped ingredients and sauté for 2 minutes. Add the tomatoes, season with salt and pepper and simmer for 15 minutes, adding about ½ cup cold water as needed. The sauce should be of medium thickness.

Drain the crabs, rinse them under cold running water and add them to the skillet. Let simmer for 15 minutes. Taste for salt and pepper, sprinkle on the parsley, transfer the contents of the skillet to a serving platter and serve hot.

Serves 6.

LA LUMINARIA ·
THE ILLUMINATION OF THE CITY

Each June 16 and 17 I try to interrupt my busy schedule to visit Pisa for the Regata di San Ranieri, the boat race named for the patron saint of Pisa (see page 250), and the Luminaria, the illumination of the city held on the eve of the race (see photograph on pages 182–183). For the ceremony of the "night before," this leisurely city is transformed into its "evening dress" with thousands of tiny lights—actually shot glasses holding tiny candles inside of them—strung up, around and across all the public buildings, private houses and palazzi.

This custom of illuminating the city has a long and extraordinary history. It began as a simple practice of the Middle Ages— transferring the candles from the inside of the church to the outside for special occasions, Then, in 1318, the city fathers extended the practice beyond the immediate neighborhood of the church when they called for "temporary lights" to be placed in every house, street and shop in honor of the Feast of Santa Maria Annunciata. In 1337, the Luminaria was moved from its old association with the Feast of the Assumption to its present place of honor— commemorating the feast-day of San Ranieri.

The custom of "lighting up" Pisa continued through the years, though only for the most exceptional occasions. One of the most spectacular was in 1688, to celebrate the transfer of the remains of San Ranieri to the newly completed chapel built in his honor. Against the candlelight backdrop of the Luminaria, a most spectacular "funeral" procession brought out all the church dignitaries in their most elaborate vestments. Only a few years before, another occasion produced a similarly inspiring Luminaria. When the bride of Cosimo II of Florence arrived in Pisa, a battery of shots was fired, at which point the people lit up all the palazzi, *churches, public buildings and private homes to produce the stunning "illumination." But most dazzling of all were the lights reflected in the Arno. All the city monuments were multiplied, as if by magic, in the water.*

By the eighteenth century, the effects were more theatrical. Not only did the Luminaria show off the architecture of a building, but another configuration was superimposed upon it to create a new surface. When the royal family of Naples visited Pisa in the nineteenth century, the Pisans produced exotic Chinese façades, an entire cloister, three portals with high columns, and the coat of arms of Pisa illuminated by 15,000 candles! Such an act was hard to follow and, in 1867, for an unexplained reason, the Luminaria was abolished. In 1937, the tradition was restored, though never again to the extent of a royal performance. It became, instead, an annual event to precede the Regata di San Ranieri.

P O L P O I N G U A Z Z E T T O

Octopus in Sauce

After taking the photographs of the Luminaria, *we went to my favorite restaurant in Pisa, where I enjoyed* Polpo in Guazzetto, *octopus cooked to tenderness and dressed with a delicious green sauce. This dish is traditionally served with boiled vegetables.*

4 small octopuses, about 8 ounces
    each, cleaned and left whole
    or 1 larger (2- to 2 ½-pound)
    octopus, cleaned and cut into
    very large pieces (see Note)
1 lemon
Coarse-grained salt
2 tablespoons red wine vinegar
1 carrot, scraped
1 small red onion, cleaned
1 celery stalk
1 tablespoon tomato paste

FOR THE SAUCE
15 sprigs Italian parsley, leaves only
2 small cloves garlic, peeled
½ cup olive oil
Salt and freshly ground black pepper
Lemon juice (optional)

TO SERVE
Boiled asparagus, boiled carrots
    and radicchio leaves

Place the octopuses in a bowl of cold water with the lemon cut in half and squeezed and a little coarse salt, and soak for ½ hour.

Bring a medium-sized pot of cold water to a boil over medium heat, and when the water reaches a boil, add coarse salt to taste, the vinegar, all the vegetables cut into large pieces and the tomato paste. Simmer for 20 minutes, then drain the octopuses, rinse under cold running water and add to the pot of vegetables. Cover and simmer for 30 minutes. If the octopuses are not larger than 8 ounces each, 30 minutes should be enough; otherwise cook a little longer, until soft. If using 1 large octopus, it could take up to 1½ hours.

Meanwhile, prepare the sauce: Finely chop the parsley and garlic together. Mix the chopped ingredients in a small bowl with the olive oil and season with salt and pepper. Add a few drops of lemon juice, if desired.

When ready, drain the octopuses and arrange each one on an individual plate (if the one large octopus was used, then cut it into smaller pieces), along with some asparagus, carrots and radicchio on the side. Pour some of the sauce over each portion and serve. This dish can be served at room temperature as well.

Note: The smaller octopuses are available for only part of the year. The larger ones (though not too large) may be used, but require a much longer cooking time, approximately 1½ hours. When fresh octopuses are not available, frozen ones can be used instead.

Cleaning octopus—that is, removing the tough outer skin— can be laborious, especially when they are large, but parboiling them for about 3 minutes first usually loosens the skin. It is, of course, best to buy them already cleaned.

Serves 4.

FISH

Because mackerel, the larger cousin of anchovies and sardines, is naturally oily, it is well served when baked with lemon juice and just a touch of olive oil. In Sgombro al limone con olive, a dish that is eaten all over Tuscany, it is prepared in this fashion and served with a type of gremolada made of chopped olive, grated lemon peel and parsley.

Coda di rospo (known in some dialects as pescatrice), or monkfish, has long been a favorite in Mediterranean countries, but has only recently been "discovered" by fishermen in the Atlantic. Its dense consistency is similar to that of lobster meat. In Italy, the tail section (called the coda), where most of the meat is concentrated, is cut into slices around the bone. Outside of Italy, it is often boned and cut into two long halves that can then be cut into slices. Either form can be used in Coda di rospo al vino bianco, a satisfying and substantial main course in which the fish is lightly flavored with garlic and rosemary.

Cooking fish in a bag is a favorite Tuscan technique. In Trancia di tonno alla versigliese, tuna is flavored with rosemary, parsley and garlic and baked in a bag made out of aluminum foil or parchment paper. White wine is added during the last 10 minutes of cooking. The density of the meat and the flavorings of this dish are reminiscent of the classic arista (roasted pork loin) of Florence. In Cernia marinata al cartoccio, grouper is bathed in an onion marinade before it is baked. Some of the marinade is then used to make a warm caper sauce.

SGOMBRO AL LIMONE CON OLIVE

Mackerel Baked with Lemon Juice and Olives

ALL OVER TUSCANY

Wash the fish carefully under cold running water.

Very lightly oil a glass baking dish. Arrange the fish in the dish. Squeeze the juice of the lemons into a bowl, add salt and pepper to the juice, mix very well and pour over the fish. Cover the baking dish with plastic wrap and refrigerate overnight.

When ready, preheat the oven to 400 degrees, remove and discard all but 2 tablespoons of the lemon juice and pour the 4 tablespoons of oil all over the fish. Bake for 15 minutes.

As the fish is cooking, finely chop the olives and parsley together. Add the lemon peel and mix very well. Sprinkle this mixture over the fish for the last minute of cooking. Remove from the oven and serve with the lemon slices and parsley.

Serves 4.

Fillets of 2 mackerels (about
    2 pounds)
5 lemons
Salt and freshly ground black pepper

PLUS
4 tablespoons olive oil
4 ounces large black Greek olives,
    preserved in brine, pitted
20 sprigs Italian parsley, leaves only
Grated peel of 1 lemon

TO SERVE
Lemon slices and Italian parsley
    leaves

CODA DI ROSPO AL VINO BIANCO

Monkfish in Wine Sauce

ALL OVER TUSCANY

2 pounds monkfish, in one piece
    (only the tail is used) with
    bone, or 2 boneless fillets
Coarse-grained salt
1 lemon
About ½ cup unbleached
    all-purpose flour
6 tablespoons olive oil
3 cloves garlic, peeled
2 tablespoons rosemary leaves,
    fresh, preserved in salt or dried
    and blanched
1 cup dry white wine
Salt and freshly ground black pepper

TO SERVE
Rosemary sprigs
1 lemon, cut into slices

Place the fish in a bowl of cold water with a little coarse salt and the lemon cut in half and squeezed, and soak for ½ hour.

Drain the fish, rinse it under cold running water and dry it with paper towels. If using one piece of fish, cut it into 6 (1-inch) slices (called *nodini*: slices of fish that include the bone in the center); if using fillets, cut them into 12 slices. Lightly flour the fish slices.

Heat the oil in a skillet over medium heat, and when the oil is warm, add the whole cloves of garlic and the rosemary. Sauté for 1 minute, then add the fish and sauté for 1 minute on each side. Add the wine and season with salt and pepper. Cook for 6 to 10 minutes. By that time the fish should be soft and the wine should be evaporated by half.

Use a slotted spoon to transfer the fish to a serving platter, then immediately strain the sauce and discard the garlic and the rosemary leaves. Pour the sauce back into the skillet and reduce for 1 minute more. Pour the sauce over the fish and serve hot with rosemary sprigs and lemon slices.

Serves 6.

TRANCIA DI TONNO ALLA VERSIGLIESE

Fresh Tuna with Rosemary

VERSILIA

2 pounds fresh tuna, in one piece
    (about 3 ½ inches thick)
Coarse-grained salt
1 lemon
5 tablespoons rosemary leaves,
    fresh, preserved in salt or dried
    and blanched
5 sprigs Italian parsley, leaves only
2 cloves garlic, peeled
½ cup unseasoned bread crumbs,
    preferably homemade
Salt and freshly ground black pepper

TO BAKE
1 tablespoon olive oil
½ cup dry white wine

TO SERVE
Fresh peas, boiled and sautéed
    in olive oil and garlic and
    seasoned with salt and pepper,
    or Caper Sauce (see page 289)

Place the whole piece of tuna in a bowl of cold water with a little coarse salt and the lemon cut in half and squeezed, and soak for ½ hour.

Finely chop the rosemary, parsley and garlic on a board. Place the bread crumbs in a small bowl, add the chopped ingredients and salt and pepper to taste, and mix very well.

Remove the fish from the water, rinse it under cold running water and lightly pat it dry with paper towels. Completely coat the tuna with the prepared bread crumbs.

Prepare a piece of parchment paper or aluminum foil (shiny-side up) and grease it with the oil. Place the tuna in the middle of the foil and wrap it completely. Place the "package" in the refrigerator.

Preheat the oven to 400 degrees. Bake the tuna wrapped in foil for 60 minutes. Open the bag, pour the wine in, close again and bake for 10 minutes more.

Remove the bag from the oven, transfer the fish and its juices to a serving platter and serve, slicing the fish like a steak, with the peas or the Caper Sauce.

Serves 4 to 6.

CERNIA MARINATA AL CARTOCCIO

Marinated Grouper Baked "in a Paper Bag"

1 whole grouper or red snapper,
    about 4 pounds, cleaned, with
    the head and tail attached
Coarse-grained salt
1 lemon

FOR THE MARINADE
1 cup olive oil
2 large lemons, squeezed, keeping
    both juice and squeezed
    lemon halves
1 small red onion, cleaned
6 large cloves garlic, peeled
15 sprigs Italian parsley, leaves only
Salt
Freshly ground black pepper

FOR THE SAUCE
2 tablespoons capers, preserved in
    wine vinegar, drained
2 tablespoons unbleached
    all-purpose flour
2 ½ cups chicken broth, preferably
    homemade
Salt and freshly ground black pepper

TO SERVE
Italian parsley sprigs

Wash the fish well, place it in a bowl of cold water with a little coarse salt and the lemon cut in half and squeezed, and soak for ½ hour.

Prepare the marinade: Pour the olive oil and lemon juice in a bowl. Finely chop the onion, garlic and parsley all together on a board. Add the chopped ingredients to the bowl with the oil-lemon mixture, season with salt and lots of pepper and lightly mix all the ingredients together.

Drain the fish and rinse it under cold running water. Place the fish in a large crockery or glass tureen and pour all the marinade and the lemon halves on top. Let the fish marinate in a cool place or in the bottom of the refrigerator for 2 hours, turning the fish over twice.

Preheat the oven to 375 degrees and cut a large piece of aluminum foil or parchment paper to serve as a "bag" for cooking the fish. Transfer the fish onto the shiny side of the prepared foil or onto the parchment paper, pour three-quarters of the marinade over it and wrap everything in the foil or paper. Place the bag on a jelly-roll pan and bake for 40 minutes, turning the fish over once. Discard lemons.

With the remaining one-quarter of the marinade, prepare the sauce to be served with the fish: Heat the marinade with the capers in a medium-sized saucepan over low heat. When the oil starts sizzling, add the flour, mix very well and cook for 1 minute. Remove the saucepan from the heat, then heat the broth in a second saucepan. When the broth reaches a boil, immediately place the saucepan with the marinade mixture over medium heat and add to it all of the boiling broth. Mix very well with a wooden spoon to be sure no lumps form, then let simmer for 15 minutes, stirring every so often with a wooden spoon and tasting for salt and pepper.

When the fish is ready, transfer it to a large serving platter. Arrange the solid part of the marinade (from the foil or parchment paper) all over the fish, but discard the juices. Serve immediately with additional parsley sprigs, passing the prepared sauce at the table.

Serves 6 to 8.

SBURRIDA O SBURITA

Fish Soup

Our first Tuscan fish soup is from the island of Elba. It represents the true local soup, today prepared only by the longtime residents in private homes. The restaurants, preferring to cater to Elba's affluent summer visitors, prepare a generic "national" fish soup, like those served in seaside resorts all over Italy.

This recipe goes back to the days centuries ago when, at different times, ancient Pisa and Genoa ruled the island. It is, therefore, understandable that it resembles Burrida, the old Ligurian soup made with dried salted fish. The Elba soup differs from the Ligurian version in its use of nepitella, *a type of wild mint, and hot red pepper, both of which are flavorings characteristic of dishes of the Tuscan coast.*

3 pounds dried salt cod
3 quarts cold water
8 medium-sized cloves garlic, peeled and crushed
20 *nepitella* or fresh mint leaves
1 small whole hot red pepper or 1 heaping teaspoon hot red pepper flakes
¾ cup olive oil
Coarse-grained salt

TO SERVE
6 large slices crusty Tuscan bread, toasted and rubbed with garlic
Italian parsley leaves
Freshly ground black pepper

Soak the cod in cold water for 24 hours, changing the water at least six times. The best way to soak it is to place it in a strainer under slowly running cold water. After 24 hours, rinse the cod under cold running water, dry it with paper towels and cut it into 3-inch slices.

Fill a medium-sized stockpot with the water and place over medium heat. When the water reaches a boil, add the garlic, *nepitella* or mint, and the hot pepper or red pepper flakes. Let simmer for 1 hour. Add the olive oil and cod, and simmer for 25 to 45 minutes, depending on the dryness of the cod. In Europe, the cod is dry and it takes 45 minutes. It is important to check regularly, as once the fish is done, additional cooking will only toughen it. Taste for salt.

Place the bread in a soup tureen and place the cod pieces on top of it. Pour a little broth over the bread and cod and sprinkle with the parsley. Let rest for at least 5 minutes before serving with the freshly ground black pepper.

Serves 6.

Fish Soup from Argentario

1 pound octopus, cleaned, from
    small tender octopuses, if
    possible (see Note under
    Polpo in guazzetto, page 197)
8 small cuttlefish (inksquid) or
    squid, cleaned
1 pound grouper or John Dory,
    cut into 2-inch slices
1 pound bass, cut into 2-inch slices
1 lemon
Coarse-grained salt
1 large red onion, cleaned
20 sprigs Italian parsley, leaves only
1 small clove garlic, peeled
6 tablespoons olive oil
3 tablespoons tomato paste
1 cup dry white wine
Salt and freshly ground black pepper
A large pinch of hot red pepper
    flakes
About 2 cups chicken broth,
    preferably homemade

PLUS
6 large slices crusty Tuscan bread,
    toasted and rubbed with garlic

TO SERVE
15 sprigs Italian parsley, leaves only

Each Mediterranean port has its own special fish soup, and the natives of the Argentario peninsula do not like their Caldaro to be confused with any others, especially the Cacciucco of nearby Livorno. As is the case with the fish soup from Elba, this dish is not prepared authentically in the chic restaurants that cater to tourists (most of which are located in the peninsula's main town of Porto Santo Stefano). It is only the fishermen here who stick to the native recipe.

We cannot authentically reproduce any of these fish soups away from their native waters, but we can come close. For Caldaro, the emphasis should be on octopus, cuttlefish (inksquid) and Mediterranean flatfish. John Dory is one authentic flatfish that can be found; grouper and bass are reasonable substitutes for the others, which are unavailable beyond the Mediterranean. This soup contains no shellfish, an important distinction.

Cut the octopus and cuttlefish into 1-inch-wide strips. Place all the fish in a bowl of cold water with the lemon cut in half and squeezed and a little coarse salt, and soak for ½ hour.

Finely chop the onion, parsley and garlic all together on a board.

Heat the olive oil in a large casserole, preferably made of terra-cotta, over medium heat. When the oil is warm, add the chopped ingredients and sauté for 10 minutes, stirring every so often with a wooden spoon. Add the tomato paste, then remove the octopus and cuttlefish from the water, rinse them under cold running water and add them to the casserole. Sauté for 10 minutes more, then add the wine and cook for 10 minutes longer, adding salt, pepper and the hot red pepper flakes. If the octopus and cuttlefish are not yet cooked and soft, start adding the broth a little at a time as needed. When ready, drain the grouper and bass, rinse under cold running water, then start adding the grouper, which generally requires a longer cooking time, to the casserole. After 2 minutes, add the bass. After about 8 minutes more, when all the fish should be cooked, the sauce should be reduced to a rather thick consistency.

Arrange the bread slices on individual plates and ladle the fish and sauce over them. Sprinkle the parsley over each serving and serve hot.

Serves 6.

VEGETABLES

In Tuscany, as all over Italy, vegetables are full courses by themselves and, with a few exceptions, not simply accompaniments to the main course. They can be served separately, on their own plate, after the main course, or at the same time as the main course. Salad is considered an alternative to the vegetable course and is appropriate only to certain grilled or fried main dishes. Included here is a sampling from the vast repertory of Tuscan vegetable recipes. Tuscans think as highly of these dishes as they do of their recipes for pastas, soups or main dishes.

Heads of Savoy cabbage with their wrinkled dark green leaves.

Preceding pages: This towering allegorical figure of the Apennine Mountains by the sixteenth-century sculptor Giambologna is all that remains of what was once the most important villa of the Medici family. Known as Pratolino, it was a huge Manneristic fantasy of grottoes, legendary gardens, and elaborate waterfalls and fountains. Pratolino was destroyed by the Hapsburg-Lorena dynasty in 1814 but was rebuilt with a new plan in 1872 by the Russian prince Demidoff. After World War II, it was purchased by the last king of Greece and became a place of refuge for much of Europe's deposed royalty. It has now been passed to the Italian government, which has initiated another restoration.

For the photograph, we filled the trough in the foreground with fruits and vegetables in an attempt to recreate the sense of abundance that the gardens here once symbolized.

ASPARAGUS

In *Asparagi in salsa verde, asparagus are dressed with a green sauce made with capers, parsley, garlic and olive oil. While it is the thin asparagus that are commonly preferred, the succulent thicker ones from Pescia are used when they can be found. These prized asparagus can be seen in the photograph of Asparagi all'uovo sodo on page 210. The sauce for this dish is made golden with the addition of hard-cooked egg yolks.*

ASPARAGI IN SALSA VERDE

Asparagus in Green Sauce

ALL OVER TUSCANY

Tie the asparagus in a bunch, keeping all the tops even. Trim the white stems evenly, leaving about 4 inches of the white part on. This way the asparagus bunch can stand up in the boiling water.

Set a pot of cold water over medium heat and when the water reaches a boil, add coarse salt to taste, then the bunch of asparagus, standing up so the tips are not in the water and will be cooked by the steam. Cook for about 10 minutes, depending on thickness. When ready they should still have a "bite." Transfer the asparagus to a serving platter.

While the asparagus cook, prepare the sauce: Place the capers, parsley, garlic and anchovy, if using, on a board or in a food processor or blender, and finely chop all the ingredients together. Transfer the chopped ingredients to a bowl, add the olive oil and salt and pepper to taste and mix very well with a wooden spoon.

Transfer the sauce to a sauceboat. Arrange the warm asparagus and the parsley sprigs on a platter or individual serving plates.

Serves 6.

2 pounds thin asparagus
Coarse-grained salt

FOR THE SAUCE
4 tablespoons capers, preserved in
    wine vinegar, drained
20 sprigs Italian parsley, leaves only
1 very small clove garlic, peeled
½ cup olive oil
Salt and freshly ground black pepper

OPTIONAL
1 anchovy, preserved in salt, or
    2 anchovy fillets, packed in
    oil, drained

TO SERVE
Italian parsley sprigs

ASPARAGI ALL'UOVO SODO

Asparagus in Yellow Sauce

Remove the tough white part from the asparagus and soak them in a bowl of cold water for ½ hour.

Bring a large pot of cold water to a boil and add coarse salt to taste. Drain the asparagus, tie them in a bunch and place in the boiling water, standing up so the tips are not in the water and will be cooked by the steam. Asparagus when ready (after about 10 minutes) should still have a "bite."

Transfer the asparagus onto a round serving platter and arrange them like the spokes of a wheel with the tips in the center. Cover the platter with foil to keep the asparagus warm.

Immediately separate the egg yolks from the whites. Coarsely chop the whites with the parsley on a board.

2 pounds thick asparagus
Coarse-grained salt
2 hard-cooked eggs
15 sprigs Italian parsley, leaves only
4 tablespoons (2 ounces) sweet
    butter
1 tablespoon lemon juice
2 tablespoons olive oil
Salt and freshly ground black pepper

TO SERVE
Lemon zests (see Appendix,
    page 292)

Mash the yolks with a fork on a plate. Melt the butter in a small saucepan over low heat and when the butter is completely melted, add the egg yolks and mix very well with a wooden spoon. Remove from the heat and, mixing constantly, add the lemon juice, olive oil and salt and pepper to taste.

Sprinkle the egg-white mixture all over the asparagus, then pour the yellow sauce (egg-yolk mixture) mainly over the tips of the asparagus. Arrange the lemon zests all over and serve. This dish should be served while still quite warm, not at room temperature.

Serves 6.

Left: A sumptuous platter of Asparagi all'uovo sodo (Asparagus in Yellow Sauce) opening onto Pescia's great country market.

C A R C I O F I   A I   C A P P E R I

Artichokes in Caper Sauce

ALL OVER TUSCANY

4 large artichokes
1 lemon
Coarse-grained salt
5 tablespoons olive oil
5 tablespoons capers, preserved in
    wine vinegar, drained
Salt and freshly ground black pepper

TO SERVE
10 sprigs Italian parsley, leaves only

It is the large artichokes from the Empoli area of the Arno Valley that are used for Carciofi ai capperi, cut-up artichokes parboiled and then sautéed with coarsely chopped capers and parsley. This dish may be eaten hot, as a vegetable course, or at room temperature as an appetizer.

Place the artichokes in a bowl of cold water with the lemon, cut in half and squeezed, and soak for ½ hour.

Bring a medium-sized casserole of cold water to a boil over medium heat.

Meanwhile, clean the artichokes (see instructions on page 78) and cut the artichokes into fourths. As you clean each artichoke, place it back in the acidulated water.

When the water in the casserole reaches a boil, add coarse salt to taste, then the artichoke and lemon halves, and boil for 5 minutes. Drain, discard the lemon and cool the artichokes under cold running water.

Heat the oil in a skillet over medium heat. Coarsely chop the capers on a board. When the oil is hot, add the artichokes, sauté for 4 minutes, turning them over two or three times. Season with salt and pepper.

Use a slotted spoon to transfer the artichokes onto a serving platter. Add the chopped capers to the skillet, raise the heat and sauté for 1 minute. Pour the sauce over the artichokes, sprinkle with the parsley and serve.

Serves 4.

Beans, one of the trademarks of Tuscan cooking, are not only incorporated into soups, minestrones, pasta and bean dishes, but are also often part of the vegetable course. In Ceci con spinaci o bietole in "inzimino," *chick-peas are combined with spinach or Swiss chard. Dishes that are labeled* inzimino *or* zimino *always combine greens with another ingredient, such as chick-peas (as in this recipe), cuttlefish or squid, and are always highly spiced.*

Fagioli al coccio, the second recipe in this grouping, employs cannellini, the white kidney beans that are sometimes called Tuscan beans. This dish is traditionally prepared in a terra-cotta pot that is called a coccio *in the Tuscan vernacular. Tuscans are strongly attached to their terra-cotta cooking vessels (which are made from the baked earth of their region) and have been since Etruscan times, as they believe these dishes give food a special rounded flavor.*

In Timballi di fagioli e rape, *the cannellini beans are puréed with broccoli raab, baked in soufflé molds and served with a light tomato sauce.*

This photograph shows food so indicative of Florence that no Italian would even need to see Brunelleschi's immense red dome or Giotto's bell tower in the background to know where it was taken. On display are cannellini beans, fresh and still green, spinach and chick-peas for the inzimino, *a bottle of rich green olive oil, a pork loin already threaded on the skewer, a full-bodied red wine plus lemons, bay leaves, sage and rosemary.*

CECI CON SPINACI O BIETOLE IN "INZIMINO"

"Inzimino" of Chick-Peas with Spinach or Swiss Chard　　FLORENCE

Soak the chick-peas in a bowl of cold water overnight.

The next morning, drain them and add them to a stockpot with 3 quarts of cold water, the whole clove of garlic and 1 tablespoon of the olive oil. Set the pot over medium heat and boil for about 45 minutes. By that time the chick-peas should be cooked through but still firm. Drain them, transfer to a crockery or glass bowl, cover with a wet towel and let rest until needed.

Clean the spinach and cook it in a large pot of salted boiling water for about 5 minutes. Drain the spinach, cool it under cold running water and squeeze gently. Coarsely chop the spinach on a board.

Coarsely chop the onion and carrots all together on a board. Place a skillet with the remaining 5 tablespoons of oil over medium heat and when the oil is warm, add the chopped onion-carrot mixture and sauté for 5 minutes. Season with salt and pepper and the hot red pepper flakes. Add the wine and let evaporate for 5 minutes. Add the spinach and chick-peas, mix very well and taste for salt and pepper.

Dissolve the tomato paste in the broth and add it to the skillet. Let cook for 10 minutes, mixing every so often with a wooden spoon. Sprinkle the parsley all over, add the lemon juice, mix very well, transfer to a serving platter and serve hot.

Serves 6 to 8.

1 cup dried chick-peas
1 large clove garlic, peeled and
    left whole
6 tablespoons olive oil
2 pounds spinach or Swiss chard,
    large stems removed
Coarse-grained salt
1 medium-sized red onion, cleaned
2 medium-sized carrots, scraped
Salt and freshly ground black pepper
A large pinch of hot red pepper
    flakes
1 cup dry white wine
2 tablespoons tomato paste
1 cup chicken or meat broth,
    preferably homemade
10 sprigs Italian parsley, leaves
    only, coarsely chopped
2 tablespoons lemon juice

Local farmers sell a cornucopia of fruits and vegetables from their stands.

Bunches of scorzabianca (*salsify*), a root vegetable that is very popular in Pescia, Lucca and along the entire coast.

Pescia's immense wholesale flower market, one of the most important flower markets in Italy, is among the world's largest sources of carnations. Long-stemmed carnations are the most popular and plentiful flower in Tuscany.

FAGIOLI AL COCCIO

Beans Cooked in a Casserole

Soak the beans in a bowl of cold water overnight.

The next morning, drain the beans, rinse them under cold running water, then place them in a medium-sized stockpot with 3 quarts of cold water. Set the pot over medium heat and simmer for about 45 minutes. By that time the beans should be cooked through but still quite firm. Add coarse salt to taste and simmer for 1 minute more. Drain the beans, saving 2 cups of the bean water. Place the beans in a crockery or glass bowl and set wet paper towels over them.

Peel the potato and cut it into less than ¼-inch-thick slices. Place the slices in a bowl of cold water. Slice the onion in the same way and add it to the bowl with the potato. Cut the pancetta into tiny pieces, coarsely chop the parsley and finely chop the garlic.

Place the oil in a medium-sized casserole (preferably made of terra-cotta) over medium heat. When the oil is warm, add the pancetta, parsley and garlic, and sauté for 3 minutes. Drain the potato and the onion and add them to the casserole. Sauté for 10 minutes, stirring every so often with a wooden spoon. Season with salt and pepper, then add the beans, mix very well, cover the casserole and cook for about 20 minutes more, adding the saved bean water as needed. The beans should be soft but still retain their shape. Taste for salt and pepper before serving. If desired, sprinkle the *Parmigiano* over each serving.

Serves 8.

2 cups dried cannellini beans
Coarse-grained salt
1 large potato (about ½ pound)
1 large red onion, cleaned
3 ounces pancetta or prosciutto,
    in one piece
10 sprigs Italian parsley, leaves only
2 medium-sized cloves garlic, peeled
4 tablespoons olive oil
Salt and freshly ground black pepper

OPTIONAL
¾ cup freshly grated *Parmigiano*

TIMBALLI DI FAGIOLI E RAPE

Timbales of Puréed Beans and Broccoli Raab

1 cup dried cannellini beans
1½ ounces pancetta, in one piece
1 tablespoon olive oil
1 small red onion, peeled and
    left whole
Salt and freshly ground black pepper

FOR THE BROCCOLI RAAB
¾ pound broccoli raab
    (broccoletti), cleaned, large
    stems removed
Coarse-grained salt
1 large clove garlic, peeled
2 tablespoons olive oil
Salt and freshly ground black pepper

PLUS
2 extra-large eggs
2 tablespoons freshly grated
    Parmigiano
2 tablespoons heavy cream

FOR THE TOMATO SAUCE
1½ pounds very ripe fresh
    tomatoes or 1½ pounds
    drained canned tomatoes,
    preferably imported Italian
2 tablespoons olive oil
1 small clove garlic, peeled and
    left whole
4 fresh basil leaves
Salt and freshly ground black pepper

TO SERVE
8 fresh basil leaves

Soak the beans in a bowl of cold water overnight.

The next morning, drain and rinse the beans very well, place them in a medium-sized casserole and pour in enough cold water to reach 1 inch above the beans. Add the pancetta, oil and onion, and set the casserole over medium heat to cook for about 1 hour, adding warm water as more liquid is needed. By the time the beans are cooked through, most of the liquid should have been absorbed. Season with salt and pepper, transfer the contents of the casserole to a crockery or glass bowl and let rest until cold. Discard the onion and pancetta.

Meanwhile, soak the broccoli raab in a bowl of cold water for 30 minutes. Bring a large quantity of cold water to a boil, add coarse salt, then drain the broccoli raab and add it to the boiling water to cook for about 10 minutes, or until very soft. Drain the broccoli raab again and cool it under cold running water. Lightly squeeze out the excess liquid and coarsely chop.

Cut the garlic into tiny pieces. Place a skillet with the oil over medium heat and when the oil is warm, add the garlic and sauté for 1 minute. Add the broccoli raab, season with salt and pepper and sauté for 4 minutes more. Remove the skillet from the heat and let stand until needed.

Pass the beans and their juices through a food mill, using the disc with the smallest holes, into a large bowl. Then pass the broccoli raab through the food mill into the same bowl.

Preheat the oven to 375 degrees and prepare a roasting pan by placing paper towels or a cotton dish towel on the bottom and adding lukewarm water to create a *bagno maria* (water bath).

Add the eggs, *Parmigiano* and cream to the bean mixture, mix very well and taste for salt and pepper.

Butter eight miniature soufflé molds (ramekins). Ladle a little more than ½ cup of the mixture into each mold and place the molds in the water bath. The level of the water should reach the level of the thick batter in the molds. Bake for 45 minutes.

Meanwhile, prepare the tomato sauce: If fresh tomatoes are used, cut them into pieces. Put the fresh or canned tomatoes into a medium-sized saucepan with the oil, garlic and basil, and simmer over low heat for 20 minutes. Pass the contents of the saucepan through a food mill, using the disc with the smallest holes, into a second, clean saucepan. Place over low heat, season with salt and pepper and reduce for 15 minutes more.

Remove the *timballi* from the oven and let them rest outside the water for 5 minutes before unmolding them onto individual dishes. Serve immediately with a basil leaf over each one and a little tomato sauce on the side.

Serves 8.

FAGIOLINI ALL'ERBA CIPOLLINA

String Beans in Chive Sauce

Chives, which grow wild in Italy, are rarely seen in herb gardens. Still, they are sold at certain high-grade greengrocers and are used in a few select dishes. In Fagiolini all'erba cipollina, *they blend beautifully with string beans and wine vinegar. Like* Carciofi ai capperi, *this dish may be served hot, as a vegetable course, or at room temperature as a piquant appetizer.*

Soak the beans in a bowl of cold water for ½ hour.

Meanwhile, bring a large pot of cold water to a boil over medium heat. Clean the beans, removing both ends, and if they are very large, cut them into two pieces. When the water reaches a boil, add coarse salt to taste, then the beans and par-boil them for 10 minutes; they should still be very firm.

As the beans cook, thinly slice the onion and place a skillet with the oil over medium heat. When the oil is warm, add the onion and sauté for 5 minutes. When the beans are ready, transfer them directly from the boiling water to the skillet. Do not

1½ pounds string beans
Coarse-grained salt
1 medium-sized red onion, cleaned
5 tablespoons olive oil
Salt and freshly ground black pepper
1 ounce fresh chives, cleaned
15 large sprigs Italian parsley,
    leaves only
2 tablespoons red wine vinegar

mix. Season with salt and pepper, cover the skillet and cook, over low heat, for 15 minutes, until the beans are cooked through but still have a bite.

Meanwhile, coarsely chop the chives and parsley on a board. Add the aromatic herbs to the beans, mix very well, taste for salt and pepper and cook for 1 minute more. Use a slotted spoon to transfer the solids from the skillet to a serving dish. Add the vinegar to the skillet and let reduce for 20 seconds. Pour the juices over the beans, mix very well and serve hot.

Serves 4 to 6.

P A T A T E   A I   C A R C I O F I

Potatoes with Artichoke Sauce   TUSCAN COUNTRYSIDE

Patate ai carciofi *is an unusual dish in that an artichoke is cooked for about 20 minutes, until it becomes soft enough to "melt" and form a sauce for the potatoes. The sharp-tongued Tuscans sometimes call this dish* Carciofi scappati *because the artichoke, the more noble of the two vegetables, is stretched by the frugal cook to the point where it has simply "escaped."*

1 large artichoke
1 lemon
2 pounds all-purpose potatoes
15 sprigs Italian parsley, leaves only
2 medium-sized cloves garlic, peeled
5 tablespoons olive oil
Salt and freshly ground black pepper

Place the artichoke in a bowl of cold water with the lemon cut in half and squeezed, and soak for 30 minutes. Clean the artichoke (see instructions on page 78), removing the tough green leaves and the choke. Cut the cleaned artichoke into pieces that measure less than ½ inch and put the pieces back into the acidulated water.

Peel the potatoes, cut them into 1½-inch cubes and soak them in a bowl of cold water until needed.

Finely chop the parsley and garlic together on a board. Heat the oil in a casserole over medium heat and when the oil is warm, add the chopped ingredients and sauté for 2 minutes.

Drain the artichoke, add it to the casserole, cover and cook for 5 minutes, stirring several times with a wooden spoon. (If the artichoke is still tough after 5 minutes, add a little water and cook longer, until very soft.) Season with salt and pepper to taste. Drain the potatoes, add them to the casserole without mixing, cover and cook for 2 minutes. Add 1 cup cold water and cook, covered, for 15 minutes more. By that time the potatoes should be cooked through and the artichoke almost puréed. Taste for salt and pepper, mix very well and cook for 20 seconds, uncovered. Transfer to a serving dish and serve hot.

Serves 6.

TORTINO DI MELANZANE ALLA FIORENTINA

Eggplant Baked in Batter

There has been some confusion regarding the difference between a frittata and a tortino. Although they are both bound with eggs, the true tortino is cooked in the oven, not on the stovetop. The most famous tortino is probably the Tortino di carciofi (made with artichokes); just as good but less popular is the Tortino di melanzane. In this version, the melanzane (eggplant) is layered with a tomato- and egg-based batter flavored with Parmigiano and basil.

Clean the eggplants, discarding the stems, then peel and cut them horizontally into slices less than ½ inch thick. Make a layer of eggplant on a platter, sprinkle on some of the coarse salt, then add layers of eggplant and salt until all the eggplant is used up. Place a dish on top of the eggplant (to help squeeze out the bitter liquid) and let stand for ½ hour.

Meanwhile, prepare the tomato sauce: If using fresh tomatoes, cut them into large pieces. Place the fresh or canned tomatoes in a medium-sized saucepan with the whole clove of garlic, the olive oil and basil, and set the pan over medium heat for 20 minutes, stirring every so often with a wooden spoon. Pass the contents of the saucepan through a food mill, using the disc with the smallest holes, into a second saucepan. Reheat the strained sauce, season with salt and pepper, simmer for 15 minutes, then transfer the sauce to a crockery or glass bowl and let cool for about ½ hour.

When the eggplants are ready, rinse them under cold running water many times (to be sure to remove all the salt), then pat them dry with paper towels.

Heat the vegetable oil along with the olive oil in a frying pan. Place a small jar or a glass in the center of a platter, then put paper towels on top of the jar (or glass) as well as all over the platter, so that after you fry the eggplant slices, you can lean them around the outside of the covered jar (or glass) to allow the extra oil to drain.

When the oil reaches about 375 degrees, lightly flour the eggplant slices and fry them, a few at a time, until golden on both sides. Transfer to the prepared serving dish. When all the slices are on the serving platter, place paper towels over them.

4 medium-sized eggplants, about 2 pounds
2 tablespoons coarse-grained salt

FOR THE TOMATO SAUCE
1 pound very ripe fresh tomatoes or 1 pound drained canned tomatoes, preferably imported Italian
1 medium-sized clove garlic, peeled and left whole
2 tablespoons olive oil
5 large basil leaves, fresh or preserved in salt
Salt and freshly ground black pepper

TO COOK THE EGGPLANTS
1 quart vegetable oil (⅔ corn oil, ⅓ sunflower oil)
½ cup olive oil
1 cup unbleached all-purpose flour

PLUS
5 tablespoons unseasoned bread crumbs, preferably homemade
3 whole extra-large eggs
3 extra-large eggs, separated
4 tablespoons freshly grated *Parmigiano*
Salt and freshly ground black pepper

Lightly oil a 13½-by-8¾-inch glass baking dish and dust the bottom and sides with some of the bread crumbs. Preheat the oven to 375 degrees.

Add the eggs and the egg yolks to the cooled tomato sauce, along with the *Parmigiano* and the leftover bread crumbs. Season with salt and pepper, and mix very well. Using a copper bowl and wire whisk, beat the egg whites until stiff, then gently fold them into the tomato sauce mixture.

Line the bottom of the baking dish with half of the eggplant slices, pour in half of the batter, then repeat the procedure to make another layer of eggplant and batter. Bake for about 20 minutes. Remove from the oven and cool for 2 to 3 minutes before cutting the *tortino* into squares and serving.

Serves 8 to 10.

LASAGNINO IN INSALATA

Shredded Cabbage Salad

CHIANTI AREA

1 pound tender cabbage, green
    leaves and tough parts removed
5 tablespoons red wine vinegar

FOR THE DRESSING
½ cup olive oil
5 to 8 tablespoons red wine vinegar
Salt and abundant freshly ground
    black pepper

TO SERVE
Several fresh basil leaves

The wrinkly-leafed Savoy cabbage (called cavolo verzotto or verza in Italian) is by far the most widely used cabbage in Italy. It is not chosen for salads, though, as the other common type of cabbage, lasagnino, is preferred for the tenderness of its leaves when they are left uncooked. Lasagnino has smooth, tightly wrapped leaves that are whiter than the leaves of Savoy cabbage.

In this recipe, the shredded cabbage is marinated in olive oil and vinegar and seasoned with salt and pepper. When I first traveled outside of Italy I was surprised to see that the most common dressing for cabbage was mayonnaise. I still prefer the lighter touch of a simple oil and vinegar combination.

Use a knife or a mandolin to thinly slice the cabbage. Rinse it many times under cold running water, then place it in a large bowl, adding enough cold water to cover. Pour in the 5 tablespoons of vinegar and let rest for 1 hour.

Drain the cabbage and season it with the oil, vinegar and salt and pepper. Cover the bowl and refrigerate for at least 1 hour. Before serving, sprinkle on the basil leaves.

Serves 6.

ZUCCHINI

In Italy, *a vegetable prepared* a funghetto *is either cooked in the style of mushrooms (cut into pieces) or with mushrooms. Zucchini* a funghetto, *in which dried porcini and large pieces of zucchini are cooked in a seasoned tomato mixture, is an example of the latter.*

Zucchini ripieni *from Lucca features a Parmigiano stuffing flavored with lemon verbena. In Italy, round zucchini, which have less flavorful pulp than long zucchini, are usually chosen for stuffing, but they are infrequently found abroad.*

Lunch in front of a wonderful Tuscan farmhouse, Fattoria Rampolla, in Chianti. The kind of stones that were used to build this house are found in the Chianti soil.

ZUCCHINI A FUNGHETTO

Zucchini with Mushrooms

Put a little coarse salt in a bowl of cold water. Clean the zucchini, discarding both ends, and soak them in the water for ½ hour.

Prepare the sauce: Coarsely chop the carrots and onion together on a board. Place a medium-sized skillet with the olive oil over medium heat and when the oil is warm, add the chopped ingredients and sauté for 10 minutes, stirring every so often with a wooden spoon.

Soak the mushrooms in a bowl with the water for ½ hour. Finely chop the parsley and garlic together on a board.

Coarse-grained salt
6 medium-sized zucchini
2 medium-sized carrots, scraped
1 medium-sized red onion, cleaned
4 tablespoons olive oil
1 ounce dried porcini mushrooms
3 cups lukewarm water
15 sprigs Italian parsley, leaves only
2 cloves garlic, peeled
1 pound very ripe fresh tomatoes,
    cut into pieces, or 1 pound
    drained canned tomatoes,
    preferably imported Italian
Salt and freshly ground black pepper

TO SERVE
Italian parsley leaves

Pass the fresh or canned tomatoes through a food mill, using the disc with the smallest holes, into a crockery or glass bowl. Add the tomatoes to the skillet and cook for 10 minutes more.

Drain and rinse the zucchini and cut them into large pieces. Drain the mushrooms, then clean them very well, making sure no sand remains attached to the stems. Save the soaking water from the mushrooms, cleaning it by filtering it through paper towels several times.

Add the mushrooms (without chopping them) and ¼ cup of their water to the skillet. Cook for 10 minutes. Add the zucchini and ½ cup more of the mushroom water. Cover the skillet and cook for 20 minutes more, adding additional liquid as needed. When the zucchini are almost cooked, add the chopped parsley and garlic, mix very well and taste for salt and pepper. Serve hot with the parsley leaves.

Serves 6.

ZUCCHINI RIPIENI

Stuffed Zucchini

Soak the zucchini in a bowl of cold water for ½ hour. If using round zucchini, cut off the tops as you would a tomato. Clean the long ones by removing both ends, making sure that the wider end is flat enough to stand up. Measure 3 inches from the wider end and cut it off. Save the thinner part for the stuffing.

Use a knife and small spoon to scoop out the pulp of the twelve 3-inch pieces; be sure to remove all the seeds and to leave

6 round zucchini or 12 medium-
    sized long zucchini, widest
    part measuring 2 inches
    in diameter
Salt
4 extra-large eggs
4 tablespoons freshly grated
    Parmigiano
Freshly ground black pepper
1½ teaspoons dried lemon
    verbena, crumbled
1 medium-sized clove garlic,
    peeled, and 5 sprigs Italian
    parsley, leaves only, finely
    chopped together
About ½ cup unseasoned bread
    crumbs, preferably homemade

TO BAKE THE ZUCCHINI
1 tablespoon olive oil
1 cup chicken or meat broth,
    preferably homemade

a border of about ¼ inch. Rinse the "containers" in running water, then sprinkle a little salt inside and turn them upside down.

Prepare the stuffing: Use a hand grater to coarsely grate the thinner part of the zucchini. Measure out 1½ cups of the grated zucchini and put it in a bowl.

Preheat the oven to 375 degrees. Add the eggs and *Parmigiano* to the bowl with the grated zucchini, season with salt and pepper and crumble over the dried lemon verbena. Add the chopped garlic and parsley, and mix very well with a wooden spoon.

Fill each zucchini "container" with the prepared stuffing. Sprinkle the bread crumbs over the stuffing.

Use the tablespoon of oil to grease a 13½-by-8¾-inch glass baking dish, then arrange all the zucchini in it. Pour the broth into the dish and very loosely cover with aluminum foil so that the tops of the zucchini are not even touching the foil.

Bake for 45 minutes, or until the zucchini containers are soft. Remove the foil and bake for 15 minutes more, until the tops are golden. Serve hot or after 1 hour (at room temperature).

Serves 6.

POMODORI RIPIENI DI FAGIOLI IN INSALATA

Tomatoes Stuffed with Borlotti Beans   ALL OVER TUSCANY

¾ cup borlotti beans (Roman beans)
2 tablespoons olive oil
1 celery stalk
2 cloves garlic, peeled
2 medium-sized carrots, scraped
Coarse-grained salt
15 fresh basil leaves, torn into thirds

(continued on next page)

In this recipe, hollowed-out tomatoes serve as containers for speckled borlotti (Roman) beans that have been seasoned with a sauce featuring scallions, garlic and parsley. The tomatoes should be lined with a bitter green radicchio, but if it is unavailable, arugula leaves can be used instead. This is another vegetable dish that may also serve as an appetizer.

Soak the beans in a bowl of cold water overnight.

The next morning, drain the beans, rinse them under cold running water and place them in a medium-sized stockpot with 3 quarts cold water. Add the olive oil, celery, garlic and carrots to the pot and set over medium heat. Let the beans simmer for about 45 minutes. By that time the beans should be cooked and rather soft but should still retain their shape. Add coarse salt to taste and simmer for 1 minute more. Drain the beans, place them in a crockery or glass bowl to cool and cover with wet paper towels.

PLUS
6 large ripe but not overripe
    tomatoes
Salt

FOR THE SAUCE
4 small scallions, green part removed
1 small clove garlic, peeled
10 sprigs Italian parsley, leaves only
½ cup olive oil
1 tablespoon red wine vinegar
Salt and freshly ground black pepper

TO SERVE
Arugula leaves
Olive oil

Prepare the sauce: Finely chop the scallions, garlic and parsley all together on a board. Place the chopped ingredients in a small bowl, add the olive oil and vinegar and season with salt and pepper. Mix very well. When the beans are cool, discard the celery, garlic and carrots, add the sauce and mix very well. Refrigerate for at least 1 hour before serving.

Prepare the tomatoes: Cut off the top part of the tomatoes (about 1½ inches from the top), then scoop out the pulp and seeds from the bottom part. Carefully wash the six tomato containers, sprinkle some salt inside and place them upside-down on paper towels for ½ hour.

When the beans are ready, place the tomatoes on a large serving platter. Line the inside part of the tomatoes with the arugula leaves, allowing the leaves to stick out of the tomatoes. Add the basil leaves to the beans, mix again and stuff the tomatoes. Pour on a few drops of oil (use any oil that remains in the bowl used for the beans, if possible) and serve at room temperature.

Serves 6.

TORTA DI ERBI

Sweet Vegetable Torte

In the Torta di erbi from Lucca, a Swiss-chard-and-Parmigiano-based filling, flavored with raisins, pine nuts, sugar, nutmeg and brandy, sits in a slightly sweet crust accented with lemon peel. The complex combination of sweet and savory is intriguing. This torte may be served as an appetizer or a light snack.

Start to prepare the filling: Cut the chard into 1-inch strips and soak them in a bowl of cold water for ½ hour.

Heat the butter and oil in a casserole over medium heat, and when the butter is melted, drain the chard and add it to the casserole. Sauté for 15 minutes, stirring every so often with a wooden spoon.

Meanwhile, soak the bread in the milk for 15 minutes. When the chard is ready, transfer the contents of the casserole to a crockery or glass bowl to cool completely.

Prepare the crust: Place the eggs and sugar in a bowl, along with the lemon peel, and mix very well with a wooden spoon. Add the butter and keep mixing until the sugar is completely dissolved and the butter is amalgamated with the other ingredients.

Place the flour in a mound on a board. Make a well in the flour and place the butter mixture in the well. Add the salt, then start rapidly incorporating the flour from the edges of the well into the butter mixture to form a ball of dough. Sprinkle on the baking powder, knead the dough for 30 seconds, wrap it in plastic wrap and refrigerate for at least 1 hour before using.

Finish the filling: Squeeze out and discard the milk from the bread. Add the bread to the bowl with the chard, then add the eggs, *Parmigiano*, raisins and pine nuts. Season with the sugar, nutmeg and salt. Add the brandy and mix very well with a wooden spoon.

Preheat the oven to 375 degrees and lightly butter a 10-by-1½-inch round cake pan with a removable bottom.

Using a rolling pin, between two pieces of plastic wrap, stretch the pastry into a disc about 15 inches in diameter. Peel the top piece of plastic wrap off the pastry and flip the pastry into the prepared pan. Remove the remaining piece of plastic wrap. Press the pastry down all around the bottom of the pan, then pour in the prepared filling. Cut off the overhanging pastry, not to the level of the filling, but a little bit above it. This way you can pinch the pastry, producing large flutings similar to those in the completely sweet version of this dish, which is called *Torta co' becchi* or *Torta co' bischeri* (page 243). Bake for 1 hour.

Remove the *torta* from the oven and let it rest for 30 minutes before transferring it to a serving platter. Serve slightly warm or at room temperature.

Serves 6 to 8.

FOR THE FILLING

2 pounds Swiss chard, cleaned, large stems removed
4 tablespoons (2 ounces) sweet butter
1 tablespoon olive oil
6 slices white bread, crusts removed
1 cup whole milk
2 extra-large eggs
4 tablespoons freshly grated *Parmigiano*
4 tablespoons raisins
2 tablespoons pine nuts (*pinoli*)
4 tablespoons granulated sugar
Pinch of freshly grated nutmeg
Pinch of salt
¼ cup brandy

FOR THE CRUST

3 extra-large eggs
5 ounces granulated sugar
Grated peel of 1 large lemon with thick skin (see Appendix, page 292)
10 tablespoons (5 ounces) sweet butter, at room temperature
10 ounces unbleached all-purpose flour
Pinch of salt
1 teaspoon baking powder

DESSERTS

Desserts in Tuscany, as in all of Italy, recall folklore, seasons and festivals more than any other grouping of dishes in Italian cuisine. In the past, certain desserts were so inextricably connected to one celebration or holy day that they were rarely if ever eaten during the rest of the year. Furthermore, many of these desserts were part of the traditions of just one particular town or village and were not prepared outside of that locality. In modern times, of course, these restrictions have loosened as people have chosen to prepare their favorite dolci more often and people from different towns have shared their recipes with the rest of the country.

Still, Tuscans do try to hold on to some of each dessert's original meaning or importance. Desserts with very ancient origins have most often come to be associated with a rite rather than a specific date—baptism, for example. For the great traditional celebrations that continue in the ancient towns, there is usually a dish that is an integral part of the history of the festival. I have tried to show this in the festival features that appear throughout this book.

And if desserts have lost their connection to one specific day—some desserts have traveled so far from their place of origin that people do not even remember with which holidays these sweets were once associated—Tuscans do try to retain at least their seasonal significance. I have for that reason organized this chapter around the seasons.

Preceding pages: Two transparent crystal jars, much like those used in old pharmacies, show off the bright color of the Pesche alla menta (Marinated Whole Peaches with Mint). In the background is the airy figure of Salome performing her dance in a fresco by Lippi, known as both "The Dance of Salome" and "The Feast of Herodias." The priest here in Prato's cathedral was at first reluctant to allow us to take this photo, but once he saw how full of life it would be he was quite happy. This cathedral is among the treasures that many of the tourists who visit Prato do not take the time to explore.

Two Lenten desserts, alphabet-shaped Quaresimali cookies and Dolce di mandorle all'arancio (Orange Almond Cake), a recipe whose Lenten origin has been obscured by the ingredients that have been added to enrich it.

LENTEN DESSERTS

Especially for Lent (Quaresima in Italian), the Tuscans make Quaresimali, cookies that use only the whites of the eggs and no shortening, possibly so that something has been "given up" for Lent. The batter is formed into alphabet shapes and baked until quite hard, which again may be considered appropriate for the season. These cookies are made especially for children.

Another dessert appropriate for Lent is Gonfiotto di mandorle, *a cake made with ground almonds and a minimal amount of flour, the sacrificed ingredient. Originally, this dessert was served with only a little powdered sugar; at some point, backsliders added whipped cream, and today two layers of* gonfiotti *are often filled with custard cream. The result:* Dolce di mandorle all'arancio.

Q U A R E S I M A L I

Lent Cookies   ALL OVER TUSCANY

4 extra-large egg whites,
    at room temperature
A large pinch of salt
4½ ounces confectioners' sugar
2 ounces unbleached all-purpose
    flour
1 ounce bittersweet cocoa powder

PLUS
Butter and flour for the cookie
    sheets

Preheat the oven to 200 degrees. Beat the egg whites until stiff, using a wire whisk and a large copper bowl. Add the salt. Sift the sugar over the egg whites, then gently fold in the flour and the cocoa.

Lightly butter and flour two cookie sheets.

Place the batter in a pastry bag with a round tip (about ¼ inch) and form letters of the alphabet directly on the cookie sheets.

Place the cookie sheets in the oven, leaving the oven door halfway open, and bake for about 20 minutes or more, until quite hard, being careful not to let the top of the *quaresimali* become too dark. (Overcooked *quaresimali* will taste bitter.) Detach the cookies from the cookie sheets with a metal spatula and let them cool completely before serving.

Quaresimali can be prepared several days in advance and stored in an airtight container.

Makes about 16.

DOLCE DI MANDORLE ALL'ARANCIO

Orange Almond Cake

Preheat the oven to 375 degrees. Coarsely chop the almonds on a board, transfer them to a cookie sheet, toast them for 10 minutes, then let them rest until cooled.

Place the water in a medium-sized saucepan, add the sugar and lemon peel, then set the pan over medium heat. When the water reaches a boil, add the chopped almonds and simmer until a thick syrup forms (this is called the soft-ball stage), about 30 minutes. Brush the inside part of the saucepan with a brush dampened with cold water to prevent the sugar from crystallizing.

Lightly butter the same cookie sheet that you used to toast the almonds, pour the complete contents of the pan onto it and let cool completely, about ½ hour.

When the sugar-almond mixture is cooled and hardened, preheat the oven to 375 degrees and lightly butter and flour two 12-inch round cake pans.

Use a metal spatula to remove the hardened sugar-almond mixture from the sheet, break it into pieces and put the pieces in the bowl of a blender or food processor. Add the flour, milk and egg yolks, and grind everything together until a smooth batter forms, then transfer the batter to a crockery or glass bowl.

Use a wire whisk and a copper bowl to beat the egg whites until stiff. Fold the whites into the batter with a spatula, incorporating them well. Pour the batter into the pans and bake for 45 minutes.

If after 20 minutes, the tops of the cakes become too brown, cover them with aluminum foil.

Remove the cakes from the oven and let rest for a few minutes before unmolding onto a serving dish. Let cool for at least ½ hour.

Prepare the custard cream: Bring water to a boil in the bottom of a double boiler. Put the egg yolks in a crockery or glass bowl. Add the sugar and stir, always in the same direction, with a wooden spoon, until the sugar is completely incorporated and the egg yolks turn a light yellow color. Slowly add the wine, then the orange extract, stirring constantly. When the water in the bottom part of the double boiler starts to boil, transfer the contents of the bowl to the top part of the double boiler and insert over the bottom. Cook, stirring constantly, always in the same direction, until thick enough to coat the spoon. Do not let the cream boil! Immediately remove the top part of the double boiler from the heat and continue to stir for 2 to 3 minutes. Transfer the cream to a crockery or glass bowl and let rest, covered, until completely cooled, about ½ hour.

Cut a piece of parchment paper to fit on an ovenproof cake stand or serving dish, then cut the parchment paper in half. Fit

FOR THE CAKES (*GONFIOTTI*)
12 ounces almonds, blanched
4 cups cold water
2 cups granulated sugar
Peel of 2 large lemons, cut into pieces
1 cup unbleached all-purpose flour
1 cup whole milk or heavy cream
8 extra-large eggs, separated

FOR THE CUSTARD CREAM
4 extra-large egg yolks
4 tablespoons granulated sugar
½ cup dry white wine
1 teaspoon domestic orange extract or 4 drops imported Italian (without water or alcohol)

FOR THE GLAZE
8 ounces confectioners' sugar
2 tablespoons freshly squeezed orange juice, strained very well
A large pinch of ground saffron
1 tablespoon cold water

TO SERVE
Orange zests (see Appendix, page 292)

the two halves of paper on the cake stand or serving dish and place one of the prepared cakes on top of the paper. Spread the cooled cream all over the cake, then place the other cake over the cream. Be sure the two cakes are even all around.

Preheat the oven to 250 degrees.

Prepare the glaze: Sift the sugar onto a board, then transfer it to a small saucepan. Add the orange juice, then dissolve the saffron in the tablespoon of water and add it to the pan. Mix very well with a wooden spoon. Set the saucepan over low heat and stir constantly with the spoon for a few minutes, until the sugar is completely dissolved.

A sculpture from the Manneristic/Baroque gardens of the Villa Garzoni (see pages 144–145).

Use a metal spatula to spread the glaze all over the top and sides of the cake. Let the glaze dry completely, then remove the parchment paper from underneath the cake and place the detachable top of the cake stand or the serving dish, with the cake on it, in the preheated oven for 2 minutes. This will make the glaze very shiny and translucent.

Remove the cake from the oven, transfer the cake to a serving platter and decorate the top with the orange zests.

Variation
GONFIOTTO DI MANDORLE
(Fluffy Almond Cake)

Prepare one Fluffy Almond Cake using half the quantity for each ingredient listed for the Orange Almond Cake. Omit the custard and the glaze, and prepare the lemon-flavored whipped cream: Whip the cream with the granulated sugar, confectioners' sugar and lemon extract in a chilled metal bowl.

Slice like a cake and serve with a sprinkling of confectioners' sugar and some of the lemon-flavored whipped cream on the side.

Serves 10 to 12.

FOR THE LEMON-FLAVORED
WHIPPED CREAM
1½ cups heavy cream
2 tablespoons granulated sugar
2 teaspoons confectioners' sugar
1 teaspoon domestic lemon extract
    or 1 drop imported Italian
    (without water or alcohol)

TO SERVE
Confectioners' sugar

Rice Fritters

St. Joseph, who was a carpenter by profession, is, in fact, the patron saint of carpenters and woodworkers. He is one of Italy's most beloved saints, and his feast day, March 19, is celebrated all over the country. On this day, it is traditional to eat different types of fritters, perhaps because fritters used to be sold from carts similar to those traditionally used by carpenters. Today in Tuscany, the fritters are made of rice and different seasonal fruits, such as apples and pears. Fritters made with the herb borage, once extremely popular, have started to make a comeback. Nettle, another herb that is being rediscovered, is added to pasta dough.

4 cups whole milk
8 ounces raw rice, preferably
    Italian Arborio
Salt
2 tablespoons (1 ounce)
    sweet butter
2 tablespoons granulated sugar
Peel of one-fourth of a lemon
    or orange
6 extra-large eggs, separated
6 to 8 tablespoons unbleached
    all-purpose flour

TO DEEP-FRY
1 quart vegetable oil (⅔ corn oil,
    ⅓ sunflower oil)
½ cup olive oil or 3 ounces lard

TO SERVE
Granulated sugar

Bring the milk to a boil in a medium-sized pot over medium heat. Add the rice, a pinch of salt, the butter, sugar and the lemon or orange rind. Lower the heat and simmer for 20 minutes, stirring every so often with a wooden spoon, until the rice is completely cooked and the milk almost totally absorbed.

Transfer the contents of the pot to a crockery or glass bowl and let stand, covered, until all of the liquid is completely absorbed and the mixture is very firm, about 2 hours.

When ready, discard the lemon or orange peel, add the egg yolks, one at a time, and the 6 tablespoons of flour, mixing very well with a wooden spoon.

Heat the vegetable oil with the olive oil or lard in a large iron skillet over medium heat.

Meanwhile, use a copper bowl and a wire whisk to beat the egg whites until stiff. Gently fold the whites into the rice mixture.

When the oil is hot, about 375 degrees, spoon one heaping tablespoon of the mixture into the oil and cook until lightly golden all over, about 1 minute. If the fritter does not hold together, add the remaining 2 tablespoons flour to the mixture. Cook the remaining fritters.

Transfer the cooked fritters to a serving dish lined with paper towels. When all the fritters are cooked, remove the paper, roll each fritter in the granulated sugar and serve hot.

Serves 8 to 10.

Fresh borage leaves, once used in a wide variety of sweet and savory dishes, are making a comeback in Italy.

Nettle leaves, which are regaining popularity as a flavoring, grow wild all over Italy.

BUCCELLATO DI LUCCA

Luccan Dessert Bread

FOR THE SPONGE
2 cups plus 1 tablespoon
    unbleached all-purpose flour
1 ounce compressed fresh yeast or
    2 packages active dry yeast
1 cup lukewarm or hot milk,
    depending on the yeast
Pinch of salt

FOR THE DOUGH
5 tablespoons raisins
5 tablespoons candied orange rind
1 cup lukewarm milk
3 cups unbleached all-purpose
    flour plus ¼ cup for kneading
6 ounces granulated sugar
Grated peel of 2 large lemons
    (see Appendix, page 292)
3 extra-large eggs
1 tablespoon aniseeds
4 tablespoons (2 ounces) sweet
    butter, melted

TO BAKE THE *BUCCELLATO*
Butter and flour to lightly butter
    and dust a cookie sheet
1 egg
1 tablespoon water
2 tablespoons granulated sugar

The history of buccellato, one of the enduring symbols of Lucca, goes back to the ancient Romans, whose military bread was called buccellatum. The present-day citizens of Lucca, an Etruscan and later a Roman town, simply say that this dessert bread has always existed there. A description of this bread in a medieval manuscript shows that it has not changed much over time.

Flour, yeast, sugar and aniseed are the main ingredients of this bread, but there are also many variables, such as the addition of eggs, butter, sweet wine or spirits (Marsala and rum have replaced older sweet wines), milk, orange or lemon rind, raisins, and candied fruit, such as orange or citron. The most rustic versions employ water but no wine or spirits, candied fruit, eggs or butter: The result is more like a bread than a cake. When milk and some of the other enriching ingredients are added, buccellato becomes a typical, not-too-sweet Italian dolce. Buccellati are most often made either in loaves (filini) or rings (ciambelle). The loaves traditionally include large raisins called zibibbi; aniseeds are usually added to the rings.

For the religious confirmation ceremony that used to take place during Lent (but which now happens at another time), the people of Lucca traditionally compete to see who can make the largest round buccellato. The finished products are often of monstrous size.

Place 2 cups of the flour in a medium-sized bowl and make a well in the center. Dissolve the yeast in the lukewarm or hot milk and pour it into the well, along with the salt. Mix with a wooden spoon, incorporating the flour little by little. When all the flour is absorbed, sprinkle the remaining tablespoon of flour over the sponge, cover the bowl and let the sponge rest, in a warm place away from drafts, until it has doubled in size, about 1 hour. (Two signs that the sponge has doubled in size are the disappearance of the tablespoon of flour or the formation of large cracks on top.)

Soak the raisins and candied orange rind in the lukewarm milk for 1 hour.

Arrange the 3 cups of flour in a ring on a board. Put the

An impressive arrangement of the two types of Buccellati (*Luccan Dessert Bread*): the loaf-shaped filini *and the* ring-shaped ciambelle. *The other typical Luccan dishes displayed on the table* are Torta di erbi (*Sweet Vegetable Torte*) *and* Castagnaccio alla lucchese (*Flat Chestnut Cake*). *In the background is the side of the S. Michele in Foro church in the Piazza S. Michele in Lucca.*

sugar, lemon peel, eggs, aniseeds and butter in a small bowl and mix very well with a wooden spoon.

When the sponge is ready, place it in the center of the ring of flour and start mixing with a wooden spoon, incorporating very little flour. Pour the contents of the bowl with the egg mixture into the ring and keep working, incorporating more flour. When almost all the flour is used up, start kneading the dough with your hands, in a folding motion.

Drain the raisins and the candied orange rind and add them to the dough. Sprinkle the remaining ¼ cup of flour on the board and keep kneading the dough until all the fruit is very well incorporated.

Lightly butter and flour a cookie sheet. Divide the dough into two pieces and shape each piece into a 15-inch-long loaf, making sure that the ends are very thin. Transfer the loaves to the prepared cookie sheet, cover them with a cotton dish towel, and let them rest, in a warm place away from drafts, until doubled in size, about 1 hour.

Preheat the oven to 375 degrees and mix the egg, water and sugar in a small bowl. When ready, brush the tops of the loaves with the egg mixture and bake for 55 minutes. By that time the *buccellati* should be golden brown and completely baked. Remove from the oven and let rest on a rack for at least 1 hour before serving.

Makes 2 loaves.

LO SCOPPIO DEL CARRO ·
CHARIOT EXPLOSION

My childhood days in Florence were full of mystery, color and ceremony, more than most childhoods and most cities, I think, because of the special way that the Florentines identify with their city and enshrine their pride through preservation of old customs. Lo scoppio del carro, literally "chariot explosion," as the local Easter rite is called, is an example of just such a custom.

It is a celebration, really, and the centerpiece of this Easter Sunday event is an ornate carriage, or carro, piled high with fireworks, which is ignited between two famous doors, Ghiberti's "Porta del Paradiso" on the Baptistry and the main door of the Duomo, located across the piazza. A fire in the shape of a small dove (called the colombina) is launched from inside the church, and lands in the awaiting carriage, causing the carriage as well as its cargo of fireworks to ignite, blaze and sparkle to the oohs and aahs of the crowd. This ceremony of fire has its origin in an old Florentine tradition of commemorating the Resurrection by lighting the Easter candle and spreading the sacred fire— fuoco benedetto—throughout the city.

Though the rite in some ways dates back to pagan times, the history of the Christian practice begins in 1101 when Pazzino de' Pazzi, a Crusader and a member of one of Florence's most prominent families, brought back from Jerusalem the rite of the fuoco benedetto and two stones, supposedly from the Sacred Sepulchre (Christ's tomb), which were used to generate the friction that, in turn, produced the sacred flame.

The ceremony has changed over the centuries—the flame is no longer passed around the city and the original stones from Jerusalem have been removed to a place of safety inside the church—and the rite has taken on a civic rather than purely religious meaning. It is a celebration complete with coats of arms, processions, music, costumes, banners and the sorteggio, or lottery, to decide the order to the soccer games of another festival, the annual Calcio in costume. It is a day when Florentines, their neighbors from the nearby Tuscan countryside and tourists from all over the world gather together in the Piazza del Duomo to watch as a miniature history of Florence flashes and sparkles before them.

Carrying the standard past the line of costumed drummers on the day of the Scoppio del carro. In the background is Florence's Baptistry with its golden doors by Ghiberti. Michelangelo called these "the doors of paradise."

Opposite: The "sacred fire," in the shape of a dove, is moved along a wire that leads from the cathedral's grand altar to the chariot full of fireworks that waits outside. If the dove's course from the altar to the chariot is a smooth one, it is considered the omen of a good harvest and a lucky year.

Facing the smoking chariot: two men in Renaissance costume and two policemen.

IL PANETTONE DI PASQUA FIORENTINO

Easter Panettone

The special Florentine Easter cake called Panettone di Pasqua is better known locally as Panettone della "Passione." A typical Tuscan play on words, passione stands not only for "the passion of Christ" but also for the passionate—three-day—commitment that was once required in order to make this cake and have it emerge from the oven at noon on Easter Sunday, in time to celebrate the Resurrection. Nowadays, passion has dimmed and the panettone is usually made in one day.

Prepare the sponge: Place the 2 cups of flour in a large crockery or glass bowl and make a well in the center. Dissolve the yeast in the lukewarm or hot milk and pour it into the well. Add a pinch of salt, then use a wooden spoon to start incorporating the flour into the well, a little at a time, until all the flour is absorbed. Sprinkle the remaining tablespoon of flour over the sponge, cover the bowl with a cotton towel and let rest, in a warm place away from drafts, until doubled in size, about 1 hour. (Two signs that the sponge has doubled in size are the disappearance of the tablespoon of flour or the formation of large cracks on top.)

When ready, soak the raisins in the milk for 15 minutes.

One ingredient at a time, add to the bowl containing the sponge, the pine nuts, the grated peel of the lemon and the orange, the eggs (one at a time), confectioners' sugar, granulated sugar, butter, Vinsanto or Marsala, aniseeds and nutmeg. As you add each ingredient, mix constantly with a wooden spoon and don't add the following ingredient until the previous one is incorporated.

Drain the raisins, discarding the milk, and add them to the sponge mixture. Mix again, then start adding the flour, a little at a time, constantly mixing with a wooden spoon. When all the flour is absorbed, cover the bowl with a cotton towel and let rest, in a warm place away from drafts, until doubled in size, about 1 hour.

When ready, add the egg and olive oil to the risen dough and mix very well with a wooden spoon. Add the milk and finally the flour and mix very well. Cover the bowl with a cotton towel and let rest, in a warm place away from drafts, until doubled in size, about 1 hour.

With ½ tablespoon of the butter, grease a 5-quart *panettone* mold or a double cake pan (a cake pan with high sides). Preheat the oven to 375 degrees.

FOR THE SPONGE
2 cups plus 1 tablespoon
   unbleached all-purpose flour
1½ ounces fresh compressed yeast
   or 3 packages active dry yeast
1 cup lukewarm or hot milk,
   depending on the yeast
Pinch of salt

FOR THE SECOND RISING
8 tablespoons raisins
1 cup lukewarm milk
4 tablespoons pine nuts (*pinoli*)
Grated peel of 1 large lemon with
   thick skin (see Appendix,
   page 292)
Grated peel of 1 large orange with
   thick skin
4 extra-large eggs
4 tablespoons confectioners' sugar
½ cup granulated sugar
8 tablespoons (4 ounces) sweet
   butter, at room temperature
½ cup Vinsanto or dry Marsala
1 tablespoon aniseeds
Pinch of freshly grated nutmeg
1½ cups unbleached all-purpose
   flour

FOR THE THIRD RISING
1 extra-large egg
2 tablespoons olive oil
½ cup lukewarm milk
½ cup unbleached all-purpose flour

FOR THE FOURTH RISING
1 tablespoon (½ ounce) sweet
   butter
1 cup unbleached all-purpose flour

TO SERVE
Crystallized sugar

FOR THE SUGAR SYRUP
(OPTIONAL)
¼ cup cold water
2 tablespoons granulated sugar

Incorporate the last cup of flour into the dough, mixing very well with a wooden spoon, then transfer the dough to the prepared mold. Cover the mold with a cotton towel and let rest, in a warm place away from drafts, until doubled in size. The dough should reach the top of the mold.

Cut the remaining butter into pats and distribute on top of the *panettone*. Bake the *panettone* for 1 hour 10 minutes. If the top part becomes too dark, cover it with a piece of aluminum foil. Remove the *panettone* from the oven and let it cool for at least ½ hour before transferring to a serving platter.

Sprinkle on the crystallized sugar. Alternatively, prepare a very thin sugar syrup (see Note) and brush it on the top of the *panettone* before sprinkling on the sugar. Serve when completely cooled.

Note: To prepare a very thin sugar syrup, place the water in a small saucepan, add the sugar and set the pan over medium heat. Bring the mixture to a boil, then simmer until a thin syrup forms, brushing the inside part of the saucepan with a brush dampened with cold water to prevent the sugar from crystallizing.

Serves 10 to 12.

TORTA CO' BISCHERI

Antique Pisan Torte

PISA

A little after Easter, to celebrate their patron saint's day, the people in the villages along the Serchio River make a torta with prominent flutings. Some people believe these flutings resemble the crenellations of a castle (called becchi) while others compare them to the pegs used to tighten the strings of a violin (bischeri in Italian). These two comparisons have given rise to two names for the same dessert: Torta co' becchi, used more around Lucca, and Torta co' bischeri, used in the Pisa area. (Bischero is one of the most common words in Tuscan slang. It has a slightly derogatory meaning—"dolt" or "fool"—but is really more humorous than insulting.) A third torta of this type is made in the area around Pistoia. In all three variations, the filling includes a little rice as well as chocolate, but each one boasts its own selection of glazed fruits and nuts. None of these variations should be confused with Torta di erbi (page 227) from Lucca. Though it boasts similar crenellations in the crust and is slightly sweet, Torta di erbi is stuffed with spinach or Swiss chard and is served as an appetizer or vegetable course.

Begin the filling: Bring the milk and water to a boil in a medium-sized pot over medium heat. When the milk reaches a boil, add the butter and salt. When the butter is completely melted, add the rice, stir very well and cook for about 18 minutes. By that time the rice should be soft. Drain the rice, discard the liquid and let the rice rest in the colander, covered, until completely cooled.

Prepare the crust: Sift the flour onto a board. Place the butter, superfine sugar and confectioners' sugar in a bowl and stir very well with a wooden spoon, until the butter is amalgamated with the other ingredients. Place this mixture on top of the flour, adding the egg yolk, whole egg, orange peel and rum. Use a metal dough scraper to quickly mix all the ingredients and form a ball of dough. Wrap the dough in plastic wrap and refrigerate for 1 hour.

Finish the filling: Transfer the cooled rice to a crockery or glass bowl and add the sugar, candied orange peel, citron, eggs, heavy cream, grated orange rind, pine nuts, and chocolate. Mix very well with a wooden spoon, then add the rum and mix again.

Lightly butter a 10- or 11-inch round cake pan with a removable bottom.

Sprinkle the baking powder over the dough and lightly knead it.

Preheat the oven to 375 degrees. Between two large pieces of plastic wrap, using a rolling pin, stretch the cooled pastry into a 15-inch disc. Peel off the plastic wrap on top of the pastry, flip the pastry into the prepared cake pan, remove the second piece of plastic wrap, press the pastry down on the bottom, then cut off and save the dough hanging over the side. With a fork, prick the pastry on the bottom of the mold and bake for 15 minutes. Remove from the oven and cool for 15 minutes.

With the remaining pastry, roll out one long strip and make "pinches" along one of the edges to resemble large fluting. Attach the non-fluted edge of this strip of pastry to the pre-baked pastry shell. Pour the filling into the mold.

Using the remaining dough, prepare 1-inch-wide strips of pastry, cutting them with a scalloped pastry cutter. Criss-cross the strips of pastry 2 inches apart over the filling.

Bake the *torta* for 1 hour. Remove from the oven and cool for ½ hour before transferring it to a serving platter.

Cool the *torta* for an additional 1 hour before serving it with confectioners' sugar sprinkled over the top.

Serves 6 to 8.

FOR THE FILLING
1 quart whole milk
1 cup cold water
2 tablespoons (1 ounce)
    sweet butter
Pinch of salt
¾ cup raw rice, preferably
    Italian Arborio
6 ounces granulated sugar
3 ounces candied orange rind
2 ounces glacéed citron
5 extra-large eggs
1 cup heavy cream
Grated peel of 1 large orange with
    thick skin (see Appendix,
    page 292)
3 ounces pine nuts (*pinoli*)
4 ounces coarsely grated
    semisweet chocolate
1 tablespoon light rum

FOR THE CRUST
1 pound unbleached all-purpose
    flour
8 tablespoons (4 ounces)
    sweet butter
8 ounces superfine sugar
2 tablespoons confectioners' sugar
1 extra-large egg yolk
1 extra-large egg
Grated peel of 1 orange
    (see Appendix, page 292)
1 tablespoon light rum
1 teaspoon baking powder

TO SERVE
Confectioners' sugar

Torta co' bischeri (*Antique Pisan Torte*), *with its heavily fluted crust resembling the pegs that tune the strings of a violin, set against Pisa's remarkable Baptistry and, further back, the façade of the cathedral. Not in view is the celebrated leaning tower, which is also located in this piazza, the Piazza dei Miracoli.*

CILIEGE AL VINO ROSSO

Cherries Baked in Red Wine

We end our sampling of spring desserts with this simple treatment of cherries, the first of the spring fruits to appear in the Tuscan markets.

Preheat the oven to 375 degrees.

Wash the cherries very well and place them in a glass baking dish. Pour the wine over the cherries and sprinkle with the sugars. The wine should cover the cherries completely. Bake for 45 minutes, until the cherries are cooked through but still firm. Add the brandy and bake for 5 minutes more.

Transfer the fruit to a serving platter, using a slotted spoon, and pour the liquid into a medium-sized casserole. Place the casserole over medium heat and simmer until the wine is reduced by half, about 35 minutes. Pour the reduced wine over the cherries and let rest until cool, about 1 hour. Serve with sprigs of fresh mint.

This dish is even better if prepared one or two days in advance and allowed to rest, covered, in the refrigerator.

Serves 8 to 10.

2 pounds ripe but not overripe
    cherries, stems removed
3 cups full-bodied red wine
2 tablespoons granulated sugar
1 tablespoon confectioners' sugar
2 tablespoons brandy or rum

TO SERVE
Fresh mint sprigs

Ciliege al vino rosso (*Cherries Baked in Red Wine*) surrounded by geraniums. In the background are Florence's Arno River and the palaces that line its south bank.

PESCHE ALLA MENTA

Marinated Whole Peaches with Mint

Coarse-grained salt
8 large perfect peaches
    (with no blemishes), ripe but
    not overripe
4 to 5 cups dry white wine
½ cup brandy
3 tablespoons granulated sugar
4 or more large fresh mint sprigs

TO SERVE
Fresh mint leaves

During the summer in Tuscany, there is an abundance of ripe, delicious fruit. Although most of the time it is enjoyed unadorned, there are a few special recipes that showcase its flavor. For Pesche alla menta, whole fresh peaches are blanched and peeled, then allowed to macerate in white wine to which a little sugar and sprigs of fresh mint have been added.

In the photograph on pages 230–231, which was taken in Prato's cathedral, we see transparent jars of these luscious peaches set against the mysterious Dance of Salome, *one of Filippo Lippi's greatest paintings and among the most important frescoes of the early Renaissance.*

Place a large pot of cold water over medium heat and when the water reaches a boil, add a pinch of coarse salt, then the peaches. Blanch for 1 to 3 minutes, depending on the type of peaches you are using and the season.

Carefully transfer the peaches from the boiling water to a bowl of cold water. Use a paring knife to carefully remove the skin from the peaches. As the first peach is ready, place it in a crockery or glass bowl and immediately pour 4 cups of the wine and the brandy over it. When all the peaches are in the bowl, add more wine if they are not completely covered. Add the sugar and at least 4 sprigs of the mint, cover the bowl and refrigerate for at least 5 or 6 hours before serving.

When ready to serve, discard the mint from the marinade. Serve each peach with some of the marinade and a fresh mint leaf.

Serves 8.

REGATA DI SAN RANIERI ·
THE PALIO ON WATER

If you are like most people, the Palio means Siena and the summer spectacle that transforms the main square there into the world's most colorful racetrack. But you may not know the other Palio—Pisa's equally colorful and historical "palio on the water" or Regata di San Ranieri. This festive boat race takes place on June 17, the day after the candlelight display of the Luminaria (see page 182). On a beautiful June day, I can think of nothing more exciting than watching Pisa put on her medieval dress for the occasion and joining the crowds along the Arno to cheer on the galleys skimming the water in the race to finish first.

   This "water palio" originated with the medieval love of contests, and it was only natural for a seafaring power like Pisa to

The four main ships in the Pisan regatta represent the naval powers of the medieval Mediterranean (Venice, Genoa, Pisa and Amalfi) and are accompanied by smaller noncontending vessels. The crowds on the river bank and the bridge shout their support.

prefer that these contests take place upon the water. The historical record begins on August 1, 1292, with the fanfare that announced the public celebration of the Feast of the Assumption: The leading young noblemen of the city, in their most elegant dress, mounted twenty horses draped in rich scarlet cloth, and rode, two by two, through all the streets of Pisa, followed by trumpeteers who announced the events that would take place on this most important of church holidays. And, as might be expected in Pisa, all roads led to the finale along the Arno—the water palio. The race was the highlight of the festivities.

   The name "palio," no matter whether a land or water competition, originally referred to the prizes given to the winner. These were magnificent gifts—luxurious silks, satins, velvets and brocades that at one time were actually draped over the head of a visiting sovereign as a sign of respect for the crown before being presented to the winner. But gradually the name referred no longer to the prize but to the competition itself. And even the prizes changed as the years went by. For the Pisan regatta, animal gifts were added to the royal silks and satins. Thus a pig, a goat, a water buffalo, or a rooster were part of the winner's purse, while a goose was awarded to the last galley to cross the finish line.

The water palio was observed in the usual fashion until 1406 when the Florentines conquered Pisa and decided the regatta would take on the function of commemorating the Florentine victory over the Milanese, which must have been particularly upsetting to the Pisans. As though appropriation of a treasured Pisan tradition were not enough, Florence stopped the regatta altogether in 1509.

The tradition was revived in 1635 when a true patriot of Pisa willed "50 scudi" (gold pieces) to the city with the stipulation that they be used to revive the annual regatta. In 1718 the regatta was for

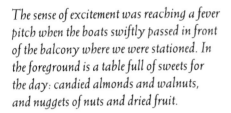

The sense of excitement was reaching a fever pitch when the boats swiftly passed in front of the balcony where we were stationed. In the foreground is a table full of sweets for the day: candied almonds and walnuts, and nuggets of nuts and dried fruit.

the first time dedicated to San Ranieri, the patron saint of the city, thus losing its age-old identification with the Feast of the Assumption and underscoring a more purely Pisan aspect of the celebration.

While the prizes today include a calf, the main emphasis is on the pair of geese that form the booby prize for last place. Geese, of course, are known for their slowness. They are also good to eat, and goose paired with homemade pappardelle (see page 115) is an appropriate Pisan dish with which to celebrate the regatta. When we went to Pisa to take photographs of the race, I would have liked to have gone to a restaurant to enjoy this dish, but since we had neglected to make reservations several months in advance, we were instead destined to make it for ourselves at home. During the race, I did manage to fill up on the sweets shown in the photograph, all of which are sold on the carts lining the riverbank throughout the day of the festivities.

CHILLED AND FROZEN DESSERTS

In *Italy*, gelati *and* semifreddi *are mainly summer desserts, and* semifreddi *are more commonly served at the end of a dinner. The custard, meringue and whipped cream used in* semifreddi *do not completely freeze, hence the name, which means "half-frozen."*

In Semifreddo di uvette, *the cream-based ice is flavored with raisins soaked in rum.* Crema zabaione *is related to* semifreddo *but it is simpler both in taste and preparation. The use of Vinsanto instead of Marsala as a flavoring makes this dessert typically Tuscan. During the summer, it is common to serve this dessert with fresh berries.*

SEMIFREDDO DI UVETTE

Raisin Semifreddo

4 ounces seedless raisins
½ cup light rum
8 extra-large egg yolks
4 tablespoons granulated sugar
1 tablespoon confectioners' sugar
¼ cup dry Marsala
¾ cup dry white wine

FOR THE SYRUP
½ cup granulated sugar
½ cup cold water
2 or 3 drops lemon juice

FOR THE MERINGUE
4 extra-large egg whites
2 tablespoons granulated sugar

FOR THE WHIPPED CREAM
2 cups heavy cream
2 tablespoons granulated sugar
2 teaspoons confectioners' sugar

Place the raisins in the rum in a small crockery or glass bowl and soak for ½ hour.

Meanwhile, mix the egg yolks with the granulated sugar and the confectioners' sugar in a crockery or glass bowl, using a wooden spoon, and when the egg yolks turn a lighter color, add the Marsala and the wine and mix very well. Drain the raisins, discarding the rum, add them to the egg mixture and mix again. Cook the custard cream, using a copper bowl over a pot of boiling water (or a double boiler). When the cream is quite thick, transfer it to a crockery or glass bowl and let rest until completely cooled, about 1 hour.

Prepare the syrup: Dissolve the sugar in the cold water, add the lemon juice and transfer to a medium-sized saucepan. Place the pan over medium heat and simmer until a very light colored syrup forms. Brush the inside of the pan, above the level of the syrup, with cold water to prevent the sugar from crystallizing.

Meanwhile, beat the egg whites for the meringue, using a wire whisk and a copper bowl, adding the sugar a few minutes after you start beating the whites. Beat the whites until stiff.

Transfer the already prepared syrup to a glass measuring cup to cool slightly, then start pouring it, in a thin stream, into the beaten egg whites, continuously beating the whites with the syrup, until all the syrup is incorporated.

Whip the cream with the granulated sugar and confectioners' sugar using a wire whisk and a chilled metal bowl.

When ready, assemble the *semifreddo*: Incorporate the cooled custard cream into the whipped cream, using a whisk, then gently fold in the egg white mixture, using a spatula so that a lot of air is incorporated into it. Transfer the *semifreddo* to a bowl or to individual cups and place in the freezer, covered, for at least 2 hours before serving.

Semifreddo can be prepared up to three days in advance and stored in the freezer until ready to serve.

Serves 10 to 12.

CREMA ZABAIONE AL VINSANTO

Zabaione with Whipped Cream

Put water in the bottom of a double boiler and bring to a boil.

Place the egg yolks in a crockery or glass bowl and add the sugar. Stir with a wooden spoon, always in the same direction, until the sugar is completely incorporated and the egg yolks turn a lighter color. Slowly add the Vinsanto, mixing steadily, then transfer the contents of the bowl to the top part of the double boiler.

When the water in the bottom part of the double boiler reaches a boil, insert the top part. Stir the egg mixture constantly with a wooden spoon, always in the same direction. The moment before the mixture starts boiling, when it is thick enough to stick to the wooden spoon, remove it from the heat and stir the contents for 1 minute more. Transfer the *zabaione* to a crockery bowl to cool for about 1 hour.

When the *zabaione* is cold, prepare the whipped cream (*panna montata*) using the heavy cream and sugars. When the whipped cream is ready and very stiff, gently fold in the cold *zabaione* and mix very carefully but thoroughly with a whisk. Cover the bowl and place it in the refrigerator until needed. Serve with fresh berries, such as raspberries or mulberries.

Serves 8.

4 extra-large egg yolks
5 tablespoons granulated sugar
¾ cup dry Vinsanto

PLUS
2 cups heavy cream
2 tablespoons granulated sugar
1 teaspoon confectioners' sugar

TO SERVE
Fresh berries

Silkworms must compete with the Tuscans for the delicious summer mulberries.

MERINGATO FIORENTINO

Florentine Meringue Cake

FLORENCE

Meringato fiorentino is an elaborate meringue cake of the type that were served at court dinners throughout the centuries. In the photograph, we see this cake sitting in the window of Il Museo Alberto della Ragione, which is located on the Piazza della Signoria, Florence's central public square. The window gives on to a spectacular view of the Palazzo Vecchio (Florence's city hall), the Biancone fountain and the Loggia dei Lanzi, an arcade sheltering Cellini's Perseus *and a collection of ancient Roman sculpture. Not entirely visible in the photo is the copy of Michelangelo's* David *that stands in place of the original in front of the Palazzo Vecchio. The original* David *now stands in the Accademia museum.*

FOR THE CHOCOLATE MERINGUE
5 large egg whites
8 ounces confectioners' sugar
1 tablespoon bittersweet cocoa
    powder

FOR THE WHITE MERINGUE
8 large egg whites
13 ounces confectioners' sugar

TO BAKE THE MERINGUE
Sweet butter
Unbleached all-purpose flour

PLUS
2 cups heavy cream
2 tablespoons confectioners' sugar
2 ounces bittersweet chocolate,
    coarsely chopped

For this cake you must prepare three different layers of meringue: The base is chocolate meringue, the middle layer is white meringue and the top layer is a ring of white meringue. Several "dots" of white and chocolate meringue are needed also.

Preheat the oven to 250 degrees.

Lightly butter and flour three cookie sheets and mark a 10-inch disc on each one.

To prepare the meringue: Place the egg whites (for the chocolate meringue base) in a large copper bowl and start beating with a wire whisk. After a few seconds, add 1 tablespoon of the sugar. Mix the remaining sugar with the cocoa and when the egg whites are airy and stiff, start sifting the sugar-cocoa mixture directly into the copper bowl. Never stop beating the egg whites until all the sugar-cocoa mixture is incorporated. Transfer the beaten egg whites to a pastry bag with a tip that measures ½ inch in diameter.

Make the meringue base on one of the marked discs by piping the egg white mixture in concentric circles, moving from the outer edge toward the center. With the remaining egg white mixture, prepare several "dots" on the same cookie sheet.

Use the same technique and the ingredients listed (left) to prepare the white meringue for the middle and top layers of the cake, preparing one layer in exactly the same manner as the chocolate layer, and the ring by piping only three of

This photograph of Meringato fiorentino (Florentine Meringue Cake) *and glasses of Vinsanto was taken from a window in the Museo della Ragione.*

DESSERTS 257

the concentric circles. Pipe some additional "dots" with the white meringue.

Place all the pans in the preheated oven for 2 hours. By that time all the meringues should be very crisp and light.

Whip the cream in a chilled metal bowl with a wire whisk, adding the sugar when the cream has some resistance and the chocolate when it is whipped and ready.

Assemble the cake: Transfer the bottom layer from the pan onto a flat round serving platter. Spread on a ½-inch-thick layer of the prepared cream, then add the second meringue. Add one more layer of cream, and finally put on the ring. Fit the remaining cream into the hole of the ring and arrange the "dots" of meringue all over the top of the cake. Put in the freezer for at least 5 hours before serving.

Serves 8 to 10.

CETRIOLI MARINATI

Marinated Cucumbers

TUSCAN COUNTRYSIDE

Each summer in Italy, when the wheat harvest is over, hearty celebratory dinners are served, and Marinated Cucumbers are often on the menu. To make this humble dessert, I use very small cucumbers that have almost no seeds.

3 thin cucumbers
Juice of half a lemon
¾ cup granulated sugar

Peel the cucumbers, cut them into slices less than ¼ inch thick and place them in a crockery or glass bowl. Pour over the lemon juice, then sprinkle on the sugar. Do not mix. Cover the bowl and refrigerate for at least 2 hours before serving.

When ready, mix very well and serve the cucumbers and the juice together.

Serves 6.

Humble Cetrioli marinati (Marinated Cucumbers) gets the respect it deserves when served in crystal bowls against a backdrop of antique ceramics. The large yellow-and-blue serving platter is from Montelupo Fiorentino, a ceramics center in the Arno Valley. The white dishes came from Arezzo, where they were made for only a short time in the mid-eighteenth century.

LA FESTA DELLE RIFICOLONE

*O*n *September 7, hundreds of people from the country join the city folk in Florence at Piazza Santissima Annunziata, Florence's most harmonious Renaissance square. They come for the festival of the rificolone, a celebration of (depending on which of two reasons you go with) either the birth of the Virgin Mary or Cosimo I's conquest of Siena, the last Tuscan city-state to hold out against Florentine rule. In years past, the crowds of people coming to celebrate the evening festival carried homemade candlelit lamps made of brightly colored paper that had been formed into fanciful shapes, the most common of which was a watermelon, or* cocomero. *These*

Overview of the Piazza Santissima Annunziata during Florence's festival of the rificolone. Note the basilica in the background and Brunelleschi's Hospital of the Innocents to the right.

lamps on sticks first lit the way for the immense parade of people descending from the hills into the river valley and were then set to float down the Arno. (The sight of the river illuminated at night by these floating paper lanterns, once seen, is never forgotten.) Many country people came down from the hillsides the night before in carriages loaded with fresh ingredients to be sold in the square—their own sheep's cheeses; dried mushrooms; cookies such as the thin anise-flavored wafers called brigidini; *a flat cake prepared with abundant egg yolks, sugar, and anise or fennel seeds, called* berlingozzo; *and cookies made from different kinds of nuts. But the king of the festival was watermelon; the sweet red part was eaten, of course, but the white part was treasured by the*

Parents buying paper lanterns, called *rificolone*, for their children.

A group of very young children sit on the church steps, bewildered by all the activity going on around them.

Cotton candy is king! It is by far the favorite candy at the festival.

country girls as a beauty mask. They rubbed this inside rind all over their faces and arms, and it was reputed to keep their skin light in color, even under the hot sun.

The Piazza Santissima Annunziata, the square where the festivities are held, is known for its Renaissance architecture. The great architect Brunelleschi designed the basilica church there, and also the immense arched hospital for foundling children, the Ospedale degli Innocenti, where babies were once routinely abandoned. They were left at night on a huge wheel, which carried them anonymously into the hospital.

Today, the celebrations are quieter and perhaps a little less colorful than they once were, but when I was a child it was my favorite festivity. I still remember my father holding me by the arm, and parading up and down the streets from the square to the cathedral, trying to avoid the exuberant groups of children running away from their parents.

Cutting the fresh nut brittle.

No festival is complete without a luscious suckling pig, called porchetta in Italian.

Anise-Flavored Wafers

These crisp wafer-like cookies are a common sight at the festival of the rificolone.

Place the flour in a bowl and make a well in the center. In a small bowl, combine the eggs, sugar, aniseeds and salt, then pour everything into the well of flour. Using a wooden spoon, start incorporating the flour from the rim of the well, then, when a rather thick dough forms, start kneading it on a board. Keep kneading until the dough is smooth, adding more flour as needed. Divide the dough into 1 tablespoon pieces and shape each piece of dough into a small ball.

   Place the *schiaccia* (see Note) over medium heat for 5 minutes, then turn it over and heat the other side for 5 minutes more. When ready, open the *schiaccia* and place one of the small balls in the center. Close the *schiaccia*, place it over the heat for about 30 seconds, then turn it over and keep it on the heat for 30 seconds more. Open the *schiaccia* and remove the cooked *brigidino*. Repeat the same procedure with the remaining balls of dough, but without heating the *schiaccia*.

   Note: A *schiaccia* is an old-style wafer iron made up of two connected pieces, each of which must be heated over a fire. The ridges on the inside of the iron leave a design on the wafer. When used for the first time, the iron must be seasoned with oil.

Makes about 25 wafers.

2 cups unbleached all-purpose flour
5 extra-large eggs
12 tablespoons granulated sugar
2 tablespoons aniseeds
Pinch of salt

FALL AND WINTER FRUIT DESSERTS

Each of these desserts is made with fruit. The Crostata di uva, *a grape tart, differs from summer* crostate *in that the fruit is baked in the crust rather than being added after the crust is baked. This is a less rustic dessert than the* Schiacciata con l'uva *that appears in my* Foods of Italy *book. In that recipe, the grapes are baked in a pizza-like flat bread.*

   In Dolce di diosperi, *puréed persimmons are combined with ground almonds, walnuts, hazelnuts, and pine nuts to produce a spectacular, moist cake that can be served with or without persimmon cream. (Alternatively, the cream can be served as a dessert on its own.)*

There are two types of persimmons in Italy. They look alike and are both very sweet, but one is not eaten until it is very soft whereas the other, known as the persimmon apple, can be eaten while it is still chewy. Either kind may be used for Dolce di diosperi. A curious sight in Italy is the persimmon tree in the winter, when all the leaves are gone but the orange fruit remains on the tree to ripen.

C R O S T A T A   D I   U V A

Grape Tart

FOR THE CRUST
8 ounces unbleached all-purpose
  flour
4 ounces superfine sugar
8 tablespoons (4 ounces) sweet
  butter, at room temperature
  and cut into pieces
2 ½ extra-large egg yolks
Grated peel of 1 lemon
Pinch of salt
1 ounce crisp ladyfingers
  (Italian *savoiardi*)

FOR THE FILLING
1 pound seedless red grapes
1 tablespoon unbleached
  all-purpose flour
3 tablespoons granulated sugar
1 tablespoon grappa
2 extra-large eggs
1 extra-large egg yolk
1 cup heavy cream

Prepare the crust: Place the flour in a mound on a board and make a well in the center. Place the sugar, butter, egg yolks, lemon peel and salt in the well, and using a fork, start amalgamating all the ingredients into the well. Then begin incorporating the flour a little at a time. When all the flour but 3 or 4 tablespoons is incorporated, start working with your hands, absorbing all the remaining flour and forming a ball of dough. This should be done very quickly; otherwise, the pastry will fall apart while it is baking. Wrap the pastry in plastic wrap and refrigerate for at least 1 hour.

Prepare the filling: Remove the stems from the grapes, rinse the grapes under cold running water and dry them with paper towels. Place the flour and the granulated sugar in a medium-sized crockery or glass bowl, add the grappa and mix very well with a wooden spoon. Add the eggs and the egg yolk and mix very well. Add the cream and mix again.

Finely grind the ladyfingers for the crust, and lightly butter a 10½-inch fluted tart pan with a removable bottom. With a rolling pin, roll the pastry between two large pieces of plastic wrap into a disc with a diameter of about 13 inches.

Preheat the oven to 375 degrees.

Remove the top layer of plastic wrap from the pastry and invert the second layer with the pastry over the prepared pan. Peel off the plastic wrap, press down the pastry all around the edges, then roll your rolling pin over the pan to cut off the pastry hanging over the sides. Lightly dust the bottom and sides of the pastry with the ground-up ladyfingers. Remove and discard the leftover crumbs. Arrange the grapes all over the pastry, then pour in the egg mixture. Bake for 1 hour 5 minutes.

Remove the *crostata* from the oven and allow it to rest for 10 minutes before removing it from the tart pan and transferring it to a serving platter. Serve the *crostata* at room temperature or, better yet, when completely cooled.

Serves 8.

Persimmon Cake

Wash the persimmons very well, then remove the stems, skin and any seeds (some persimmons do not have seeds.) Measure out exactly 2 pounds of pulp and pass it through a cone-shaped sieve or very fine strainer into a large bowl.

Finely chop all the nuts together, along with the granulated sugar and vanilla-flavored sugar. (If using a food processor, combine the pulp, nuts, and sugars, and grind very well, using the standard metal blade.)

Transfer the ground ingredients to a large bowl, add the 5 tablespoons of sugar, 6 tablespoons of the flour and the eggs and mix all the ingredients together with a wooden spoon.

Preheat the oven to 375 degrees. Using the tablespoon of butter, heavily grease the bottom and sides of a 10-inch spring-form pan. Flour the pan very well with the remaining flour and discard what is left over. Add the baking powder to the batter in the bowl, mix very well and transfer the contents to the prepared pan.

Bake for 1 hour. Remove the cake from the oven and let rest on a rack until completely cool, about 1 hour. Open the form, transfer the cake onto a round serving dish and serve in slices.

Alternatively, prepare the persimmon cream to serve with the cake: Wash the persimmon very well, then remove the stem, skin and any seeds. Remove any tough fibers mixed with the pulp. Pass the pulp through a food mill, using the disc with the smallest holes, into a crockery or glass bowl. Be sure that only the soft pulp has passed through. If any fibers remain, strain again using a finer strainer. Measure ¼ pound of the puréed pulp and discard the leftover.

Bring water to a boil in the bottom of a double boiler (preferably made of copper).

Put the egg yolks in a crockery or glass bowl and add the sugar. Stir with a wooden spoon, always in the same direction, until the sugar is completely incorporated and the egg yolks turn a light yellow color. Then add the persimmon purée and mix very well to incorporate the fruit evenly.

Transfer the contents of the bowl to the top part of the double boiler. When the water in the bottom part is boiling, insert the top and stir constantly with a wooden spoon, always in the same direction. Just before it boils, the custard should be thick enough to coat the spoon. Immediately remove the top part of the double boiler from the heat and stir the contents for 1 minute longer.

6 large and very ripe soft
  persimmons (2 pounds
  after skin, stems and seeds
  are removed)
4 ounces blanched almonds
4 ounces blanched walnuts
4 ounces blanched hazelnuts
2 ounces pine nuts (*pinoli*)
4 ounces granulated sugar
2 tablespoons vanilla bean-flavored
  sugar, or 1 teaspoon vanilla
  extract and 2 tablespoons
  granulated sugar

PLUS
5 tablespoons granulated sugar
8 tablespoons unbleached
  all-purpose flour
3 extra-large eggs
1 tablespoon (½ ounce)
  sweet butter
1 teaspoon baking powder

PERSIMMON CREAM
1 very ripe persimmon
3 extra-large egg yolks
5 tablespoons granulated sugar

PLUS
¾ cup heavy cream
1 tablespoon granulated sugar
1 teaspoon confectioners' sugar

Transfer the custard to a crockery or glass bowl to cool, about ½ hour. Then cover the bowl and place in the refrigerator.

Chill a metal bowl (stainless steel, not copper) and a wire whisk for preparing the whipped cream. Add the sugars to the cream and whip with the chilled whisk. Remove the persimmon custard from the refrigerator and gently fold it into the whipped cream. Transfer the persimmon cream into a crockery or glass bowl, cover and refrigerate until needed.

Serves 8 to 10.

EPIFANIA

When I was a child, Epiphany was a day of celebration. We would receive gifts from La Befana, the Good Witch, in honor of the presents that the Three Kings gave to the infant Jesus, and we were allowed to play all day and eat all the sweets we wanted. All year long, we reminded ourselves that on the eve of January 6, La Befana would ride from one chimney to the next on her broomstick and either punish us by leaving no presents, or reward us with gifts, depending on our behavior at home and at school. In those days, before the Christmas tree became popular in Italy, we would hang our stockings from the hood of the stove before going to bed and wake up to find that La Befana had filled the socks with cookies, chocolates and dried fruits.

Epiphany was always on the last day of our winter vacation from school. The celebration put a damper on my birthday, though, which was the next day. Not only did I have to go back to school, but I received only one gift—meant to serve for my birthday and Epiphany.

Though some of the gift-giving has since been moved to Christmas, Epiphany is still celebrated all over Italy. Each region has its specialty dishes, mainly desserts, which are prepared only for this occasion. The most famous of these are semolina fritters and winter fruits, mainly pears and apples, poached with different spices in red or white wine.

Corbezzole, *the berries of the so-called strawberry tree (a type of evergreen), turn from green to yellow to bright red as they ripen. They are ready to eat in early winter and are often used to make jams. Strawberry trees, really bushes, were in the past used to line boulevards.*

DESSERTS FOR EPIPHANY

While I was growing up, the real winter festivities centered around Epiphany, not Christmas. Each family had its own favorite desserts for the festive day, and my family's specialties included Torta di mele alle mandorle, *an apple-nut tart, and* Brutti ma buoni, *the cookies that are "ugly but good." Although these cookies have become so popular that they are available commercially I still prefer them homemade.*

The desserts most associated with Christmas—not only in Tuscany but all over Italy—are those of Siena, specifically panforte *and* ricciarelli, *both of which have become so famous that they are not only eaten all year long but are produced commercially and exported to other countries.*

TORTA DI MELE ALLE MANDORLE

Apple-Nut Tart

FLORENCE

Cut the apples into quarters, then peel and core them. Cut the lemon in half and squeeze it into a large bowl, discarding all of the seeds. Slice the apple quarters widthwise into very thin pieces, using a knife or mandolin. As each piece of apple is sliced, put it in the bowl with the lemon juice.

If you blanched the almonds yourself, be sure they are very dry; if necessary, place them in a 375-degree oven for 15 minutes.

Place the orange peel, almonds, sugar and flour in a food processor or blender and blend until the almonds resemble flour. Add the milk and eggs and blend again until a very smooth batter forms.

Preheat the oven to 375 degrees. Transfer the batter to the bowl with the apples and mix very well. Heavily butter the bottom and sides of a 13½-by-8¾-inch glass baking dish, then line it with the 2 tablespoons of sugar.

Transfer the contents of the bowl to the prepared baking pan, spreading the apple slices all over, and bake for 35 minutes. Remove the tart from the oven and let cool for a few minutes before sprinkling on the confectioners' sugar. Cut into squares and serve hot or at room temperature (after 1 or 2 hours).

Serves 6 to 8.

2 large yellow Delicious apples,
    ripe but not overripe
1 large lemon
Grated peel of 1 orange
    (see Appendix, page 292)
4 ounces blanched almonds
4 tablespoons granulated sugar
2 tablespoons unbleached
    all-purpose flour
½ cup whole milk
4 extra-large eggs

TO BAKE THE TART
2 tablespoons (1 ounce)
    sweet butter
2 tablespoons granulated sugar

TO SERVE
⅓ cup confectioners' sugar

Torta di mele alle mandorle, *the apple-nut tart favored by my family for the celebration of Epiphany. Mandarins and other types of oranges are the featured fruits of this holiday; here, to amuse the children, the oranges are presented with silver heads, arms and legs.*

BRUTTI MA BUONI O BRUTTI E BUONI

Ugly but Good Cookies

1¼ pounds almonds or hazelnuts
   or a combination of the two,
   blanched and lightly toasted
½ pound granulated sugar
6 extra-large egg whites,
   at room temperature
A large pinch of ground cinnamon
½ teaspoon domestic vanilla
   extract or 2 drops imported
   Italian (without water
   or alcohol)

TO BAKE THE COOKIES
Butter and flour for the
   cookie sheets

Finely chop ¾ pound of the nuts with 4 tablespoons of the sugar. Chop ¼ pound of the remaining nuts somewhat coarsely and the remaining ¼ pound very coarsely. Mix the finely ground and the coarsely ground nuts together.

Preheat the oven to 250 degrees.

Use a wire whisk and a copper bowl to beat the egg whites until soft peaks form. Start adding the remaining sugar, a little at a time, constantly beating the egg whites. Then start adding the ground nuts, heaping tablespoons at a time. Add the cinnamon and the vanilla extract. Transfer the contents of the bowl to a large casserole and place the casserole over medium heat for about 2 minutes, mixing constantly with a spatula, to "dry" the pastry.

Lightly butter and flour two cookie sheets, then spoon out 2 tablespoons of the batter to form little mounds on the cookie sheet. Bake for 45 minutes. Raise the heat to 300 degrees and bake for 40 minutes more. By that time the cookies should be golden and rather crisp. Remove the cookies from the oven, detach them from the sheet with a metal spatula, transfer them to a wire rack and let them rest for ½ hour until cold. By that time they should be very crisp. These cookies can be stored in an airtight container for several days.

Makes about 26 cookies.

Brutti ma buoni (*Ugly But Good Cookies*) sit on Prato's beautiful Bacchus fountain, which was executed by the seventeenth-century sculptor Ferdinando Tacca; he was also responsible for the twin fountains in Florence's Piazza Santissima Annunziata and a sculpture called The Moors *in Livorno. This fountain stands in front of the Palazzo Communale, the old City Hall, now home to a civic art museum. Natives of Prato claim that their* Brutti ma buoni *are the sister cookie to the celebrated* biscotti *or* cantucci *almond cookies.*

CHESTNUT-FLAVORED DESSERTS

The three recipes that follow all employ either chestnuts or chestnut flour, important staple ingredients during the winter when they are used in sweet and savory dishes, especially in the more rugged parts of Tuscany. The very rustic Necci, thin pancakes made from thick batter on a special pancake iron, are usually spread with fruit preserves, ricotta, or a soft cheese and then rolled up. This is a dessert to prepare in front of the fireplace on a cold winter night. From Lucca, there is the flat chestnut-flour cake called Castagnaccio, which is a bit different from its famous Florentine cousin of the same name in that grated orange peel and freshly ground black pepper (a medieval touch) are added to the batter. Torta di marroni al cioccolato relies on the perfect marriage of the chocolate and the chestnuts. This cake can be made with or without a glaze.

Necci (Chestnut Flour Pancakes) are made in the special two-part necci iron shown here. The antique Luccan design on the plate holding the rolled-up necci is called zampe di gallina (hen's feet) because the brown spots recall the bird's footprints. In the upper right of the photograph is a terra-cotta mold with a prominent scalloped edge, the kind of mold originally used to make Torta co' bischeri.

N E C C I

Chestnut Flour Pancakes

GARFAGNANA

Sift the flour to remove all the lumps. Place the flour in a bowl and make a well in the center. Start adding the water, little by little, mixing with a wooden spoon and very gradually incorporating the flour. When all the water is used up, add a pinch of salt and mix again. Be sure there are no lumps at all in the batter. Cover and let the batter rest for ½ hour in a cool place or on the bottom shelf of your refrigerator.

Heat the two parts of the *necci* iron over medium heat. When they are hot, about 375 degrees, season them very well with olive oil. Reheat the irons and when you are ready to prepare the *necci*, oil again. Pour ¼ cup of the batter in the center of one part of the iron, let the batter set, then oil the other iron again and place it on top of the half-cooked *neccio*. Let cook for 2 minutes, turning the whole thing over once. Transfer the prepared *neccio* to a platter and stuff it with either fruit preserves or cheese. *Necci* must be eaten as they are cooked, one after the other, stuffed and rolled up.

Repeat this procedure for as many *necci* as you need, oiling the iron each time.

Serves 8 to 10.

1½ cups Italian chestnut flour
1 cup cold water or whole milk
Pinch of salt

FOR THE STUFFING
Fruit preserves or homemade ricotta or other very soft cheese

CASTAGNACCIO ALLA LUCCHESE

Flat Chestnut Cake

Place the raisins in a small bowl with ½ cup of the milk and let rest for ½ hour.

When ready, drain the raisins and mix them with 2 table-spoons of the chestnut flour.

Place the remaining flour in a large crockery or glass bowl (if it is very lumpy, sift it first) and preheat the oven to 375 degrees. Make a well in the center of the flour and add the sugar, pine nuts, orange peel, salt and pepper. Start pouring in the remaining milk, a little at a time, mixing constantly with a wooden spoon, until all the milk is used up. Add the raisins and mix again.

With 3 tablespoons of the oil, grease a 14-inch round baking dish (preferably made of tin-lined copper).

Pour the contents of the bowl into the prepared dish and sprinkle the remaining olive oil all over. If desired, sprinkle the rosemary leaves over the batter. Bake for about 40 minutes. Remove from the oven and let cool for a few minutes before slicing. Serve with the orange zests.

Serves 8.

6 tablespoons raisins
4½ cups whole milk
3½ cups Italian chestnut flour
2 tablespoons granulated sugar
3 tablespoons pine nuts (*pinoli*)
    or walnuts
Grated peel of 1 orange
    (see Appendix, page 292)
Pinch of salt
Pinch of freshly ground black
    pepper
7 tablespoons olive oil

OPTIONAL
1 tablespoon fresh rosemary leaves

PLUS
Orange zests (see Appendix,
    page 292)

TORTA DI MARRONI AL CIOCCOLATO

Chestnut Torte with Chocolate

Soak the fresh chestnuts in a bowl of cold water overnight. The next morning, boil them in lightly salted water for about 1½ hours or until very soft. Drain the chestnuts and immediately peel them, removing both skins, then pass the fresh or canned chestnuts through a food mill, using first the disc with the largest holes, then the disc with the smallest holes, into a crockery or glass bowl. (You should have 10 ounces of riced chestnuts.)

Place a medium-sized stockpot of cold water over medium heat. Place the butter and chocolate in a large metal bowl. When the water reaches a boil, remove the pot from the heat and place the bowl with the butter and chocolate on top. When the chocolate is completely melted, after about 15 minutes, remove the bowl from the pot and use a wooden spoon to thoroughly mix together the chocolate and butter. Start adding the egg yolks, one at a time, constantly mixing, and when all the egg yolks are incorporated, add the rum and mix again.

Preheat the oven to 375 degrees.

Add the espresso and 5 tablespoons of the sugar to the riced chestnuts, mix very well, then pour in the prepared choco-

1 pound fresh chestnuts, preferably
    Italian *marroni*, or 10 ounces
    canned whole chestnuts
Coarse-grained salt
6 tablespoons (3 ounces)
    sweet butter
6 ounces bittersweet chocolate,
    in one piece
5 extra-large eggs, separated
3 tablespoons light rum
¾ cup espresso
6 tablespoons granulated sugar

PLUS
1 tablespoon (½ ounce)
    sweet butter
2 ounces butter cookies or
    tea biscuits, pulverized in a
    food processor

late mixture. Keep mixing until a very smooth but fairly thick batter forms.

Heavily butter a 10-inch springform pan, then line it with the cookie crumbs, discarding the excess crumbs.

Use a wire whisk and a copper bowl to beat the egg whites with the remaining tablespoon of sugar, until soft peaks form, then gently incorporate them into the chestnut mixture, using a spatula.

I made the chocolate leaves for this Torta di marroni al cioccolato *(Chestnut Torte with Chocolate) with the delicate leaves of a chestnut tree. The veins on these leaves are almost invisible, but, fortunately, an impression of them came through clearly in the chocolate. The plate in this photograph is an antique from Montelupo.*

FOR THE GLAZE
4 ounces bittersweet chocolate,
    cut into pieces
4 tablespoons (2 ounces)
    sweet butter
3 teaspoons light corn syrup

Pour the contents of the bowl into the prepared form and bake for 45 minutes. If the top of the torte starts to become too dark, place a piece of aluminum foil over it. Remove the torte from the oven and let it rest on a rack for about 15 minutes before opening the form and transferring the cake to a wire rack lined with parchment paper.

When the cake is almost cool, after about 25 minutes, prepare the glaze by placing the chocolate, butter and syrup in a small saucepan over medium heat. Mix constantly with a wooden spoon until all the ingredients are well combined and a very smooth sauce forms. Keep stirring as you start pouring the sauce all over the cake, being sure to completely cover both the top and the sides of the cake. Let the glaze harden before transferring the cake to a large round serving platter. The torte may be served with a dab of whipped cream.

Serves 8.

TORTA DI FARRO

Wheat Berry Cake

Farro (a type of soft wheat berry and an ingredient that survives from ancient times) is employed not only in the famous Zuppa di farro from Lucchesia, but also in the Torta di farro. For this cake, the soaked wheat berries are boiled with orange and lemon peel, then added to a ricotta-based batter. This version does not include a crust, which I prefer for two reasons: The cake is lighter and there is nothing to compete with the texture of the berries.

Rinse the farro under cold running water until the water runs clear, then soak it in a bowl of cold water for ½ hour.

Pour the milk and water into a medium-sized stockpot, set the pot over medium heat and when the mixture reaches a boil, add the butter, sugar, lemon peel, orange peel and salt. Drain the farro and add it to the pot. Stir constantly for 2 minutes, until it reaches a boil again. Simmer for 1 hour, stirring every so often to be sure the wheat does not stick to the bottom of the pot. Drain the wheat, discard the liquid and let the wheat rest in the colander, covered, until cool, about ½ hour.

Place the ricotta, granulated sugar, confectioners' sugar, eggs and grated orange peel in a large crockery or glass bowl. Mix very well with a wooden spoon, then discard the lemon and orange peel from the cooled wheat and add the wheat to the bowl with the other ingredients. Mix very well with a wooden spoon.

Preheat the oven to 375 degrees and heavily butter, with the 1 tablespoon of butter, a 10-inch springform pan. Line the bottom and sides of the pan with the ground cookies and discard the excess crumbs.

Pour the wheat mixture into the prepared form and bake for 1 hour 25 minutes. Remove the cake from the oven and let it rest for 20 minutes before opening the form and transferring the cake to a serving platter. Let the cake rest until completely cold before serving.

To serve, sprinkle confectioners' sugar over the top of the cake and cut it into wedges.

Serves 8 to 10.

TO COOK THE FARRO
8 ounces farro (soft wheat berries)
6 cups whole milk
1 quart cold water
2 tablespoons (1 ounce)
    sweet butter
2 tablespoons granulated sugar
Peel of 1 lemon
Peel of 1 orange
Pinch of salt

FOR THE CAKE
15 ounces ricotta, drained very well
6 ounces granulated sugar
4 tablespoons confectioners' sugar
6 extra-large eggs
Grated peel of 1 orange with
thick skin

TO BAKE
1 tablespoon (½ ounce)
sweet butter
3 ounces finely ground crisp
ladyfingers (Italian *savoiardi*)
or any other hard cookie,
such as champagne puffs

TO SERVE
Confectioners' sugar

*The dining room of Lucca's
Bucadisantantonio restaurant with its
beautiful collection of copper and brass
pots and implements. This was once an
important stop for travelers in search of
food and wine, and there still exists a
document that was posted there in 1782
by the Duchy of Lucca prohibiting the
restaurant from serving foreign wines.
On the table in front are three servings of
Torta di farro (Wheat Berry Cake).*

Livorno-Style Bomboloni

The cooked potato that is added to the yeast dough differentiates bomboloni *made in Livorno from those made in other parts of Tuscany. While you do not taste the potato, it affects the outcome quite a bit, yielding softer, moister bomboloni. Bomboloni are extremely popular and are found at every Tuscan fair.*

Boil the potato (with the skin on) in salted water, until very soft.

Meanwhile, prepare the sponge: Place the ¾ cup of flour in a small bowl and make a well in the center. Dissolve the yeast in the lukewarm or hot milk, then pour it into the well along with the salt. Start taking the flour from the edges of the well, a little at a time, using a wooden spoon, until all the flour is incorporated into the dissolved yeast. Sprinkle over the remaining tablespoon of flour, cover the bowl with a towel and let rest, in a warm place away from drafts, until doubled in size, about 1 hour. (Two signs that the sponge has doubled in size are the disappearance of the tablespoon of flour or the formation of large cracks on top.)

Melt the butter in a large metal bowl over boiling water, then remove the bowl from the heat and let cool for about 15 minutes.

When the potato is ready and the sponge has almost doubled in size, peel the potato and pass it through a food mill, using the disc with the smallest holes, into a crockery or glass bowl. Measure out 8 ounces of the riced potatoes and discard the rest.

Add the lemon peel to the melted butter, mix very well, then start adding the eggs, one at a time, constantly mixing with a wooden spoon, always in the same direction. Add the sugar, then add the sponge and the potato and mix until a thick but very smooth batter forms. Start adding the flour, ¼ cup at a time, constantly mixing, and when all the flour but ½ cup is used up, stir in the milk followed by the remaining flour. The dough should be very elastic and smooth. Cover the bowl with a towel and let rest, in a warm place away from drafts, until doubled in size, about 1 hour.

Sprinkle the cup of flour all over a board, transfer the risen dough to the board, then start kneading in a folding motion, trying not to absorb a lot of the flour.

Roll the dough out gently with a rolling pin to make a sheet about ¼ inch thick, then cut out about 14 discs with a 3-inch round cookie cutter. Transfer the *bomboloni* onto a very well floured cotton dish towel and cover them with a second dish towel.

1 large all-purpose potato
   (about 8 ounces)
Coarse-grained salt

FOR THE SPONGE
¾ cup plus 1 tablespoon
   unbleached all-purpose flour
1 ounce fresh compressed yeast or
   2 packages active dry yeast
½ cup lukewarm or hot milk,
   depending on the yeast
Pinch of salt

FOR THE DOUGH
3 tablespoons (1½ ounces)
   sweet butter
Grated peel of 2 large lemons
   (see Appendix, page 292)
3 extra-large eggs
5 tablespoons granulated sugar
2 ¾ cups unbleached all-purpose
   flour
½ cup lukewarm milk

TO PREPARE THE *BOMBOLONI*
About 1 cup unbleached
   all-purpose flour

TO DEEP-FRY
1 quart vegetable oil (⅔ corn oil,
   ⅓ sunflower oil)

TO SERVE
Granulated sugar

STUFFING (OPTIONAL)
Pastry cream or chocolate pastry
   cream (see Note)

Reassemble the leftover dough into a ball. Stretch it out again with a rolling pin and repeat as before. Let the *bomboloni* rest until doubled in size, about 1 hour.

Heat the oil in a deep-fat fryer over medium heat and when the oil reaches about 375 degrees, use a spatula to transfer the *bomboloni* to the hot oil. Fry them for about 15 seconds on each side; they should be very puffy and golden.

Transfer the *bomboloni* to a platter lined with paper towels, then roll them in the granulated sugar and serve hot.

Note: If you want to stuff the *bomboloni* with pastry cream, use a syringe to insert the stuffing before rolling them in sugar.

Makes 24.

MIGLIACCIO DI FARINA GIALLA

Flat Cornmeal Cake

To *a non-Tuscan,* Migliaccio di farina gialla, *a flat cake made with cornmeal, not flour, might seem more like a savory dish as opposed to a dessert, though it is certainly sweet thanks to the addition of a generous quantity of raisins.*

9 ounces raisins
4½ cups whole milk
8 tablespoons (4 ounces) sweet butter, cut into pats
8 tablespoons granulated sugar
A large pinch of salt
1 pound fine stone-ground yellow cornmeal, preferably imported Italian
1½ teaspoons baking powder
Grated peel of 1 large lemon (see Appendix, page 292)

PLUS
2 tablespoons (1 ounce) sweet butter

TO SERVE
Confectioners' sugar

Place the raisins and ½ cup of the milk in a crockery or glass bowl and soak for ½ hour.

Place the butter in a large crockery or glass bowl, sprinkle on the sugar, then the salt, and cover everything with the cornmeal.

Bring the remaining 4 cups milk to a boil, pour it into the large bowl containing the cornmeal, mix very well with a wooden spoon and let rest until cool, about 1 hour.

Preheat the oven to 375 degrees and use the 2 tablespoons butter to heavily grease a 14-inch round cake pan (preferably made of tin-lined copper). Drain the raisins and add them to the cornmeal mixture, mix very well, then add the baking powder and lemon peel and mix again. Transfer the thick cornmeal batter to the buttered pan, making sure it is evenly distributed.

Bake the cake for 1 hour 15 minutes, until a golden crust has formed on top and the inside of the cake is completely cooked (see Note). Remove the cake from the oven and cool for a few minutes, then sprinkle with the confectioners' sugar and serve in slices.

Note: The baking time will be much shorter if you are using an aluminum or other metal pan, rather than a tin-lined copper pan. Bake the *migliaccio* until a toothpick inserted in the center comes out completely dry.

Serves 12.

CIOCCOLATA IN TAZZA

Florentine-Style Hot Chocolate

FLORENCE

One of the joys of winter in Florence is spending the afternoon in one of the old cafés, slowly sipping a cup of rich hot chocolate topped with a mound of freshly whipped cream. In these days of powdered mixes, it is a relief to see that real hot chocolate is still being served there.

4 ounces semisweet chocolate,
    cut into small pieces
1 tablespoon (½ ounce)
    sweet butter
½ cup whole milk
2 cups heavy cream

PLUS
1 cup heavy cream
1 tablespoon granulated sugar
1 teaspoon confectioners' sugar

Place the chocolate, butter, milk and heavy cream in a medium-size saucepan over medium heat. When the mixture reaches a boil, start stirring with a wooden spoon until the chocolate is completely melted. Serve immediately or simmer longer to reduce it to a very dense, brownish hot chocolate.

Serve in heated cappuccino cups with tablespoons of whipped cream, made with the heavy cream, granulated sugar and confectioners' sugar, on top.

Serves 4.

TORTA DI RISO AL LIMONE

Tart Filled with Rice Custard

The Italian winter season ends with Carnevale, the burst of merriment that lightens the gloom of February and prepares us for the sacrifices of Lent. In the past, the holiday included masked balls and theatrical and operatic performances as well as disguised revelers celebrating in the streets. The great capitals of Venice,

A major event of Carnival in Florence used to be the great race of the carriages of the nobility, beginning, as seen in this nineteenth-century painting by Signorini, in the Piazza Santa Croce, and continuing through the city streets to the finish line at the S. Trinita bridge. These races were so popular that half of the grand entrance stairway to Florence's old abbey church, the Badia Fiorentina, was destroyed to create more space on the street to accommodate the racing carriages.

Naples and Florence were the scenes of the most elaborate celebrations, and many foods—multilayered pasta dishes and grand desserts—were reserved just for this occasion. Today, there are fewer public events but the holiday spirit still lives, especially in family celebrations.

For our Carnevale dessert, my family, with our fondness for the little Florentine rice cakes (called budini di riso), has always chosen Torta di riso al limone, more elaborate than the budini but reminiscent of them. During Carnevale, the little fried pastry snacks called cenci (or rags), because of their misshapen appearance, are popular with all Florentines.

Place the milk in a medium-sized saucepan over medium heat. When the milk reaches a boil, add the rice, along with the lemon peel, salt, sugar and butter. Let simmer for 20 minutes, then drain the rice and let it rest in the colander for 1 hour, covered with plastic wrap to prevent it from drying out.

Prepare the crust: Finely grind the almonds with the sugar in a food processor or blender. Transfer the almond mixture to a board, then add the egg, flour, confectioners' sugar, butter, lemon extract and salt. Use a metal dough scraper to quickly amalgamate all these ingredients, then refrigerate, wrapped in plastic wrap, for as long as possible, even overnight.

Prepare the custard: Bring water to a boil in the bottom of a double boiler. Put the egg yolks in a crockery or glass bowl. Add the sugar and stir, always in the same direction, with a wooden spoon, until the sugar is completely incorporated and the egg yolks turn a light yellow color. Slowly add the cream, milk, and grated lemon peel, stirring constantly. When the water in the bottom part of the double boiler starts to boil, transfer the cream mixture in the bowl to the top part of the double boiler and insert over the bottom part of the double boiler. Cook, stirring constantly, always in the same direction, until thick enough to coat the spoon. Do not allow to boil! Immediately remove the top part of the double boiler from the heat and continue to stir for 2 to 3 minutes; then transfer the custard to a crockery or glass bowl and let cool completely, about ½ hour. Combine the cooled custard with the rice, discarding the large piece of lemon peel.

Preheat the oven to 375 degrees and lightly butter a 10-inch fluted tart pan with a removable bottom. Lightly knead the pastry for the crust on a floured surface, then place the pastry between two large pieces of plastic wrap and use a rolling pin to stretch it into a disc about 13 inches in diameter. Peel off the top piece of the plastic wrap, then invert the bottom part onto the prepared pan. Peel off the plastic wrap and gently press down the pastry all around the pan. Cut off any excess pastry that hangs over the side of the pan.

Fill the tart with the prepared rice mixture and bake for 40 minutes. Remove from the oven, transfer to a rack and let cook for 15 minutes before removing the tart from the pan.

Serve hot or at room temperature. Sprinkle with confectioners' sugar just before serving and slice like a pie.

To reheat the tart, wrap it in aluminum foil and place it in a 375-degree oven for 15 minutes.

Serves 8.

3 cups whole milk
½ cup raw rice, preferably
    Italian Arborio
Large piece of lemon peel
Pinch of salt
1 tablespoon granulated sugar
1 tablespoon (½ ounce)
    sweet butter

FOR THE CRUST
2 ounces blanched almonds
4 tablespoons granulated sugar
1 extra-large egg
¾ cup unbleached all-purpose flour
2 tablespoons confectioners' sugar
4 tablespoons (2 ounces)
    sweet butter
1 teaspoon domestic lemon extract
    or 1 drop imported Italian
    (without alcohol or oil)
A large pinch of salt

FOR THE CUSTARD
4 extra-large egg yolks
4 heaping tablespoons granulated
    sugar
1 cup heavy cream
1 cup whole milk
Grated peel of 2 medium-sized
    lemons with thick skin
    (see Appendix, page 292)

TO SERVE
Sifted confectioners' sugar

Although neither Zuccotto all'alkermes nor Torta della zia is associated with a specific holiday, both are commonly served at special family celebrations in Tuscany. When unmolded, the dome-shaped Zuccotto all'alkermes reveals its striking red color, the result of soaking the spongecake in the Medici liqueur known as Alkermes. This dessert is often compared to Brunelleschi's great terra-cotta-colored dome on Florence's cathedral. Because Alkermes is difficult to find, I have included instructions for making it in the recipe.

Different varieties of Torta della zia, a ricotta-custard cake, are found all over Italy. This version is flavored with rum as well as raisins, pine nuts and almonds.

ZUCCOTTO ALL'ALKERMES

Zuccotto with Alkermes

FLORENCE

FOR THE SPONGECAKE
(*BOCCA DI DAMA*)
6 extra-large eggs, separated
8 ounces granulated sugar
Grated peel of 1 large orange
    (see Appendix, page 292)
2 ounces potato starch
2 ounces unbleached all-purpose
    flour
Pinch of salt

FOR THE STUFFING
2 ounces candied orange peel,
    cut into ½-inch pieces
½ cup light rum
3 extra-large eggs, separated
6 tablespoons granulated sugar
2 tablespoons confectioners' sugar
¾ cup dry white wine
1½ cups heavy cream

(continued on next page)

Prepare the sponge cake up to two days in advance: Place the egg yolks in a crockery or glass bowl. Add the sugar and orange peel. Mix with a wooden spoon until the sugar is completely incorporated and dissolved and the eggs are lighter in color.

Mix the potato starch and flour together. Add the salt. Add this mixture to the egg yolk mixture, a little at a time, mixing constantly with a wooden spoon. When all the flour is used up, lightly butter a 10-inch round cake pan. Preheat the oven to 375 degrees.

Beat the egg whites, in a copper bowl with a wire whisk, until stiff, then gently fold them into the batter with a rubber spatula. Pour the contents of the bowl into the prepared pan and bake for about 45 minutes. Remove the cake from the oven and let it rest for at least 20 minutes before unmolding onto a rack. Invert the cake and let cool completely.

The following day prepare the stuffing: Soak the orange peel in the rum for ½ hour.

Place the egg yolks in a crockery or glass bowl, add 3 tablespoons of the granulated sugar and 1 tablespoon of the confectioners' sugar, and mix very well with a wooden spoon, until all the sugar is completely dissolved.

Meanwhile, set a pot of cold water over medium heat. Add the wine to the egg mixture and mix again. When the water in the pot reaches a boil, transfer the egg mixture to a lined or unlined copper bowl and fit the bowl over the boiling water. Be sure the water does not touch the bottom part of the insert. Drain the orange peel, discarding the rum, and add the peel to the egg mixture. Stir continuously with a wooden spoon until the egg mixture is quite thick. Immediately remove the insert

(c o n t i n u e d)

from the boiling water, mix the egg mixture and transfer it to a crockery or glass bowl. Let the egg mixture cool completely, about 1 hour.

Meanwhile, prepare a syrup: Place the ½ cup cold water, the sugar and lemon juice in a small saucepan over low heat. When it starts to boil, stir lightly to keep the sugar from sticking to the sides. Brush the inside part of the pan, just above the level of the syrup, with cold water to prevent the sugar from crystallizing, and continue to cook until a syrup forms.

Meanwhile, in a copper bowl with a wire whisk, beat the 3 leftover egg whites with 1 tablespoon of the remaining granulated sugar and ½ tablespoon of the remaining confectioners' sugar, until stiff.

Transfer the prepared syrup to a glass measuring cup to cool it slightly, then start pouring it, in a thin stream, into the beaten egg whites, continuously beating the whites with the syrup, until all the syrup is incorporated.

Whip the cream with the remaining granulated sugar and confectioners' sugar using a chilled wire whisk and a chilled metal bowl. Incorporate the cooled custard cream into the whipped cream, using a whisk, then gently fold in the egg whites, using a rubber spatula so that a lot of air is incorporated. Add the walnuts and refrigerate, covered, until needed.

Assemble the *zuccotto*: Cut the completely cold *bocca di dama* into ½-inch-thick slices and cut the slices in half. Lay the slices on a large serving platter and sprinkle the Alkermes all over. Line an 8-inch *zuccotto* mold (if you do not have a *zuccotto* mold, use an 8-inch dome-shaped glass mold) with the slices of sponge cake, placed vertically, so that the darker crusts of the slices make vertical ribs. Use the best slices and reserve the others for the top part of the mold, which will actually be on the bottom of the cake once it is unmolded. Place the prepared stuffing in the mold and make a layer of sponge cake with the remaining slices.

Cover the mold with its lid or with aluminum foil and place the mold in the freezer for ½ hour. Then refrigerate for at least 2 hours before unmolding the *zuccotto* onto a serving platter. The *zuccotto* should be uniformly red (as a result of the Alkermes that was poured all over); if it isn't, pour on more of the liqueur. Slice it like a cake and serve.

Note: Cochineal, which is used more for its red color than for its flavor, can be replaced by a vegetable coloring. Already prepared essence of Alkermes is available at Milan Laboratory, 57 Spring Street, New York, New York 10012. The essence must be mixed with grain alcohol or unflavored vodka. See the instructions on the bottle for proportions.

Serves 8 to 10.

The ingredients for making Alkermes, the red-colored Medici liqueur, in one of the rooms in the Bardini museum in Florence. The chest, taken from a church sacristy, dates back to the fifteenth century; the Madonna and Child is the work of the fifteenth-century sculptor, Benedetto da Maiano. This museum, which was once a palace, is located on the Piazza de' Mozzi. It is one of the hidden treasures of Florence.

FOR THE SYRUP
½ cup cold water
½ cup granulated sugar
2 drops lemon juice

PLUS
2 ounces walnuts, coarsely chopped

FOR ASSEMBLING THE *ZUCCOTTO*
¾ cup Alkermes (see recipe on page 283, or purchase at a liquor store)

ALKERMES (See Note)

12 grams cinnamon

10 grams coriander seeds

7 grams cochineal

3 grams mace

2.5 grams whole cloves

5 grams dried orange peel

3 grams aniseed

10 pods cardamom

½ vanilla bean

3 cups grain alcohol or unflavored
  80-proof vodka

3½ cups cold water

1¾ pounds granulated sugar

½ cup rose water

Preparing Alkermes at Home

This recipe makes about 7 cups of Alkermes. You will only need
¾ cup for the recipe for Zuccotto all'Alkermes.

To prepare the Alkermes, place all the spices except for the
vanilla bean in a marble mortar and grind them very well with
the pestle. Cut the vanilla bean into five pieces.

Place the ground spices and vanilla pieces in a glass jar with
a screw top. Add the grain alcohol or the vodka and 1½ cups of
the cold water, then close the jar and let it stand for one week,
shaking the jar once a day.

When ready, dissolve the sugar in the remaining 2 cups of
cold water. Add the water with the dissolved sugar to the jar,
cover and let rest for one more day, shaking the jar twice during
this period.

Strain the contents of the jar through a coffee filter into a
large crockery or glass bowl. Add the rose water to the bowl,
then transfer the contents to two bottles. Close the bottles and
let them rest for one more day.

Ricotta Custard Cake

Wet a medium-sized casserole with a few drops of cold water before adding the milk, so that the milk will not stick to the bottom of the casserole. Bring the milk to a simmer over medium heat, lower the heat, then add the vanilla bean and cook for 15 minutes.

Meanwhile, soak the raisins with 4 tablespoons of the rum in a small crockery or glass bowl.

When ready, remove the milk from the heat, pass it through a cheesecloth into a crockery or glass bowl and let cool for ½ hour.

Prepare a very light golden caramelized sugar to line the mold: Place the sugar and water in an enamel or unlined copper saucepan set over medium heat and stir with a wooden spoon until the mixture starts to bubble. Add the lemon juice and simmer, allowing the thick syrup to melt into a smoother one, until it turns a light golden color. Brush the inside part of the saucepan with a brush dampened with cold water to prevent the sugar from crystallizing. This process should take about 15 minutes.

Lightly butter a 3-quart ring mold before lining it with the caramel.

Preheat the oven to 400 degrees and prepare a *bagno maria* (water bath), using a large baking pan that is lined on the bottom with a cotton towel or several layers of paper towels.

Finely grind the soaked raisins (they should have absorbed all of the rum by this point) and coarsely grind the pine nuts and almonds together. Add the raisins (plus any rum that the raisins haven't absorbed) and nuts to the bowl of milk; then add the ricotta, the remaining 4 tablespoons of rum, and the granulated and confectioners' sugars. Mix very well with a wooden spoon. Start adding the eggs and egg yolks, one at a time, continuously stirring with the wooden spoon. When all the eggs and egg yolks are incorporated, transfer the mixture to the prepared mold and place it in the baking pan with enough lukewarm water to reach the height of the mixture in the mold. Bake for 1½ hours.

Remove the cake from the oven and let cool on a rack for 15 minutes. When ready, invert the mold onto a large round serving platter but do not lift it off. Refrigerate the cake, with the mold over it, for at least 2 hours. Lift off the mold and cut into wedges to serve.

Serves 8 to 10.

4 cups whole milk
1 (2-inch) piece vanilla bean
4 ounces raisins
8 tablespoons white rum
4 ounces pine nuts (*pinoli*)
2 ounces blanched almonds
15 ounces whole-milk ricotta, drained very well
5 tablespoons granulated sugar
2 tablespoons confectioners' sugar
6 extra-large eggs
3 extra-large egg yolks

FOR THE MOLD
1 cup granulated sugar
½ cup cold water
5 drops lemon juice

TORTA MANTOVANA O LA MANTOVANA

Tuscan Pound Cake

1 extra-large egg
3 extra-large egg yolks
8 ounces granulated sugar
12 tablespoons (6 ounces)
    sweet butter
8 ounces unbleached all-purpose
    flour
Grated peel of 1 orange or lemon
    (see Appendix, page 292)

TO BAKE
Butter and flour for the ring mold
1 ounce almonds, blanched and
    finely ground with 1 tablespoon
    granulated sugar

TO SERVE
Confectioners' sugar

Prato, near Florence, is quite far from Mantova in Lombardy, so it is interesting to consider just why a cake from Prato would be called Montovana (see photograph of the cake on page 41). The current favorite theory recalls that Isabella d'Este, married to the Duke of Mantova, often visited the Medici in Florence. It is thought that during one of Isabella's visits she shared the recipe for Torta Paradiso *(a favorite Mantova cake named after one of her palaces) with the Medici. Over the centuries, the people of Prato and Pistoia developed this somewhat different cake, but remembered its inspiration from Mantova. The original* Torta paradiso *is still made in Mantova but is never called* Torta Mantovana.

Both Torta Montovana *and* Torta paradiso *resemble the English and American pound cake in their near equal proportions of flour, butter, sugar and eggs, and it seems likely that the origins of both of these cakes, as well as the related English plum cake, lie in the* Mantovana *and the* Paradiso.

Place the whole egg, egg yolks and sugar in a crockery or glass bowl or in the bowl of a food processor or blender. Blend or mix with a wooden spoon until the sugar is completely incorporated into the eggs and the mixture resembles a whipped custard cream.

Melt the butter in the top of a double boiler and let cool completely. Start adding the flour, a little at a time, constantly mixing or blending. Add the cooled butter and grated peel and mix again.

Lightly butter and flour a 12-inch ring mold and preheat the oven to 325 degrees. Pour the thick batter into the prepared mold, sprinkle the almonds on top and bake for 55 minutes. Remove from the oven and let the cake rest for at least 1 hour before unmolding onto a serving platter. Sprinkle with confectioners' sugar before serving.

Serves 6 to 8.

SAUCES

In this book, the basic Italian sauces, such as balsamella or salsa bianca, are presented in connection with the first recipe in which they appear, and when used again, the reader is referred to that page. Most of the other sauces are presented as part of a specific recipe for pasta, risotto, meat, fish or fowl, or even a vegetable or dessert. I chose to do it this way because these sauces are associated with a particular dish and do not exist independently.

There is, however, a body of sauces, mainly herb, green and tomato sauces, that can accompany many different recipes. I include here a small number of these sauces.

The first sauce, Pommarola all'olio, is a tomato sauce made with aromatic vegetables and herbs. It differs from the classic pommarola sauce in that the flavor of olive oil is strong and the butter is omitted. This particular version may be used with pasta as well as boiled meats (but not with fish).

Also for boiled meats are the sauce from Siena called Salsa al dragoncello con prezzemolo, which is based on the combination of tarragon (that city's favorite herb) with wine *vinegar and parsley;* Salsa al ramerino, *a green sauce featuring rosemary (*ramerino *is the Tuscan vernacular for* rosmarino, *the Italian word for rosemary); and* Mostarda alla toscana, *which is made by marinating the must of very ripe grapes with mustard seed and then combining the must with unripe pears and green apples that have been cooked in Vinsanto flavored with sugar, cinnamon and clove. In the classic version of this sauce, which comes from Mantova, only unripe fruit is used. The final sauce for meat is* Salsa d'agresto, *made with tiny unripe grapes combined with a variety of ingredients, including onion, parsley, garlic, almonds, walnuts and—to contrast with the sourness of the grapes—honey, which is a Renaissance touch.*

To be used with either meat or fish is Salsa ai capperi al limone, *which features the flavors of capers, lemon juice and vinegar. For fish only, there is* Salsa di cipolline, *in which chopped scallions are cooked in white wine vinegar and combined with chopped walnuts, capers and olive oil.*

POMMAROLA ALL'OLIO

Spring Tomato Sauce with Olive Oil

Very coarsely chop the onion, celery, garlic, carrot, parsley and basil all together on a board. If fresh tomatoes are used, cut them into large pieces.

Place the fresh or canned tomatoes in a medium-sized non-reactive casserole and add the chopped vegetables and 2 tablespoons of the olive oil. Set the casserole, covered, over low heat and cook for 1½ hours, shaking (but not mixing) every so often, to prevent the tomatoes from sticking to the bottom.

Pass the contents of the casserole through a food mill, using the disc with the smallest holes, into a second casserole. Place the casserole with the sauce over medium heat and add the remaining oil and salt and pepper. Mix very well and let reduce for 15 minutes, stirring every so often with a wooden spoon.

When ready, transfer the sauce to a crockery or glass bowl and let stand until needed. The sauce can be prepared up to two days in advance and kept, covered, in the refrigerator.

Makes about 2 cups.

1 medium-sized red onion, cleaned
1 medium-sized celery stalk
1 large clove garlic, peeled
1 medium-sized carrot, scraped
10 sprigs Italian parsley, leaves only
8 large basil leaves, fresh or
    preserved in salt
2 pounds very ripe fresh tomatoes
    or 2 pounds drained canned
    tomatoes, preferably
    imported Italian
4 tablespoons olive oil
Salt and freshly ground black pepper

SALSA AL DRAGONCELLO CON PREZZEMOLO

Tarragon Sauce with Parsley

Soak the bread in the water for 5 minutes. Squeeze the water out of the bread and place the bread in a crockery or glass bowl.

Finely chop the garlic on a board, then add the parsley and tarragon and finely chop all together. Transfer the chopped ingredients to the bowl with the bread, season with salt and pepper, then, if desired, add the egg yolk, mashing it very well. Start adding the olive oil, a little at a time, constantly mixing with a wooden spoon. When all the oil is used up, taste for salt and pepper, mix again and refrigerate, covered, for at least ½ hour before using.

When ready to serve, add the vinegar and mix very well.

Makes ¾ cup.

3 slices white bread, crusts removed
1 cup cold water
3 large cloves garlic, peeled
25 sprigs Italian parsley, leaves only
7 tablespoons fresh tarragon leaves
Salt and freshly ground black pepper
1 extra-large hard-boiled egg yolk
    (optional)
¾ cup olive oil
1 teaspoon red wine vinegar

SALSA AL RAMERINO

Rosemary Sauce

2 tablespoons fresh rosemary leaves
1 medium-sized clove garlic, peeled
3 tablespoons (1½ ounces) sweet
    butter
2 tablespoons olive oil
Salt and freshly ground black pepper
2 tablespoons red wine vinegar
3 slices white bread, crusts removed

Finely chop the rosemary and garlic together on a board. Heat the butter and olive oil in a small saucepan over medium heat and when the butter is completely melted, add the chopped ingredients and sauté for about 3 minutes. Season with salt and pepper, then add the vinegar and let it evaporate for 3 minutes. Remove the saucepan from the heat and let the sauce rest for 10 minutes.

Meanwhile, soak the bread in a bowl of lukewarm water for 5 minutes. Squeeze out the water from the bread, then put the squeezed bread and the contents of the saucepan in a blender or food processor and blend them together well.

Transfer the sauce to a crockery or glass bowl and taste for salt and pepper, then mix very well and refrigerate, covered, for at least 1 hour before serving.

Makes about 1 cup.

SALSA AI CAPPERI AL LIMONE

Caper Sauce with Lemon

2 ounces capers, preserved in wine
    vinegar, drained
4 tablespoons olive oil
Salt and freshly ground black pepper
1 medium-sized clove garlic, peeled
2 tablespoons (1 ounce) sweet
    butter, at room temperature
1 scant tablespoon unbleached
    all-purpose flour
1 cup lukewarm homemade
    chicken broth
1 tablespoon freshly squeezed
    lemon juice
1 scant tablespoon red wine vinegar

Finely chop the capers on a board and transfer them to a small crockery or glass bowl. Add the oil and salt and pepper to taste. Mix all the ingredients well with a wooden spoon. Let stand until needed.

Finely chop the garlic and transfer it to a second crockery or glass bowl. Add the butter and flour to the garlic and combine with a fork until a thick paste is formed. Add the broth, lemon juice and wine vinegar, and mix again with a wooden spoon, adding a pinch of salt and pepper.

Transfer the caper mixture to a small heavy saucepan and place it over low heat. Sauté gently for 5 minutes, stirring occasionally with a wooden spoon, then add the broth mixture and mix very well to be sure that no lumps have formed. Simmer for about 10 minutes. By that time the sauce should be ready.

Makes about 1 cup.

MOSTARDA ALLA TOSCANA

Mustard-Flavored Fruit

Clean the grapes, discard the stems and rinse thoroughly under cold running water. Pat the grapes dry with paper towels. Mash the grapes in a marble mortar with a marble pestle and transfer the juice and the skins to a crockery or glass bowl. Cover the bowl and refrigerate for 2 days.

Peel the pears and apples, core them and cut into thin slices. Place the fruit in a medium-sized saucepan, along with the sugar, cinnamon, clove and Vinsanto. Set the saucepan over low heat and cook until all the liquid has evaporated and the fruit is quite soft.

Meanwhile, strain the grape must (the mashed grapes) into a second saucepan, add the mustard seeds and cook for about 20 minutes. By that time the must should be reduced by half. Strain the must again, discarding the mustard seeds, and, while it is still very hot, add it to the saucepan with the fruit. Cook for 2 minutes more, then transfer the contents to a crockery or glass bowl and cool completely.

When the sauce has cooled, add the citron and mix well. Transfer the sauce to a glass jar, cover and refrigerate. Serve very cold.

Note: Vinsanto is a dessert wine from Tuscany.

Makes 4 cups.

4 pounds very ripe and sweet
    seedless white grapes
3 unripe Bosc pears
3 unripe green apples or Granny
    Smith apples
2 tablespoons granulated sugar
A large pinch of ground cinnamon
1 whole clove
1 cup Vinsanto or dry sherry
    (see Note)
2 tablespoons hot mustard seeds
3 ounces candied citron, cut into
    tiny pieces

SALSA D'AGRESTO

Sauce of Unripe Grapes

After removing the stems, soak the grapes in a bowl of cold water for 15 minutes.

Combine the onion, parsley, garlic, almonds and walnuts in a food processor or blender and finely chop or grind. Transfer the ground ingredients to a small saucepan.

Soak the bread in the vinegar for 10 minutes. Very lightly squeeze the bread, leaving a lot of the vinegar in it. Add the bread to the saucepan.

Set the saucepan over low heat and, mixing constantly, add the honey and season with salt and pepper. Cook for 10 minutes, adding the broth as needed. The sauce should be rather thick.

Transfer the sauce to a crockery or glass bowl and let it cool completely before serving.

Makes about 1½ cups.

1 pound unripe grapes
1 small red onion, cleaned
15 sprigs Italian parsley, leaves only
1 clove garlic, peeled
2 ounces blanched almonds
2 ounces shelled walnuts
2 slices white bread, crusts removed
½ cup red wine vinegar
2 teaspoons honey
Salt and freshly ground black pepper
About ½ cup chicken or meat
    broth, preferably homemade

SALSA DI CIPOLLINE

Scallion Sauce for Fish

20 medium-sized scallions
20 sprigs Italian parsley, leaves only
1 large clove garlic, peeled
½ cup white wine vinegar
Salt and freshly ground black pepper
2 ounces shelled walnuts
3 heaping tablespoons capers,
    preserved in wine vinegar,
    drained
4 tablespoons olive oil

Clean the scallions, removing the dark green parts. Finely chop the white parts of the scallions together with the parsley and garlic on a board.

Pour the wine vinegar into a small saucepan, then add the chopped ingredients, place the pan over low heat and simmer for 10 minutes, stirring occasionally with a wooden spoon. Season with salt and pepper to taste.

Meanwhile, use a chopper or a food processor to finely chop the walnuts. When ready, add the nuts to the pan, reduce the heat to the lowest setting and cook for 5 minutes more, stirring constantly with a wooden spoon.

Transfer the contents of the pan to a food processor or food mill and, using the disc with the smallest holes, grind everything together, adding the capers and olive oil. The sauce should be smooth and homogenous.

Transfer the sauce to a crockery or glass bowl and cool completely before serving.

Makes about 1 ½ cups.

The branch of a walnut tree. The walnuts in their shells are protected by their tough green hulls, which dry up and open as the nuts mature. The nuts are sometimes picked while they are immature and used to make a liqueur; when the liqueur is ready, the soft nuts are eaten—hull and all.

A P P E N D I X

Grating Oranges and Lemons

Place a piece of parchment paper or thick waxed paper over the holes of a hand grater. Hold the paper in place with one hand while moving the orange or lemon back and forth on the paper with the other. Work on different sections of the paper so that the paper does not wear out. Use a rubber spatula to remove the grated orange or lemon peel from the paper. Do not use what is inside the grater or any of the white bitter part of the peel.

Making Orange or Lemon Zests

Orange or lemon zests, thin strips of the colored part of the fruit, can be made most easily with a citrus zester or a vegetable peeler. Simply pull the zester from the top of the fruit to the base so that you end up with long thin strips of zest. It is important not to catch any of the white pith, as it has a bitter flavor. Strips of zest can be cut from the fruit with a knife, although it is more difficult to make thin strips and to avoid the white pith.

Preserving Aromatic Herbs in Salt

Remove the leaves of the herbs from their stems without washing them. In a mason jar, make a ½-inch-thick layer of coarse-grained salt. Add a layer of herb leaves, then salt, and continue in this manner until all the leaves are used up or the jar is full, finishing with a layer of salt. Close the jar securely and keep in a cool place. To use the herbs, wash away the salt and any dirt that may be clinging to the leaves. Some herbs, such as basil, will lose some of their color, but they will not lose any of their flavor.

Dried and Blanched Rosemary Leaves

If you do not have fresh rosemary leaves or rosemary preserved in salt, blanch dried leaves in boiling water for a few seconds. Use the same quantity of blanched leaves as you would fresh.

Making Pasta with a Manual Pasta Machine

To prepare the pasta dough, place the flour in a mound on a pasta board and use a fork to make a well in the center. Place the eggs and salt (and any other ingredients specified in the recipe) in the well and, with a fork, combine them. Still using the fork, start to incorporate the flour from the inner rim of the well with the mixture in the center, always incorporating fresh flour from the lower part, pushing it under the dough that is forming to keep it from sticking to the board. Remove the pieces of dough attached to the fork and incorporate them. Use your hands to gather the dough together.

Scrape the board with a pastry scraper, putting together all the unincorporated flour. Place the sifter on the board and using one hand, "clean" the flour by moving the sifter back and forth without lifting the sifter from the board. Discard the globules of dough that remain in the sifter. With the palm of one hand, start kneading the dough on the board, folding the dough over with the other hand, absorbing the leftover flour from the board. Do not sprinkle the flour over the dough. Continue kneading for about 2 to 3 minutes, absorbing the flour, until the dough is not wet anymore and all but 4 or 5 tablespoons of the flour have been incorporated; the remaining flour will be used for kneading the dough with the pasta machine.

Use the palm of one hand to flatten the ball of dough to a thickness of about ½ inch so it can fit between the rollers of the pasta machine (If the pasta dough is made with more than 2 eggs, divide the dough into 1 cup portions before flattening it). Set the pasta machine at its widest setting and feed the dough through the rollers. With your hand, remove the layer of dough from underneath the pasta machine. Holding the layer of dough with both hands, gently flour one side of the dough by drawing it across the flour on the board. Fold the dough into thirds (folding the two short sides toward the center), and press down with your fingers, starting from one open side toward the opposite open side, so that the three layers are melded together and no air remains between them. Using the same wide setting of the rollers, insert one of the open ends of the folded layer of dough through the rollers. Continue folding and feeding the dough through the rollers 8 to 10 times or less, until the dough is very smooth and elastic. The pasta dough is now ready to be stretched. Move the rollers to a narrower setting, following the manufacturer's instructions for your machine.

Flour the layer of pasta on both sides by drawing it across the flour on the board. When feeding the layer of pasta into the machine, stand sideways in relation to the table, holding the handle of the machine with your right hand. Hold the other hand up sideways, keeping the four fingers together and holding the thumb out. Let the sheet of pasta rest over your hand between the first finger and the outstretched thumb. Pass the dough through the rollers once; do not fold any more. Move the wheel down to the next notch, passing the dough through the rollers just once. After passing each time, sprinkle the layer of pasta with a little flour. Each successive notch will produce a thinner layer of pasta. Repeat this procedure until the layer is the desired thickness, which is indicated in each recipe. Still letting the pasta hang over one hand, pull it out to its full length. Cut into the desired shape.

How to Tie a Piece of Meat Like a Salami

To tie a piece of meat like a salami, cut a piece of string six times the length of the meat to be tied. Place the string under one of the short sides of the rolled-up meat (about 1½ inches from the end) and make a knot, leaving only enough string on one side to pull over and knot the first ring in the center. Bring the long end of the string down the meat another 1½ inches, and hold the string in place with a finger. With the other hand, pull the string under and around again to the point where the string is being held by your finger. Pass the end of the string over and then under (like a sailor's knot). Remove your finger, hold the short end of the string with one hand and pull the other end tight with the other hand. Continue this process at 1½-inch intervals until you reach the opposite end of the meat. Stand the meat on one end and put the remaining string over the top end to the underside of the meat. As the string intersects with each ring of string, pull under and over, fastening in the same way as was done on the other side (it is no longer necessary to hold the string with your finger or to pull tight on this side). After the last intersection, tie a knot using the two ends of the string. When the meat is ready, you will only need to cut the string in one place in order to remove it.

Boning a Chicken as for a Galantine

Several recipes in this book require that you bone a chicken as for a galantine, but leave the skin attached to the meat. For these recipes, follow the instructions provided here. (Note that to make a true galantine, the boned meat is separated from the skin and cut into cubes or strips.)

Use a boning knife to cut through the skin of the chicken around the leg joint. Cut through again to sever the tendons, then twist and push out the leg to free it from the thigh bone. Repeat with the other leg.

Turn the chicken breast-side down, then, use the boning knife to cut through the skin and meat attached to the spine, cutting all the way down the back as far back as the tail so that the entire back is opened. Cut the tendons that connect the upper part of the thigh to the spine and cartilage. Cut the thigh bone free from the piece of cartilage left after the removal of the leg bone. Repeat with the other thigh.

Starting at the tail end of the back, begin to free the meat on both sides of the carcass. Continue to free all the meat around the breast, being sure that all the meat is completely detached and being careful not to make holes in the skin. At this point, the meat that remains is only attached at the tail end and to the center breast bone. Insert the knife, sharp-side up, between the meat and the end of the carcass just above the tail, and cut through. The tail will come off with it. Lift off the meat at the tail end of the carcass. Cut along the breast bone to detach the meat that is still attached to the carcass. If desired, reserve the carcass for preparing stock.

Open the whole boned chicken and remove the wishbone at the top of the breast. Detach the bone connecting the whole wing to the shoulder by cutting into the joint; then detach it at the other end, where it connects to the double bone of the second section of the wing, and discard. Cut off the tip of the wing and discard. Scrape the meat off the double bone of the second section of the wing and cut off the bone from the attached cartilage. The chicken is now completely boned but unlike the classic galantine, all the meat is left in place, attached to the skin. Tuck in the legs and wings.

CONVERSION CHART

BUTTER

In the United States, butter is generally sold in a one-pound package, which contains four equal "sticks." The wrapper on each stick is marked to show tablespoons, so the cook can cut the stick according to the quantity required. The equivalent weights are:

1 stick = 115 g/4 oz
1 tablespoon = 15 g/½ oz

FLOUR

To achieve a near equivalent to American all-purpose flour, use half British plain flour and half strong bread flour.

American cake flour can be replaced by British plain flour alone.

SUGAR

American granulated sugar is finer than British granulated, closer to caster sugar, so British cooks should use caster sugar throughout.

YEAST

Quantities of dried yeast (called active dry yeast in the United States) are usually given in number of packages. Each package contains 7 g/¼ oz of yeast, which is equivalent to a scant tablespoon.

INGREDIENTS AND EQUIPMENT GLOSSARY

The following ingredients and equipment are basically the same on both sides of the Atlantic, but have different names.

AMERICAN	BRITISH
arugula	rocket
baking soda	bicarbonate of soda
bell pepper	sweet pepper (capsicum)
Bibb and Boston lettuce	soft-leaved, round lettuce
broiler/to broil	grill/to grill
celery stalk	celery stick
cheesecloth	muslin
confectioners' sugar	icing sugar
cookie sheet	baking sheet
eggplant	aubergine
fava bean	broad bean
ground beef/pork	minced beef/pork
heavy cream (37.6% fat)	whipping cream (35–40% fat)
hot red pepper flakes	dried crushed red chilli
parchment paper	nonstick baking paper
Romaine lettuce	cos lettuce
scallion	spring onion
semisweet chocolate	plain chocolate
shrimp	prawn (varying in size)
skillet	frying pan
squab	young pigeon
unsweetened chocolate	bitter *chocolat pâtissier*
whole milk	homogenized milk
zucchini	courgette

VOLUME EQUIVALENTS

These are not exact equivalents, but have been rounded up or down slightly to make measuring easier.

AMERICAN	METRIC	IMPERIAL
¼ t	1.25 ml	
½ t	2.5 ml	
1 t	5 ml	
½ T (1½ t)	7.5 ml	
1 T (3 t)	15 ml	
¼ cup (4 T)	60 ml	2 fl oz
⅓ cup (5 T)	75 ml	2½ fl oz
½ cup (8 T)	125 ml	4 fl oz
⅔ cup (10 T)	150 ml	5 fl oz (¼ pint)
¾ cup (12 T)	175 ml	6 fl oz
1 cup (16 T)	250 ml	8 fl oz
1¼ cups	300 ml	10 fl oz (½ pint)
1½ cups	350 ml	12 fl oz
1 pint (2 cups)	500 ml	16 fl oz
1 quart (4 cups)	1 litre	1¾ pints

WEIGHT EQUIVALENTS

These are not exact equivalents, but have been rounded up or down slightly to make measuring easier.

AVOIRDUPOIS	METRIC
¼ oz	7 g
½ oz	15 g
1 oz	30 g
2 oz	60 g
3 oz	90 g
4 oz	115 g
5 oz	150 g
6 oz	175 g
7 oz	200 g

AVOIRDUPOIS	METRIC
8 oz	225 g
9 oz	250 g
10 oz	300 g
11 oz	325 g
12 oz	350 g
13 oz	375 g
14 oz	400 g
15 oz	425 g
1 lb	450 g
1 lb 2 oz	500 g
1½ lb	750 g
2 lb	900 g
2¼ lb	1 kg
3 lb	1.4 kg
4 lb	1.8 kg
4½ lb	2 kg

OVEN TEMPERATURES

Consult this chart for the Centigrade and gas mark equivalents for Fahrenheit temperatures.

OVEN	°F	°C	GAS MARK
very cool	250–275	130–140	½–1
cool	300	150	2
warm	325	170	3
moderate	350	180	4
moderately hot	375	190	5
	400	200	6
hot	425	220	7
very hot	450	230	8
	475	250	9

ACKNOWLEDGMENTS

For all of their help with this book, I would like to thank the following individuals and organizations.

The Italian Government Tourist Office in New York for being a liaison with the different offices in Italy

Giovanni Brachetti Montorselli for all his help in the Chianti

Contessa Federica Piccolomini Cinelli for the gracious hospitality in her palace in Piazza Santa Croce in Florence

The Azienda del Turismo of Pisa

Balducci and Dean & DeLuca shops in New York

Marchese Piero Antinori and his collaborators, Betty Scavetta and Loris Scaffei

Mondavi Winery in California for express-mailing almost a whole olive tree to us in New York

The Azienda del Turismo of Pistoia

The Azienda del Turismo of Livorno

The Lungarno Hotels

The hilltown of Monteriggioni and its Il Pozzo restaurant

Francesca Colombini Cinelli for opening doors for us in Montalcino

The Azienda del Turismo of Lucca

Dott. Luciano Panci of the Assessorato Turismo Regione Toscana for coordinating our work with all the different Aziende

The Biliotti family, farmers in Chianti

Richard Ginori China for lending us some of their beautiful pieces

Tessilarte in Florence for all the linen

The silver and china shop of Pampaloni in Florence

The Azienda del Turismo of Arezzo and the Galleria San Giorgio antique shop

The Pecorino cheese producer, Pasquale Putzulu, in Pienza

The director of Villa Garzoni in Collodi (Lucca)

The curator of the Palazzo Vecchio and the curator of the Bardini Museum

The Azienda del Turismo of Volterra

Silvano Focardi of the *La Chiocciola contrada* in Siena

The Azienda del Turismo of Prato

The Hotel Astoria in Florence

The Fattoria Rampolla in Chianti Classico

The curator of the Museum Alberto della Ragione in Florence

The Buca di Santantonio restaurant in Lucca

Sandro, Lella, Gianna, and Peter, who even had to sweep floors while assisting me, and our driver and all my relatives, who are now scattered throughout Tuscany, fortunately for me

A special thank you to Romano Buccianti, an incredible *trovarobe*, who found so many locations and old things for us

Leslie Stoker and my ever-patient editor Melanie Falick

Henry Weinberg, as usual, for his crucial role in this book

And my strong right hand, Sara Malone

INDEX

The text was set in Weiss, composed in-house on the Macintosh IIsi in QuarkXpress 3.1,
and output on the Linotronic L300 at The Sarabande Press, New York, New York.
The book was printed and bound by Toppan Printing Company, Ltd., Tokyo, Japan.